WOMEN STAGE DIRECTORS SPEAK

WOMEN STAGE DIRECTORS SPEAK

Exploring the Influence of Gender on Their Work

by Rebecca Daniels

McFarland & Company, Inc., Publishers
Jefferson, North Carolina, and London

British Library Cataloguing-in-Publication data are available

Library of Congress Cataloguing-in-Publication Data

Daniels, Rebecca, 1949–
    Women stage directors speak : exploring the influence of gender on
their work / by Rebecca Daniels.
        p.   cm.
    Includes bibliographical references and index.
    ISBN 0-7864-0965-7 (softcover : 50# alk. paper) ∞
    1. Theater—Production and direction.   2. Women theatrical
producers and directors—United States—Interviews.   I. Title.
PN2053.D36   1996
792'.0233'082—dc20   96-28188
                                                                    CIP

Manufactured in the United States of America

*McFarland & Company, Inc., Publishers
    Box 611, Jefferson, North Carolina 28640*

ACKNOWLEDGMENTS

First and foremost, I wish to express sincere admiration for and appreciation to all the women directors who shared their artistic processes and their thoughts about gender and directing with me.

Special thanks to my dissertation adviser and good friend, Dr. Grant McKernie, Theatre Department, University of Oregon, for believing that a study about the work of contemporary women directors was important scholarship. My gratitude also goes to St. Lawrence University, whose generous research grant support allowed me to expand the study quite substantially from its original form.

I am grateful also to my supportive colleagues in the Speech and Theatre Department at St. Lawrence. Parts of this manuscript were read in draft by Grant McKernie, University of Oregon; Kirk Fuoss, St. Lawrence University; Richard M. Carp, Northern Illinois University; Mary Donahoe, Wright State University; and Nancy Klementowski, playwright. Their comments and criticisms proved invaluable in the final stages of writing.

Thanks also to the individuals and theatres that helped me gather the photographic images of these directors at work.

This book could not exist without the constant support and encouragement of my many women friends, most especially Nancy Klementowski, Vana O'Brien, Mary Mears-Haskell, and Theresa Mason.

Finally, sincere and loving gratitude to my mother, Mary Daniels, who has always encouraged me to pursue the path of excellence in my work and life.

CONTENTS

PREFACE

Between December 1991 and October 1994, I interviewed thirty-five contemporary women stage directors working in the United States to ascertain whether and in what way these women perceived gender as most significantly influencing their own artistic processes.[1] As a director myself, I saw this study as an opportunity to explore and report on the perceptions of other women working in my field. Rather than evaluating, analyzing, or theorizing about a "woman's process," it was my intent to give these articulate and insightful women an opportunity to speak for themselves about their work. I was, after all, exploring a very personal area, their perceptions about themselves and their creative work. It has been my own experience as a director that I have shared many of their opinions at various points in my career and depending on the context of the work I was doing. Furthermore, I suspect other directors, regardless of gender, may find they share many of these same perceptions and concerns.

THE STUDY, ITS SIGNIFICANCE, AND THE METHODS USED

Directing Dominated by Male Artists

The profession of directing has been heavily influenced and dominated by male artists since it first came to prominence in the nineteenth century, and most directing theory and pedagogy to date has been written by men. One can find some limited historical information about women directors, perhaps an occasional interview or biography of a particularly prominent woman celebrity, who may direct as well as produce, act, or write for the stage, or an occasional inclusion of information about women directors in theatre history sources, but even less is available about how those women directors work. For example, a 1960s source book edited by female authors on directors of the modern theatre included only two significant references to women

1

directors.[2] In 1976, another book of collected essays on contemporary directors with the stated goal of providing a guide to contemporary directing practices and procedures included no women at all.[3] In a 1988 interview book about directors and their work, only three out of twenty-one interviewees were women and one of those was primarily a choreographer.[4] Also in 1988, a book specifically about women in the theatre included only one short article dedicated solely to women directors, although it made several brief references to specific women who direct and included some directors in its look at women's backstage contributions. The article was historical rather than process oriented.[5] Happily, in 1992 a book about specific directors and their rehearsal processes actually included five women out of ten directors profiled,[6] and in 1993, a book of collected essays came out which addressed specific productions by avowedly feminist directors, stating that it wished to present ways of thinking about directing as connected to social awareness.[7] These references on women directors, while not comprising an inclusive list, are emblematic of the fact that resources like these present only a small body of historical or critical work on a group that is growing rapidly within the theatre profession. Recent figures from the Society for Stage Directors and Choreographers indicate that women now make up 20 percent of the membership roster, and there are clearly more women than that working as directors, especially in the nonprofit and academic theatres.

Women Directors in America

Although she has existed since the emergence of directing as a profession, the woman director has been almost invisible, strikingly absent from the history books because her participation has often been restricted to regional, alternative, or educational theatres that were not considered major institutions or part of the commercial mainstream. Historically, means by which women were able to find their way into directing included starting out as actresses or even as playwrights directing their own work. Rachel Crothers is an early and prolific example of the playwright-director who started with a Broadway success in 1908 and subsequently directed another twenty of her own plays prior to 1940. In the last half of the nineteenth and early twentieth century, a number of actress-managers distinguished themselves in the theatre, most notably Eva Le Gallienne, who in the 1920s created an alternative to Broadway with her Civic Repertory Theatre. In the 1930s, Hallie Flanagan was chosen by President Roosevelt to head the Federal Theater Project, and Cheryl Crawford helped create the influential Group Theatre. In the 1940s, Crawford joined forces with Le Gallienne and Margaret Webster to found the American Repertory Theatre, and in the late 1940s and early 1950s the regional theatre movement was led by Margo Jones, Nina Vance, and Zelda Fichandler. These are only a few of the women directors

Zelda Fichandler (center) directs a rehearsal of Istvan Orkeny's *Screenplay* at Arena Stage. Actors in the foreground are Stanley Anderson, Regina David, and Terrance Currier. (1983). Photo by Joan Marcus.

and producers active in the first half of the twentieth century. After World War II, however, it seemed that whatever their previous contributions to the development of American theatre, women's contributions were most often relegated to the background or fringe, and male artists took over many of the prominent positions, especially those involving significant budgets and large audiences. In the 1960s and 1970s, women were instrumental in the alternative theatre movement, often becoming producers in order to have more opportunities to direct. A 1983 study by the League of Professional Theatre Women notes that from 1977 to 1982 on Broadway, only 3 percent of plays produced were directed by women, and of 50 nonprofit theatres also studied, only 6 percent of productions were directed by women. The situation in the regional theatres started to show considerable improvement in the late 1980s, however, as more opportunities developed for women directors.[8]

As their number and visibility increase, women, including several in this book, are starting to come to prominence as artistic directors in their own theatres. Zelda Fichandler was the artistic force behind the Arena Stage for forty years, Barbara Ann Teer has directed the National Black Theatre for twenty-six years, Tisa Chang has headed the Pan Asian Repertory Theatre for eighteen years, Sharon Ott has guided the Berkeley Repertory Theatre for eleven years, Timothy Near has run the San Jose Repertory Company for eight years, Elizabeth Huddle managed Intiman Theatre in Seattle for seven years and has recently taken over leadership at Portland Center Stage, Emily Mann has been the artistic overseer at the McCarter Theatre for five years, Mary Robinson led the Philadelphia Drama Guild for five years, and JoAnne Akalaitis supervised artistic activities at the Public Theater in New York for two years, to name only a few. These women, and others like them, are making incredible contributions to the contemporary theatre, yet in spite of their growth in visibility and viability in the theatre world, there is still very little published about the woman director. This book hopes to take a step toward rendering women directors and the processes by which they work more visible.

Goals of the Present Work

This book concentrates on the creative process of directing and whether women directors perceive gender to be a significant influence on their participation in that process and on their interpretive choices as artists. Gender and gender behavior are complex sociological and cultural issues, confounding reality (nature) and illusion (social conditioning) in much the same way theatre does. Much theoretical work on gender is recent, and theories and perceptions are constantly shifting, whether it be in the fields of science, sociology, literature, or the arts, and there is often little agreement. While feminist performance theory has developed in complexity and sophistication over the last ten or fifteen years, most of the critical work has been in the analysis of literature or acting, or in evaluations of the reception of the performance event itself, rather than an exploration of what goes into the creation of a piece of theatre from a directorial point of view. My goal is not to make definitive or absolute statements about the relationship between gender and art, but rather to explore both perception and process in the hopes of exposing some expectations, issues, and images which will be relevant to directors, regardless of gender.

I explore the perceptions women directors have about their working process and what might be inferred about the profession of directing and women's participation in the directing process as a result of that awareness, starting with a primary focus on gender influences and gender expectations. I further identify influences besides gender that have a significant influence on how these women make their artistic choices, such as age, ethnicity, religious background, sexual preference, or other sociological or psychological influences. Given that artistic vision and interpretive choice are extremely subjective areas of inquiry and given that gender issues are complex and often controversial, I do not attempt to make definitive, prescriptive, or evaluative statements about the processes used by women directors. Nor do I attempt to make value judgments regarding differences between male and female directors or the superiority of one gender over the other in the artistic process. Instead, I present descriptive analyses of the way particular women work, thus providing a framework for exploring the directing process in general.

Structure of the Book

Chapter 2 introduces the women directors who participated in the study and their thoughts on origins of gender differences. Chapter 3 looks at what it means to be defined as a woman director rather than simply a director and whether the awareness of gender influences is a conscious part of the working process or simply something which can be identified and speculated about only after the fact. The responses of the women directors and the issues they identified as being influenced by gender in their work generally concerned two key qualities of a good director: leadership and the ability to collaborate. Part Two (Chapters 4 and 5) takes a closer look at issues of leadership and the role of power in the directing process. It also explores issues in the reception of a woman in authority by other artists as well as the possibilities of internal resistance or self-doubt. Part Three (Chapters 6 and 7) explores the notion of collaboration, including issues of nurturing, the use of intuition, sensitivity to feelings and emotions, and creating an environment of trust and intimacy. This section concludes with a look at the need for balance between these two important directorial qualities, leadership and collaboration. The interviews also explore certain interpretive and functional elements of the directing process. Part Four (Chapters 8, 9, 10, and 11) examines the directors' perception of the impact of gender on script selection, casting, character interpretation, visual/technical elements, and use of space. The issues explored in Chapter 11, although not specific to the artistic process, were nevertheless deemed influential gendered issues by a number of the directors. The issues include financial and career considerations and family demands.

Structure of the Interviews

The interviews on which this book is based, whether in person or by telephone, always started with one general question: "How, and in which areas of your working process, do you perceive gender to have the most significant influence on your artistic and interpretive process as a director?" Once a director answered, thereby identifying her own priorities and perceptions, a corollary question was asked about her awareness of other influences besides gender that might have equal, or more significant, influence on the development of her artistic vision. Depending on which subjects had already been addressed in the initial answer, the director was then asked for her opinion about the influence of gender in the areas of leadership, collaboration, choice of material, casting, communication with other artists, approach to characters, and use of space. Each director was also asked about her own ideas regarding gender and gender differences in an attempt to categorize the responses according to the director's position within the various feminist theoretical camps: liberal, cultural/radical, or materialist.[9] The interview also included a question about how the director believes other artists perceive her as a director and as a woman and closed with the opportunity for her to make a final statement regarding gender and her artistic work. There are social, economic, and political issues important to women who are members of any profession heavily dominated by men, such as this one. My interviews, however, were concerned only with those issues insofar as they seem to influence artistic vision and interpretive process.

Limitations of This Book

The limitations inherent in a project of this nature are several. First, because comparatively speaking, much has been written about the process of male directors and because of the inclusion of the male-dominated theoretical framework, I did not feel the need to interview male directors as part of this study. That will comprise another, equally fascinating study for some other researcher who, I suspect, may find that male directors share similar perceptions about the important elements and ultimate goals of the directing process with the women studied here. They may approach the specific artistic issues from a somewhat different point of view, however. The difficulty in comparing men and women arises in some measure because, as psychologist Carol Gilligan points out with respect to her psychological studies of gender behaviors, it is difficult to say "different" without saying "better" or "worse." When male behavior has been naturalized as the norm, it is difficult to see female behavior which diverges from that standard as anything but a lack of development or power, even if it produces the same or similar results,[10] and women are often seen as having a political agenda if they deviate too often or too far from that norm.

Also, because so many elements can be considered significant to the process of directing, I limited this book, as much as was possible, to issues of creative vision (interpretation/personal voice) and to the ways in which directors interact with other theatre artists during the process of putting a show together. Since the interviews began, however, with my asking the women directors what issues and experiences were important to them, the respondents have created their own priorities. These priorities, in turn, have created the structure of this book, and the reader will discover that many of the issues and priorities overlap, weaving in and around each other even as the directors try to evaluate and separate elements of their own process.

1. A Brief History of the Directorial Function, Theories, and Processes

Directing as a Profession

The profession of stage director is one of the most recent additions to the theatre. Throughout history, playwrights and actor-managers obviously exercised significant control over work in the theatres with which they were involved, but the director as a separate artistic identity emerged only in the latter years of the nineteenth century. The reasons for this development are varied and complex, but some general influences can be identified as central. With the advent of the electric light and other stage technologies which developed and progressed with increasing rapidity and sophistication, the theatre event became much more complex. This led quite naturally to the perceived need for a single, outside, objective eye to guide all the disparate elements into a single unified vision. The director was assumed to be the individual who would supply the unifying interpretation, one who would understand all the theatre arts and undertake to devote full energy to bringing them together in an artistic whole.

Generally considered the pioneer in this new role, Georg II, duke of Saxe-Meinengen in Germany, was the first to exercise central artistic discipline over his company, controlling the overall vision and design of each production. His attempt to define this new role was followed shortly by Konstantin Stanislavski and Vladimir Nemirovich-Danchenko in Russia, Andre Antoine and Jacques Copeau in France, and Gordon Craig in England, among many others, all of whom advocated the notion of a single, powerful, dominant controller of the theatrical event. This notion of the director as the unifying artist of the theatre has come to dominate theatrical practice over the last one hundred years, and now it would be a rare production indeed that did not employ a director.

Directing Theory

In just over a hundred years, the profession of director has grown in importance and stature, yet it still lacks a comprehensive body of theoretical material to compare with other artistic disciplines, especially acting. Generally, directing has been learned through observation, practice, or methods borrowed from other disciplines such as acting, visual arts, or literary criticism. It has been defined by and large by those who practice it, and for the most part it has been male directors who have dominated the field and set the standards for "good" directing. Most of the material written about directing tends to be very pragmatic, concerned with exploring specific details of the process rather than with creating a cohesive theoretical base. Although there is a generally accepted dominant model, this model will not necessarily represent the way all directors work. In point of fact, there may be as many methods for directing as there are individual artists. In the preface to his series of interviews of contemporary directors, Arthur Bartow asserts "there is no 'correct' method of directing. As soon as one points to a director whose technique results in success, one can then look to another director whose method contradicts the first and whose work is also recognized as significant."[1]

Most articles or texts on directing generally represent the perspectives of the individual authors, who seem to accept the idea that directing principles vary from director to director, sometimes even from production to production of a single director. The process of directing has been called a "subtle and complex art,"[2] a "world of throbbing intangibles,"[3] and "an unmapped art or an academic discipline with almost no fixed landmarks."[4] The director's function has been described as "work[ing] continuously in a problem-solving mode, dealing with each situation according to its own specific nature,"[5] doing "what[ever] they decide needs doing" to create the theatrical event,[6] or taking on a range of roles in order to be the one who "guides, orders and manages every aspect of a theatre production."[7] This lack of specificity and acknowledgment of ambiguity is usually followed by an analysis of the author's own approach, as if by working closely enough within the trees one will eventually find and be able to name the forest. In the face of this apparent lack of theoretical cohesion, there are still some points about which all who write about directing or practice it seem to agree. When one looks at the details of putting together a production, the process is comprised of similar elements, even though the emphasis and relative importance of those elements may vary greatly with each individual approach. Thus a picture begins to emerge of some principles that seem to be held in common by most directors regardless of how these principles are individually applied in the artistic working process or their relative merits debated in the realm of theory. There are two ways in which these principles manifest themselves.

QUALITIES OF A GOOD DIRECTOR

The quality variously described as leadership, clarity of vision, or being in control of the artistic process is identified by all teachers and theorists of directing as one of the necessary qualities of a good director. A second necessary quality is the ability to collaborate with other artists in the collective process of theatre. All of the women interviewed were aware of and articulate about the importance of these qualities in their working process, and they had an ongoing awareness of the need for balance between the two attributes that sometimes appear to be contradictory. They were also able to identify these attributes, or at least their perception of them, as areas influenced by gender or societal expectations of gender behavior in various ways.

One directing textbook develops a model for incorporating leadership and collaboration in the director's process by invoking the notion of dual consciousness involving what the authors call the "creator" and the "observer." While these roles do not correspond directly to leader or collaborator, the point is that a good director must be able to operate from both vantage points, sometimes simultaneously: "A good director maintains a dual consciousness rotating between the perceptions of 'creator' and 'observer' while working on a production. (S)he acknowledges the outside audience factor, while simultaneously creating from inside the world of the play. Directors who do not incorporate both vantage points may be startled by audience reactions to their work. No single formula codifies how to apply such a double awareness, but maintaining a dual consciousness throughout [the process] assists you."[8]

In a 1986 doctoral study of student actor preferences for director behavior, the factors deemed most important in judging good directors were first, inclusiveness and reasonableness, which were defined as the "open" qualities of flexibility, supportiveness, and encouragement of actor input (which can all be identified as part of the requirements of successful collaboration); and second, clarity and confidence, which were described as the more "closed" qualities of discipline and control as well as conviction of interpretation and clarity of vision and communication (all qualities identified with effective leadership). Further, the study drew the conclusion that actors seem to prefer directors who can find a way to balance the two extremes of "open" and "closed" at the same time, thereby finding the "balance of opposites that actors seem to find important—a sort of yin and yang of directing technique. As in the Oriental philosophy, so with the actors of this study, a balance between the two extremes seemed to be the desired state for the director."[9]

PRACTICAL ELEMENTS OF THE DIRECTING PROCESS

The second way in which shared principles of directing appear in the literature of directing theory and pedagogy is in the description of key practical elements of the directing process itself. In all of the source documents consulted, certain commonalities could be found, regardless of the specific emphasis or approach.[10] For the most part, these major elements take their theoretical base from other disciplines. The first element is some kind of textual interpretation, which derives from the field of literary analysis and criticism and is the basis for the director's creative vision and production concept. Most texts deal with style as a separate element of the directing process, but for the purposes of this book it will be considered as part of interpretation. The second important element involves the visual aspects of the theatrical production, including design elements, composition, stage picture, blocking, and movement. These all involve the physical translation of the text into visual patterns and derive their theoretical base from the aesthetics of visual art. A third major element in the directing process is work with actors, using methods and materials from acting theory and pedagogy. This element often stresses psychological approach, emotional context, and motivation and involves by far the most intimate and personal collaboration. These three categories can encompass all of the various pragmatic details and all other functional steps in the directing process in some way. They are also clearly modified by the qualities of a good director and her ability to communicate with fellow artists.

COMMUNICATION IN DIRECTING

The issue of communication as part of the directing process crosses all boundaries and influences all functions, especially as it seems to be influenced by gender behaviors, perceptions, and expectations in the director or the other artists. In both leadership and collaboration, human communication seems to be an implicit key to success, and yet in directing theory or pedagogy the issue of communication is often elided or simply dealt with as a practical means to an end rather than explored as a critical and creative element of the process. All agree about its importance, yet none seem to be able to do much more than acknowledge its existence in the process, even though it might seem to be part of the key to balancing the two sometimes contradictory and seemingly paradoxical qualities of a good director. Besides the lack of theoretical awareness on how communication impacts the directing process, the idea of communication itself has become controversial and problematic. Theories of language and communication have been problematized by the advent of deconstruction and the notion that meaning can never be fixed. Furthermore, feminist theories challenge the traditional model of communication as having been weighted culturally and historically toward a male, Eurocentric point of view, which has then been naturalized as holding universal meaning. It is beyond the scope of this study to explore these theories in depth, and the women in this study did not seem to question the traditional model of communication. They generally accepted the notion that communication is critical to a director, but did not often talk about it as a separate element of the process or consider it an issue of anything other than personal style. References to various communication abilities and styles run throughout the interviews and are most conspicuously present in the discussions of leadership and collaboration.

A DIRECTOR PLAYS MANY ROLES

Most of the source books on directing approach the process in a somewhat linear and chronological manner, but all maintain an awareness of the multiplicity, connectedness, and occasional ambiguity of functions, as well as their performative nature. One text states that "the range of directorial functions varies enormously" depending on many factors inherent in each production, situation, or individual,[11] another refers to the many hats a director wears,[12] and a third goes so far as to organize the material presented in terms of the various roles a director plays during the process.[13] The idea of performing many roles in life is neither new nor unusual. Because of a cultural familiarity with the elusiveness and ambiguity of identity, combined with their social position as the ones more often expected to be concerned with relationship interaction and responsive to the needs and expectations of others, women may have a more acute awareness of their ability to play those many roles ascribed to them, and most of the women interviewed were very comfortable with the multiplicity of functions and malleable roles that the directing process demands.

2. The Women Interviewed and Their Perceptions of Gender Differences

The interviews for this book were most often in person, sometimes by telephone. I was also able to observe a few of the directors in rehearsal situations. The women are well known and well regarded in their local metropolitan areas; most have regional reputations as directors and many have national or international reputations. Most make their entire living working as theatre artists, sometimes in combination with teaching or the management of artistic programs at a particular theatre company and sometimes as free-lance artists. They have devoted their lives to the theatre and have been successful in establishing themselves as esteemed professionals in the field. Because of where I have lived and worked in the last five years, the directors I talked with were concentrated in two locations. Many live and work on the West Coast between Seattle and San Francisco. The others live or work in the New York City area. These women are in no way to be considered definitive or exhaustive of women directors, and they were very careful to point out that they were speaking for themselves only, not for all women who direct. Their insights suggest, however, recurrent issues and point to important sites where gender and directing intersect.

A Brief Introduction to the Directors

Background Profile

Selection for initial contact was made by reputation or personal referral, and although most of the women observed or interviewed come from relatively mainstream theatrical situations, an attempt was made to include lesbians and women of color in the interviewing process. Because there are so few women directors, however, there are even fewer minority women who have chosen the career of director or been given the opportunity to follow that career. Of the thirty-five women directors interviewed, two are Asian American, three are African American, three are Latina, and twenty-seven are white; four "out" lesbians are included. They range in age from early thirties to late sixties, but the majority of them (71 percent) are between 40 and 50 years old. All do free-lance work in some measure; some run their own theatres. Most have a high level of education and training (31 percent have bachelor's degrees and 46 percent have advanced degrees, including three with honorary doctorates), and their careers in the theatre range from fifteen to fifty years in length, with the majority of them (83 percent) directing from ten to twenty-five or more of those years. When one looks at their professional stature in the theatre, most of the women interviewed in this study fall into the category of liberal feminists in that they have found success by avoiding issues of gender and have participated in a male-dominated system that was already in place when they began their careers. The directors deny, however, that their success is a result of simply becoming "imitation men," and most (74 percent) consider themselves feminists. Those who do not view themselves as feminists seem to equate feminism with a limited and strident political agenda or think they don't really know how to define feminism and are thus unwilling to use it as a defining term for themselves.

Because a theatrical biography is contained in Appendix B, here I will only identify the directors by their home base and any current or recent affiliations:

- JoAnne Akalaitis, New York
- Nikki Appino, Seattle, Washington
- Melia Bensussen, New York
- Michelle Blackmon, formerly based in Seattle, now working in Ashland, Oregon
- Patricia Blem, formerly based in Portland, Oregon, now temporarily retired from the theatre world
- Anne Bogart, co-artistic director of the Saratoga International Theatre Institute and associate professor of theatre at Columbia University, New York
- Julianne Boyd, New York
- Alana Byington, associate director of the Oregon Stage Company, Portland, Oregon
- Tisa Chang, founder and artistic/producing director of Pan Asian Repertory Theatre, New York
- Liz Diamond, resident director at Yale Repertory Theatre, New Haven, Connecticut, and New York

- Zelda Fichandler, founder and former artistic director of Arena Stage, Washington, D.C., currently head of the graduate acting program at New York University, New York
- Susan Finque, formerly based in Seattle, now assistant professor of theatre at Antioch University in Yellow Springs, Ohio
- Maria Irene Fornes, New York
- Rita Giomi, Seattle, Washington
- Tori Haring-Smith, dramaturg at Trinity Repertory Company and associate professor of theatre at Brown University, Providence, Rhode Island
- Pamela Hendrick, formerly based in Minneapolis, now assistant professor of theatre at Stockton College of New Jersey.
- Brenda Hubbard, formerly based in Portland and Seattle, now assistant professor of theatre at Central Washington University
- Elizabeth Huddle, producing artistic director of Portland Center Stage, Portland, Oregon
- Bea Kiyohara, former artistic director of the Northwest Asian American Theatre, presently dean of student development services at Seattle Central Community College
- Roberta Levitow, Santa Monica, California
- Emily Mann, artistic director of the McCarter Theatre, Princeton, New Jersey
- Diana Marré, Seattle, Washington
- Penny Metropulos, Ashland, Oregon
- Gloria Muzio, New York
- Timothy Near, artistic director of San Jose Repertory Theatre, San Jose, California
- Sharon Ott, artistic director of Berkeley Repertory Theatre, Berkeley, California
- Victoria Parker, adjunct professor of theatre, Portland State University, Portland, Oregon
- Adele Prandini, artistic director of Theatre Rhinoceros, San Francisco, California
- Mary B. Robinson, former artistic director of the Philadelphia Drama Guild, Philadelphia, Pennsylvania
- Seret Scott, New York
- Fontaine Syer, associate artistic director of the Oregon Shakespeare Festival, Ashland, Oregon
- Julie Taymor, New York
- Barbara Ann Teer, founder and chief executive officer of the National Black Theatre and Institute of Action Arts, Harlem, New York
- Susana Tubert, New York

• Cynthia White, associate director of play development at the Oregon Shakespeare Festival, Ashland, Oregon.

These thirty-five women have extremely varied backgrounds and have done many things in the theatre besides directing. Twenty-nine started as actors, and sixteen still act from time to time, although most of them very selectively. In fact, five stated specifically during the interviews that it was dissatisfaction with the behavior of their male directors or dissatisfaction with roles available for women that led them into directing careers. Twenty-two are experienced playwrights or have been involved in adapting material for the stage or creating original collaborative performance pieces. Twelve have worked as dramaturgs or literary managers, sometimes in conjunction with their own directing work, sometimes for other directors. Seven have significant design background. Only five began directing without any previous performance-related experience. Twenty-one have been involved in founding a theatre of their own, and twenty have been responsible for the artistic leadership of a company at one time or another in their careers (about half of these twenty have less than five years in the artistic director role, the others have from eight to twenty years, one has forty years). Twenty-eight have experience teaching some aspect of theatre (from one semester to twenty-five years, both full and part-time), primarily at the college or professional training level. Fifteen studied for or began other careers before deciding to embark on a career in the theatre; these other careers included painting and textile design, structural anthropology, pre-med and philosophy, science and engineering, Russian language translation, and the teaching of romantic poetry and creative writing. Some of these preparing for or working in other careers have worked, or continue to work, at other jobs to support themselves when directing work is scarce, including high school teaching, bookkeeping, advertising, social service work, or education administration.

In the course of our conversations, the directors also identified factors besides gender which have significant influence on their artistic identity and personal development as an artist. Material from the interviews relating directly to these other issues is included in Appendix A. Significant influences described most often by the directors include family background, cultural or ethnic identity and influence, educational background (especially a love of learning, language, and communication), political or social concerns, religious or spiritual influences, other arts, and occasionally other disciplines altogether. Many of them also look to specific role models, teachers, family members, or other artists in and out of the theatre for their inspirations and aspirations.

All directing texts discuss in one way or another the importance of directors having an eclectic and wide range of interests and knowledge. These women are clearly no exception in this regard. In fact, there are many influences on any director, and the ones identified here are by no means intended to be considered the only important influences. Each artist has a personal equation for the many factors that make up an artistic identity, and these are simply a sampling of the interesting and diverse possible influences, the ones that happened to be foremost in the minds of these directors at the time of our conversations.

POSITIONS ON GENDER DIFFERENCES

Popular Ways of Characterizing Gender Differences

Because this is a study of the perceptions of women directors about how gender might or might not affect their work as artists, it is important to know how they view gender differences in today's society before we look at other concerns. In feminist discourse on gender, the notion of fixed or natural gender identity and behavior is constantly being critiqued and often deconstructed. Nevertheless, it has been common, especially in popular culture, to express gender differences in terms of various dualities. The capacity for autonomous thinking, clear decision making and responsible action, and a self that is defined through separation are often associated with masculinity. Sensitivity to feelings, awareness of others, responsibility for caretaking and a self delineated by connection are generally valorized as feminine.

Another popular way of characterizing gender differences involves the network of relationships that inform their actions. Psychologist Carol Gilligan believes that male ways of structuring relationships tend toward the hierarchical, while women tend to work within a structure of nonhierarchical interconnections, symbolized by the image of a web.[1] Deborah Tannen, a contemporary theorist in the field of communication and linguistics, describes gender differences in terms of the differing notions of intimacy and independence: "Intimacy is key in a world of connection where individuals negotiate complex networks of friendship, minimize differences, try to reach consensus, and avoid the appearance of superiority, which would highlight differences. In a world of status, independence is key, because a primary means of establishing status is to tell others what to do, and taking orders is a marker of lower status. Though all humans need both intimacy and independence, women tend to focus on the first and men on the second."[2]

A number of the women I spoke with showed a keen interest in exploring more information about gender differences, and contemporary books on gender differences in psychology and communication seemed already to have influenced the thinking of several of them. In fact, during the interviews several of the women mentioned they had read Tannen or Gilligan on gender differences, and the ideas in their books carried much weight with these particular directors.

Applying these somewhat stereotypical but generally accepted cultural assumptions, one could identify certain elements that make up the directing process which might be considered gendered behaviors, either male or female depending on the task itself. In terms of cultural sex-role stereotypes, the easy use of intuition or the ability to understand and communicate feelings would probably be considered more female or feminine behavior. Furthermore, the need to analyze intellectually or communicate authoritatively has been viewed by society as a predominantly masculine or male behavior. According to most contemporary theorists and teachers of directing, all of these behaviors have some importance in the directing process.

Gender Complexities and Contradictions

When queried on their beliefs regarding gender differences in society, most of the directors were initially reluctant to theorize on the subject. Many of them imply, however, that they would like to see gender understood in terms of "both...and" rather than "either...or." This information provides an interesting frame for the issues these women identify as being influenced by gender in their careers as stage directors. By and large the women tend to situate themselves and their beliefs somewhere midway along a continuum between strict biological determinism and complete cultural construction of gender, with the majority giving a much greater role to social conditioning than to biology, and with only one woman out of thirty-five voicing belief in biological determinism as the stronger of the two influences. Echoing the imagery of multiplicity and ambiguity in the director's functions, they all believe the issue of gender to be equally complex and contradictory.

Susana Tubert says she believes in the existence of sexual/cultural role playing but does not want to be defined or limited by gender identity or expectations: "The psyche is bigger than that. I believe that we all have both male and female in us. It's too limiting to reduce the issue to gender differences. On the other hand, I won't hide who I am: I'm a woman and I'm proud of it; I'm a Latina and I'm proud of it; I'm a director and I'm proud of it. Some days I feel like my whole life's one big political act." This sentiment, that gender is just one more thing that defines but doesn't limit them, was expressed in one way or another by many of the women, regardless of where they positioned themselves and their beliefs about gender on the theoretical continuum from biological determinism (the radical/essentialist feminist position) to cultural construction (the materialist feminist position).

Cultural Construction as the Primary Influence

At the materialist extreme is a self-identified lesbian Marxist, Diana Marré, who believes that her family "slipped up in transmitting gender specific role stuff" to her. Marré focuses much of her directing work on the confabulation of gender roles as well as connecting gender issues with those of race and class. Several others also place themselves firmly within the materialist position. Liz Diamond was direct and to the point, saying, "I'm less of an essentialist as a feminist, or less of a cultural feminist, à la Carol Gilligan, than I am someone who sees the way we construct ourselves as women as historically determined." Nikki Appino was clearly in a stage of intense politicization of her work at the time of our conversation and maintained a strong connection between cultural construction of gender behaviors and the subculture issues of oppression by means of gender, race, and class. She emphatically identifies those issues of oppression as the primary ones she wants to foreground in her work from this point on.

Susan Finque provides an articulate awareness of gender as performative behavior and finds in that awareness an artistic advantage:

> I think that there are people who are in male biological bodies who are dealing in behavior modes in a feminine gender. I don't think that it's necessarily because I'm biologically female that leads me to having a gender behavior that is female as well. In fact, I think one of the things that makes me an effective artist is this mixture of masculine and feminine in who I am as a human being on the planet. Androgyny and its mysteries will probably continue to compel me all my life and affect my work. The question with gender is [quoting transsexual Kate Bornstein], "Why can't we count higher than two?" What is the problem here that the line is so strongly divided and the rules are so polarized that a person has to choose which battle side they're on? I find it boring. I find it as limiting as the rules that our contemporary American society has set up based on our genitals.

Anne Bogart agrees with Finque, also seeing the gender question as a complex equation, much larger than an either/or proposition: "The more I study and understand both sociology and psychology, the more complicated gender becomes. I don't believe in a clear cut division between men and women. I believe there are probably a lot more than two genders. I believe in environmental influences. I believe in complexity more than anything. All I know is that there's probably a broad spectrum upon which every individual falls in a different place. That's why I have trouble with the gender questions that you're asking. Because I feel very uncomfortable answering any of them in a clear cut way."

Masculine and Feminine in Everyone

While she does not talk about the possibility of more than two genders as Bogart and Finque do, Cynthia White is "not a strong believer in masculine and feminine corresponding to men and women." She does agree, however, that the duality "provides a convenient analytical structure" for discussion.

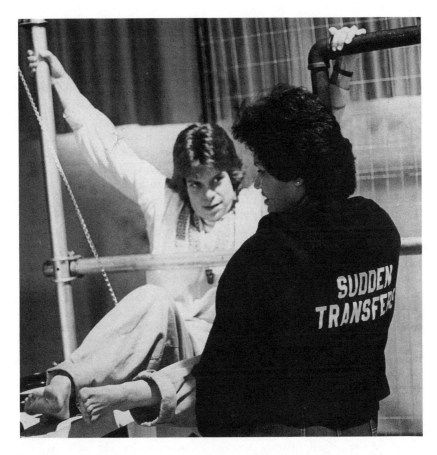

Susan Finque (left) with actress Lydia Mendoza on the set of *Sudden Transfers: A New Theatrework on Women in Prison* at the University of Santa Cruz (1981). Photo by Annice Jacoby.

Both Patricia Blem and Penny Metropulos place a great deal of importance on the notion of balance and the search for wholeness on a spiritual level, and seem to base their ideas on a loose combination of Eastern mystic philosophy and Jungian archetypes. They express the belief that we all have male and female energies within our psyches. Metropulos discusses the qualities of yin and yang in everyone. She believes that feminine qualities are not limited to women's psyches and that we must all search for a balance between the two. Blem goes into more detail: "When you open yourself up, you're getting the energy, yin and yang both, coming through you, to work with however it needs to be worked. So I think that I work with both. The tools are there for both. ... I think there is a basic difference between male and female. The energy is different. I think female energy is receiving, male energy is an outward push. I believe that every human being has both these energies in them, whether male or female."

Although she does not use the yin and yang terminology, Liz Huddle also discusses the male and female energies within her psyche, using similar suppositions about what those energies are and how they manifest in her work. "The artistic instinct within me is basically a feminine instinct. I have tremendous masculine tendencies in terms of drive and push and administrative capabilities, but as I create, it's my feminine instincts I rely on." She goes on to say the composition of gender differences in her opinion comes from "the mix of the way you're brought up within your individual culture, within a larger culture that is patriarchal, and then your predetermined biological differences and how that mix happens with a given individual."

Roberta Levitow agrees with the notion that we all have both energies in us, and she believes that how we use those energies really depends on our environmental reinforcement for certain behaviors early in our lives: "It is both the physical, physiological composition of the creature, which brings certain predispositions, and then it is how those predispositions are exercised over the next very intense number of years of life. From everything I've read, the best I can figure so far is it must be a combination, our chemicals, our gene pool, and what's exercised in our gene pool. I think that within the first ten years people are communicating to you your gender." Levitow elaborates on her position by talking about the acting training she has observed in the classroom of colleague and performer, Anna Deavere Smith, concluding with a clear statement of her personal belief in the unique combination of male and female in each of us:

> Smith's proposal is that we all live on a gender spectrum somewhere between the poles of ultimate masculine and ultimate feminine. She teaches the students to define character by picking a place on the gender spectrum, because she says we all feel like we are a certain combination of masculine and feminine and you can really build character out of that. She often does gender reversal exercises in class. I sat through a couple of them, and they are wild. All of her work is trying to find people on that spectrum, and find herself on that spectrum. I feel like I'm a woman who combines this much masculine with my feminine, and that person is a woman who combines this much feminine with her masculine. I might be closer to a man who has a mix more like my mix than with a particular woman I'm sitting next to. That's my personal philosophy about gender.

Pamela Hendrick also agrees with the notion that one could have influence from both the genders, presenting her ideas about behavioral differences in terms of tendencies and avoidances which can be reinforced in a variety of ways in our lives:

> I am one of those people who believes that the division between material feminism and cultural feminism is an artificial one. I believe that there are many

aspects of gendered behavior that are culturally constructed, based on power differences, and I also think that there are very possibly gender differences that are innate. But I also strongly believe that there are no absolutes, that gender differences, in our culture and in every culture, fall into the categories, as the sociologist would say, of avoidances and tendencies rather than absolutes. I think that women tend towards certain behaviors and tend to avoid others, and conversely men do the same. There are virtually no absolutes, and my studies of differences in speech and body language certainly bear that out. There is no gesture, there is no vocal pattern that women exclusively use and men don't use. There is no gesture or vocal pattern that men use and women don't.

These tendencies and avoidances, as Hendrick calls them, seem to be reinforced by a variety of factors in the eyes of these women. Many take a middle-of-the-road position about which influences might be stronger, seeming reluctant to define any one influence as more significant than another.

A Mix of Genetics and Environment

While she also refers to everyone having a masculine and feminine side, Alana Byington sees gender differences as a mix of genetics and environment, a "predisposition one way or another that is reinforced by environment, or not." Melia Bensussen also sees a mix of influences, saying, "This is a safe answer if not the most interesting one—my gut feeling is somewhere in the middle, but I think it depends on what aspect of life. I think in directing I would lean more towards the environmental because I don't see the physical as affecting me now, but I also don't have children right now." Adele Prandini articulates this notion about the mix of influences very strongly:

> I do think it's a combination. Men are treated differently as little people. They are taught lies about women as very little people and lies about themselves. That has to have an impact, that conditioning. And the physical differences have to have an impact. They're not allowed to be spiritual in the way that women can be spiritual. They're not allowed their intuition. Certainly they have it, and if they don't they can develop it. So all of these things must contribute to that difference because all experiences contribute to who we are. We start out with a certain set, you know, and then what do we do with it? I think that you can't assign it to one thing. It's got to be that collection.

Gloria Muzio clearly believes that social conditioning is a strong influence, but in looking at gender differences she identifies the difficulty inherent in any assumptions about gender behavior. She goes on, however, to make one herself, based on her personal experience:

> GM: It's hard as a woman to know how it's different, because we don't think but like how we think, do you know? In general, I tend to think that men are more result oriented. I'm always interested by the male/female conversation

about a woman talking about what's wrong, and a man thinking that means
he has to fix it—where for the woman, just exploring what's wrong is part of
fixing it—and that the man is more interested in "What do we *do*?" One of
my thoughts is that women are not so interested in that result, they are more
interested in the process.

RD: Do you think that comes from our biology or from our social conditioning?

GM: Oh, I think it's both. I think it's heavy social conditioning, but I also
think that there's something biological as well. I don't have any children, but
when you talk to parents they'll tell you from day one little boys are different
from the little girls. They're just different. It doesn't mean one is meant to
stay at home and one is meant to work. It just means they're different. But I
also think there is heavy social conditioning.

Like Muzio, Mary Robinson uses behavioral variations in young children as a way to talk about her opinions on gender. In our conversation, she
brings up the contrasts she has noticed between her own young son and a
friend's daughter of the same age, noting that she finds it fascinating to
observe that many of the stereotypical gender differences are already present
in the children even though both have gentle, thoughtful, nontraditional
fathers and strong mothers. Robinson also refers to Deborah Tannen's book
about male and female communication styles: "The way she says men are
looking for status and women are looking to connect is a generalization, but
I think there is some truth in it. It helped me understand a former colleague
because I was finding it difficult to understand why he worked a certain way
and I worked another way. I began to realize that neither is right, it's just
what's most right for each of us."

Although her child is a bit older, Tisa Chang also refers to gender differences she has observed in children as a way to illustrate her beliefs. She
believes those differences come from a combination of influences, but mostly
from social conditioning, and identifies sexual preference as another possible
influence in how we might think about gender:

TC: As a parent of a 14-year-old boy, and comparing notes with other parents who have little girls or boys, there's no question that little girls are, generally speaking, going to be a bit more biologically, physiologically, psychologically prepared to be more organized, a little bit more mature, a little more
sensible. Whether mother nature said this is going to be the person who is
going to be procreating and being instrumental in shaping the young, or
whether society trains them to be that way, I don't know. But generally speaking, I think that is so. It doesn't mean that there aren't exceptions to the rule.
I think boys tend to be a little bit more conformist and need communal appro-
bation a lot more. In many ways, I feel males are thinner skinned. Girls can
be embarrassed and mortified, but we can get over something, whereas I think
boys—you might even find it in adult men sometimes whose feelings have
been hurt because I've been tactless or something—really hold that grudge
for a long time.

RD: Do you think that's social conditioning? That we allow them those behaviors, or do you think that's innate, part of being a male?

TC: A lot of it's conditioning, because the minute you are a boy, you're being brought up a certain way, and if you are a girl you are being brought up a certain way. I do feel that our behavior and existence are shaped by gender differences. I think that some of that is now changing quite a bit because of external societal values changing. However, our thinking and our behavior will continue to be shaped by how we are prepared in life. No matter how liberal people get, I think this will always continue It will shape our being. I think that's for the good. I personally think gender differences and responses because of gender are very good. I think that's what makes life interesting. It would be rather boring to have everybody merged together. I don't know if we can predict what the differences would be, particularly since homosexuality and lesbianism also enters into the discussion in a very tangible, concrete fashion as a very interesting alternative, an additional layering of consideration.

Zelda Fichandler also refers to the differences one can observe in young children, wondering whether they are inborn or culturally derived: "I don't know whether this is inborn or culturally early determined, but I've noticed that little girls have more interest in what they wear and are flirtatious at age two and three. So either you get to them very fast or else they have that animal behavior. I don't know why they shouldn't have the animal behavior. It wouldn't be hard to convince me that there's some pretty hard wiring about how women and men are different." She speculates further about those differences, the difficulty in determining where they come from, and how they might manifest in her work:

I think the last person you see is yourself. To see your work is to see an objectification of your temperament, your preferences, your perceptions, your visual sense, your choreographic sense. Having said that, I would say that one of the elements—I don't know whether it's dominant or semi-dominant or recessive—but one of the elements of who you are is your gender. That's been worked upon hormonally in the womb and worked upon culturally since you left that safe place never again to return. That has got to mean something because in the play of evolution we find that gender was one of the great evolutionary tools because it allowed for mixing of genetic materials. Sexual difference was a way that nature provided for diversity and the strength for survival. We didn't decide anything about that. While we think we're determining our lives, in the long evolutionary scale we're actually determining the life of a species. I think it was terribly clever of evolution to have made two sexes. In its wisdom, evolution must have thought those differences were useful, creative, complementary. There is that Y chromosome that seems to have something to do with this, and there is that cultural injunction to behave in a certain way. Surely I was subjected to it. "You don't really need to argue with people," my mother would say. "Particularly men. You don't need to disagree all the time, you could just keep your thoughts to yourself." However, it seems to me in the work of directing, there's a wide range of what is masculine and what is feminine. Some male directors are enormously psychologically sensitive and nurturing with their people and what they bring out in a play, and some women directors are quite tough, one might say nonempathic, with their actors.

Tori Haring-Smith explains that although she is not one to believe all gender differences are biological, she definitely believes in some innate elements: "I'd like to say I'm a materialist because most of the time I believe that I learned to have a gendered vision from the culture around me. However, there's probably 25 percent of me that believes my gendered way of seeing is inherent in my biology—essential. I believe that when somebody walks on the stage with long hair and a skirt and isn't cross-dressed, people make assumptions on the basis of what they assume that person's biological sex is. So there's a part of me that thinks gender is essential, although most of me believes as a theoretician that it is materialist." This moderate position is shared in varying degrees by almost all the other women, with most, like Haring-Smith, believing the stronger influence is cultural.

Nature as the Stronger Influence

Barbara Ann Teer is the only person I talked with who believes gender is more related to biology than social conditioning, but she definitely identifies some cultural influences as well:

> For me, gender is biological, and the responsibilities that one has, one is going to do, regardless. If you have a responsibility to take care of your own, to educate your own, to transform the identity of people of African descent, you will do it. From a western point of view we are underprivileged, undercapitalized, underdeveloped; we're the third world, the colored world. That's not my reality, and when it comes to economics and materialism, perhaps we are underdeveloped, but when you look at the world from a spiritual reality, which is, as far as I'm concerned, the only way to view the world, then reality makes us not "under" or "over." We come from a different paradigm or different reality, and we are certainly equipped creatively, male and female, to constantly turn out the most awesome creative ideas in every walk of life, be it clothes, food, theatre, religion, gesture, language, because that's the way we were born. I think that could be considered creatively feminine. I don't like the word feminine, because the feminine gender is assessed as weak, "under," and "less than" in this materialistically driven culture. It's based on a reality of scarcity. People think that if you're feminine somehow you're weak or you're to be victimized, or taken over. It's all wrong-headed as far as I'm concerned. The concepts are wrong-headed, the construct is wrong-headed. It gives no dignity to the creativity of life. When you talk in terms of linear, Cartesian reality, things that are outside you, you get stuck in that box, "If it's feminine, then you've got to fight for your rights because you don't have any rights if you're a woman." None of that works for me. It's simply somebody else's idea of somebody else's world, and it's not my idea of things as they are.

In spite of her insistence on biological differences, Teer actually seems to resist making any gender distinctions at all, putting more emphasis on cultural background as a determining factor in creative endeavors, which she sees as "feminine" in nature.

Physical Differences

Although none of these women stake their beliefs on biological determinism as the primary reason for gender differences, physical issues do seem to be important to several of the women. Timothy Near speaks of the environment of the body: "Our bodies must affect our spirits in some way. If you think the environment affects your spirit, your body *is* your environment and it has to affect the spirit. The fact that, whether you become a mother or not, you are someone who is built to give birth and feed a new body from your own and take on the dependence of that creature, this must affect our spirit in some way." Brenda Hubbard believes that cycles of menstruation and childbearing have a significant effect on gender behavior, using genital imagery to talk about the difference between male focus on external and "penetrating" awareness and female focus on internal and "receiving" awareness. Even with this comment on the importance of biological rhythms, Hubbard still believes that gender behavior is "eighty percent conditioning."

Maria Irene Fornes seems at first to put strong emphasis on physical issues as a major factor in gender differences, but then goes on to define a political and socially constructed system that exacerbates those physical differences:

> The main difference has to do with physical strength. In our world, the ultimate power has to do with the strong. Among men, the weaker man doesn't have the power that a strong man has physically, and a weak man will have more power than a strong woman. But then it becomes a question of armies. A weak man is the weaker in the army of the strong, but a strong woman, who may be stronger than this weak man, belongs already to the army of the weak. So women cannot simply be moved on because they are strong, because they still belong to the army of the weak. ... So a woman has to be better than the small guy because they are both not as strong physically. They are at a disadvantage, but the woman, in relation to the weak guy, is at an additional disadvantage because she belongs to the other race, the other side, the enemy. I think it has to do with physical strength, but I think it also has to do with the fact that the world as it is today has been built by men.

One can see that even when some elements of physical difference seem to be important for these directors or even taken for granted by them, there is still a great reluctance to make definitive statements about their beliefs in the reasons for gender differences.

Shifting Perspectives

In the exploration of her beliefs about gender differences, Sharon Ott admits to changing beliefs and rather enjoys the constantly shifting perspective which she believes provides her more flexibility as an artist:

Sexuality [and by inference, gender difference] is a complex and changeable thing that manifests itself in completely different ways with different people. I don't know the answer. The one thing that always drives me nuts with some feminists is that they are so certain of what they feel. I just never feel that certain about it and, in a way, I hope nobody ever finds the real answer. In some ways there's a part of me that actually finds the mystery compelling. Because I'm a person of dramatic bent, I don't want to know. I would prefer not to actually make up my mind because then I can't deal with it artistically or deal with it subconsciously. A sense of enigma is actually desirable; it's part of what's absolutely, incredibly amazing about human animals, that kind of complicated behavior. It should be what we're doing as artists, to plummet into the psychology and the pathology. Just explore it and put up what we found in front of people.

This point of view could be interpreted by some as a quintessentially female one, with its welcoming of ambiguity and an identity that seems to be in process with itself rather than fixed, but I believe Ott and some of the others would be more inclined to see it as a creative point of view, the position of an artist engaged in a dialogue with her world.

Summary

We have seen that, although a few of these women directors believe strongly in cultural construction as the primary influence on gender and one believes biological factors are the strongest influence, a majority see gender as a moderate mix of these two factors and acknowledge environmental reinforcement and social influences on gender behavior in varying degrees in that mix. There is also substantial agreement with the notion that there are masculine and feminine traits and energies in everyone. The one issue on which there is complete agreement is the complexity of gender and the difficulty in defining its influence precisely. Furthermore, it seems that in their shared belief that gender boundaries seem more permeable and less fixed in the theatre world, these women resist being defined by gender, not wanting to be limited or marked by rigid definitions in any way.

3. GENDER MEANS EVERYTHING AND NOTHING

During the initial inquiries, strong and positive responses to my request for interviews were encountered because women artists are quite sensitive to the need for their voices to be heard. However, when first asked directly how gender influences their working process, responses varied from incredulous looks to laughter to thoughtful silence. Throughout the interviews, a paradoxical concept began to emerge that led to an early working title for this book. "Everything and Nothing" seems to be the way many of the directors are inclined to respond when asked about the extent of gender influence in their artistic work. While responses run the gamut from a constant, conscious awareness to none at all, even those directors who believe it has absolutely nothing to do with the way they make artistic choices are often put in a gendered position by others who presume that it has everything to do with their way of working. Many of those interviewed decried the need to be identified as women directors even while agreeing to answer questions about gender influence on their artistic work, and most look forward to the day when they will simply be considered directors.

RESISTING DEFINITION AS A WOMAN DIRECTOR

The Artist as a Genderless Being

The concept of the artist as a genderless being has been identified by some feminist theorists as potentially damaging to women because of its unwitting compliance with a historically male-dominated sense of aesthetics.[1] Yet the women I spoke with who support the notion of genderless artists believe it to be highly advantageous for them as professionals to resist thinking of themselves as women directors. In fact, many were initially reluctant to state any generalities regarding gender influences. They prefer to view gender as simply an element, albeit a critical one, in a complex combination of influences which shape their individual artistic identities. This sentiment is echoed in a related context by playwright Heather McDonald. The play is *Dream of a Common Language*, which was being directed at Berkeley Repertory Theatre during my observation of Sharon Ott. The character, Pola, is a woman painter who wants simply to be considered a painter:

> I simply don't believe that a woman enters a studio any differently than a man does. ... You don't go into a studio and say, Oh, here I am about to make a painting by a woman. I mean, there you are alone in this huge space and you're not thinking about your breasts and your vagina. ... You are inside yourself, looking at some object lying on a table, a velvet petal of a rose, a half-filled bottle of perfume, and this is what you are supposed to make a world out of. That is all you are conscious of. I don't believe that a man feels any differently. Does a man go striding into his studio thinking, well, here I am this marvelous man with this marvelous power of the male and this marvelous penis to inspire me? I don't believe it. When you are painting, you are inside yourself. You are looking at this terrifying unknown, and trying to feel something, trying to pull everything you can out of all your experience and make something new.[2]

Many of the directors I interviewed embrace a similar point of view, exemplified by Cynthia White, who says simply, "I really am a director first, although I do not deny the fact that I'm a woman." Penny Metropulos makes a related point, saying, "I am politically aware that I am first an artist in the theatre. There's this sense that all theatre is political. But I think part of our job is to be larger than that, to embrace those politics, to look at them and think about them and make moral decisions about the situation, but I believe part of that moral decision has to do with an awareness beyond politics—a spiritual awareness, if you will."

Nikki Appino, although almost exclusively focused on women's issues in the selection of her material and the artists and theatres she chooses to work with, expresses a distinctly different point of view when questioned about the artistic process itself: "Creatively, in the room, doing the work, I'm never, ever aware of it. I do not think that I adjust myself in any way to deal with it. Deep down inside, what the creative process is for me, it's genderless." Sharon Ott, although very interested in directing pieces like *Dream of a Common Language* because of its focus on women artists, believes gender should not be an issue in the production of art. She objects strenuously to the ghettoization of women directors, and in a recent feature article about women artistic directors, she notes ruefully that the simple fact that articles and books need to be written about women in the theatre "shows that [gender] is still an issue. It proves that there's still some way in which we're regarded differently."[3]

Reluctance to Make Gender Distinctions

Most of the women I interviewed insist they are not aware of a conscious emphasis on gender issues as they are working, but when reflecting back on the process they can identify several areas of probable influence. Some responses tend to be along certain clichéd lines (such as power being a masculine attribute and collaboration being more feminine), but most women qualify their ideas by framing their responses in terms of what they believe is usually thought about gender differences in our society. Most are reluctant to make generalities or stereotypical distinctions about gender, preferring instead to talk about personality as well as the context of behavior. Gloria Muzio points out the difficulties in analyzing one's own process in comparison to something one can only assume about the processes of others: "As a director you rarely watch other directors work. You hear from other actors how different directors work. You see their finished work, but you rarely are in on the process, you rarely sit in on other directors' rehearsals. You don't know. So it's hard to talk about, or even to start thinking about, what about my gender makes my work process what it is, not really knowing how a man's work process might be different."

Muzio continues by discussing the dangers of trying to identify gender distinctions without taking other individual differences into account. She clearly wants to use whatever she believes she can bring to the process by virtue of being a woman, without feeling limited or pigeonholed by it:

> I think it's dangerous and bad to limit—for women to be thought as a certain kind of director and for men to be thought of as another kind of director. It's always been important to me and crucial to be thought of as a good director, not as a good woman director, but unfortunately, I've been singled out at times as a woman. It's clear to me that I don't want it to be as though I'm going to direct like you would think a man would direct it. I just want to be good. I want to hold onto to what it is that makes me "me," and one of those many things is that I'm a woman. I'd like to think that's what makes different directors and different points of view, that a man is going to pick up the same script that I pick up and do a very, very different production, and only one of those factors that is going to make it a different production is that he's a man and I'm a woman. It's also going to make a different production because of all the other many things of who we are. It's a very tricky subject to me because I think there's some danger in it too. And yet, I also am very high on saying that women are different than men. We just look at things differently.

Mary Robinson also identifies difficulties in drawing comparisons between how different directors work, citing a male director who works in ways very similar to her own process: "It's all very hard to sort out. One of the reasons is because directors don't tend to know how each other works except by hearsay and reading about each other because you don't get to watch other directors. We have a resident director [at the Philadelphia Drama Guild], an African American man, and he is, if anything, even more nurturing than I. You can't possibly draw a distinction between the way the two of us work. I think he very much holds to the same beliefs I do in how he works. He's the director whose work I happen to know best because I've been able to see him at work."

Regarding her awareness of the influence of gender in her own work, Robinson also articulates a changing awareness as she grows older and her career progresses. She, like Muzio, wants to acknowledge but not be limited by her gender:

> I've been thinking about the influence of gender since I've been directing professionally, which is over fifteen years now. Ten or fifteen years ago, I would have said, "Not at all; I'm a director, I happen to be a woman who is a director." Now that I've really found my feet as a director and am very comfortable directing, I would amend that and say there are many things that make me the particular director I am, and certainly a large part of that is being a woman. But I would also say the other thing it has to do with is age. Fifteen years ago I thought, "Not only am I a woman, I'm young. I'm younger than most of the people I direct, and some of the men I direct are old enough to be my father." I think there was a defensiveness about being a young woman director. Now that I'm no longer such a young director, I think I'm much more able to embrace the fact that I'm whatever is meant by a woman director. I think that the influence of gender is a really interesting question that I'll be probably thinking about all my life. It's a question I'm far more comfortable with now than I used to be because I used to get very defensive when people would suggest that it was a possibility. But I certainly think that part of whom I've become as a director is influenced by the fact that I am a woman, a 40-year-old woman with a husband and a child, who is running a theatre. There are so many other things that go into that identity. I hesitate to get simplistic and say I work this way because I'm a woman. But it certainly is a strong factor in who I am as a person and therefore who I am as a director.

Occasionally, some of the women found it hard to talk about gender issues at all, but it was difficult to determine whether this stemmed from reluctance or lack of awareness. Many of the women are quite sensitive to the sexual/political dynamics of hiring practices and pay scales, and they are aware of wanting to select projects that provide women with a stronger cultural voice. They maintain, however, that, in spite of that awareness, once they actually start work on creating a production, the focus is on the work to be done. They are rarely aware of gender being an influence on the directing process itself, unless or until some incident or encounter occurs to remind them that their gender is creating a particular situation.

THINKING ABOUT GENDER WHEN WORKING

Gender Is Both Everything and Nothing

Most of the directors prefaced their remarks about specific instances of gender influence with a more general statement of its influence on them ranging from everything to nothing, and sometimes, paradoxically, encompassing both. Many of them believe that being a woman definitely has an influence on the way they work, but rarely are they aware of that influence or willing to admit to it on a conscious level during the process itself. In a letter prior to our interview, Roberta Levitow was the first to raise the paradox of "everything and nothing," as she explores the ways gender is constantly influencing her process but rarely in a conscious way: "What has gender meant to my career? Everything and nothing. In one sense I never think about it. My ambition as an artist has always been to express myself as fully as possible, and early on I seldom stopped to consider what gender had to do with it. As I climbed the ladder of the professional theatre, the necessity to constantly think about my gender did arise. In this sense I always think about it—as a female worker in a social political world. I am aware that my assignments, often on women's plays, and my position in business hierarchies are inevitably influenced by gender."

When asked to expand on this notion during our interview, Levitow described how conscious awareness of gender can come and go during her work. She also observes an inhibiting gender influence on the social process related to the work:

> Sometimes I don't think it has anything to do with it at all, and then at other moments, I think, "But of course, it's completely and constantly relevant. That's who I am." I tend to feel it most in a political and social sense. I feel it most in the gender politics of getting work, developing working relationships with artistic directors, designers, actors. In other words, it has a lot to do with how people see me. When I walk into the room, the fact that I'm female seems to set up certain behavior on their part, that actually I feel I'm generally accommodating to, but it's not something I necessarily intend to bring. Although I have, over the years, played around with different variations on ignoring it, using it, and having a chip on my shoulder about needing to use it, or feeling a pressure to use it, or feeling some kind of effect on my experience because of it. I think the social process between men and women is really deeply influential in everybody's business, in every way that women are interacting in the workplace. That's certainly true with artistic directors. I find when I work for women artistic directors, we tend to socialize more. When I work with male artistic directors, it's very different to go out to dinner, or go have a drink after the rehearsal, than it is with a female colleague. I think there is a real inhibiting factor in terms of women interacting in the social sense with male artistic directors. That's unfortunate because the artistic process is so much about finding kindred spirits in terms of building a core

of artists that you like to work with. It was easier when we were all younger and we had more of a brotherly/sisterly feeling. It's much harder as you get older and it gets more strict in your expectations of how men and women socialize. I find that's an important issue.

Rita Giomi believes gender has a profound influence on her work, but makes it quite clear that she only thinks about it after the fact:

> Personally, I think it influences everything, from start to finish—from selection of script, to selection of theatre to casting, to everything. I don't think there's any way to separate gender because we all carry gender bias in some way, which is not to say it's always a bad thing at all. I think it just is. I never really stop to think about it while I'm working. I don't know that anybody does. I think the minute you do, you're sunk because your focus goes to the wrong place. It goes on yourself, and that's not where your direct focus should be while you're in process. It has to be on what's in front of you and what's going on there. Because while you're flying, if you look down, if you stop to think, "How am I doing this? How am I making myself float up here?" then you fall. But clearly you learned how to fly from somewhere, so trust it. I don't stop and ask myself, "How would I be directing this if I were a man?" So, no, I'm not "conscious" of gender while I work.

While Giomi was clearly very aware of gender influence as we talked about her process, she believes that in the midst of that process she needs to trust her influences but not analyze them. This same sense of gender as "everything and nothing" was implied anecdotally throughout many of the other interviews. While no one was as specific as Levitow in naming that idea, even women who believe gender has no significant influence on their artistic choices seem to be regularly put in the position—by others—of seeming as if it has everything to do with why they work the way they do.

A Constant, Conscious Influence

Only a handful of the women I spoke with were emphatic in identifying gender as an element of artistic significance in their work. Susan Finque was one of the few who felt gender as a constant, conscious influence. She thought that this awareness was perhaps a result of her "wisdom as a lesbian," one who does not fit comfortably into traditional female models: "I think it plays into every dynamic of the theatre experience, which goes from the conception, to the creative team, to the rehearsal process, to the interpretation of the material, to the interaction with the audience. I think it affects everything. As a human being, I've become more politically and socially

Opposite: Roberta Levitow (left) with actors (from left) Ebbe Roe Smith, Barry Sherman, and Elizabeth Ruscio on the set of Marlane Meyer's *Moe's Lucky Seven* at the Mark Taper Forum Lab '91 New Work Festival (1991). Photo by Robert Hummer.

enlightened every day, but unquestionably the most profound influence in my life is my womanhood, and it comes into play in everything, whether it's a question of politics or race or gender or money or whatever. There is definitely a core there about being a woman in the theatre."

The awareness of being a woman in the theatre was also a strong influence on Tori Haring-Smith, one of the few directors who identified gender as the most significant influence on her work during our interview. She thinks this is particularly a result of the ongoing but subtle resistance she continues to encounter: "I think gender is clearly the biggest influence on me as an artist by far. The professional theatre world is so male that I feel like I'm constantly hanging onto my identity. There are other things that have influenced me, but they're not as pervasive or oppressive, so that's why gender is the major influence."

IGNORING GENDER

Why the Choice Is Made

Some of the women I spoke with seem to feel almost guilty that they don't think about gender more often, although they are now beginning to question why gender is not more of an influence on their process and to be aware that it may be a field of inquiry worth opening now that they have achieved positions of success. Timothy Near wonders whether her lack of gender awareness might serve as a protection for a woman in her position:

> These kinds of questions always come as a bit of a surprise to me, and my response is odd to me because certainly I was in the middle of the feminist movement. I was in my thirties during the "feminist seventies." My sister was and still is a feminist leader. I read the books, I listened to the music, I felt influenced. But as we moved into the eighties I let a lot of it go—I rarely think about gender differences in my daily life, in my workplace. I hear women blaming or giving credit to the difficulties and successes of their directorial work. I don't do that. I don't really think about it that much. I'm always a little embarrassed about that, but maybe I'd rather forget that gender differences exist—just let it go and do my work. I'm afraid if I dwell on it too much I will start to doubt what I'm doing or question myself in a negative way.

Liz Huddle also speaks of ignoring gender in order to achieve success in a male-dominated field. She has only recently become more aware of the positive aspects of gender as well as its emerging possibilities for her as a director: "I don't mean to sidestep the issue of gender. It's only because I think one of the reasons I have succeeded very well within the world that I've been in is because I've ignored it to a very great degree. Consequently, there is very little in me that is defensive. That's good and bad in that there are issues there that probably do need to be dealt with, or at least I should be more aware within myself. But I create fairly unconsciously, or have for many years, and am only now beginning to really bring it to consciousness and codify what happens within my process."

Anne Bogart discusses the potential negatives in ignoring gender for career reasons, pointing out that the ultimate result of that choice may be working like everyone else, which means mostly men, thereby not exploring one's unique and true artistic identity to the fullest:

> Women in the theatre world are confronted with two possibilities, to work from their gender, or to work from the traditional male methodology of making theatre. A lot of women choose the second for career reasons, whether it's conscious or subconscious. I won't name names, but there are women who have pretty fabulous careers because they have made a certain decision in their life that is survival oriented—to work like a man, not in the way I think they really are. I know these people, and they're not that way. They've made the decision, and I think it's a shame. There's always the corporate ladder out there, but what's your own ladder? I think that unless women are more true to themselves, which might help our field, then we're missing out on a lot.

The difficulty is, of course, discerning when one is being true to oneself, finding one's own voice, rather than simply imitating the work of others. The issue is doubly difficult because many young directors tend to look up to and model themselves after inspirational role models and mentors, many of whom are men.

Working Like a Man

The issue of seeming to "work like a man" in order to gain reputation and respect is a complicated one for the woman director. Several of the women can recall those words being directed at them and their work in a supposedly complimentary fashion, yet their responses are not always enthusiastic. Zelda Fichandler recounts two separate instances, the first early in her career: "I don't know whether there are different ways of thinking, I have no idea about that, but a famous director once said to me, 'You think like a man,' as the highest form of compliment. 'You think like a man, your mind has muscle.' I was 25 or so, and I think I said, 'Thank you, yours has, too.'" She goes on to describe a second, later incident during a tour to Russia: "One of the leading Russian directors said, 'Those crowd scenes look like they were directed by a man.' He said my work was very good, which I took to be four stars plus from him. He said that the organization and vigor of the crowd scenes made him think it was directed by a man." When asked if she took these comparisons to be complimentary, she replies in a way that conjures up some of the stereotypical male/female differences which are so difficult to avoid: "If they mean you think assertively and logically and clearly and effectively, if that's what they think male thought is, you can be complimented, but it's very sexist. It says women can't think except as a man, as a male attribute. Of course, when we work in the theatre, we're working with men who may have strong 'female' characteristics." This last sentiment, about gender boundaries in the theatre being less clearly defined, was repeated in several different contexts by a number of the directors.

Emily Mann expresses some ambivalence about how gender might manifest in her work and has experienced critiques of her work similar to those experienced by Fichandler. She seems to find the idea puzzling, having some difficulty knowing whether to be flattered or offended:

> I don't know how to answer the question how being female has affected my work because I do think that great directing means that you're coming from where you live inside. You have a vision, a heart and a soul, and that's why you're doing the work you're doing. It is impossible to work personally if you're not taking your own sexuality into account. Now, whether a man is using the more female side of himself, or a woman is using the more male side of herself, I don't know. But I don't think I could ever separate myself from being female. So I can't tell you if it does affect me, or if I were a man what would be different. I haven't experienced it. I'm sure I would be very different as a man. I would have experienced the world differently, but I don't know whether the source points from which I work would be different. One of the funniest statements ever said to me was by a rather eminent man of the theatre down in Louisville when *Execution of Justice* opened. He said, "I love this play. You think like a man." Now where do you begin with a statement like that? I remember being just dumbfounded. What do you say? Thank you? No words came.

Seret Scott is equally ambivalent about critics who have described her work as showing a male perspective; she believes that she is simply trying to do the best job possible: "I don't know that I'm doing things any differently than anyone else. I have been told that a lot of the results I get are from a male perspective. I don't know how to take that because a lot of the times the critics are saying it. They mean it as a compliment, which is really strange to me. It's not so much that I direct from a male perspective or in a male way. There are things that I want to say that are specific to the material. I'm not going to compromise it for myself. I'm going to go for it the best way I can to get what I want."

Roberta Levitow has had a similar experience, but in an unexpected and puzzling context because the person making the comment was also female, showing how easy it is for anyone to accept these supposed differences as normal and as some kind of value judgment: "When I did *Etta Jenks*, in New York at the Women's Project, Julia Miles came up afterwards and she said, 'Roberta, Roberta, people are talking about the work. They like it so much, they say you direct like a man.' I knew she meant it as a compliment. I knew they had meant it as a compliment. I guess it was a compliment in their terms.

For a long time, ever since that happened, I've thought, 'What did they mean by that?'"

Many of these difficulties come down to the fact that theatrical aesthetics have been naturalized as neutral and objective during a time when the field has been dominated by men. Therefore, "working like a man" can simply mean meeting the accepted standards. Working in new or uproven ways can be damaging to anyone's career, whether male or female, hence the temptation to work like everybody else in order to achieve success in the field.

No Easy Answers

Only One of Many Influences

More than half of the women interviewed say they do not think about gender at all while working. They are by no means in agreement, however, about how any subconscious gender influences or issues might manifest in their process, and most have no easy answers to offer. Patricia Blem feels certain of gender's influence but is equally certain it is not consciously brought to bear when she works: "I'm not sure that in any overt way I'm conscious that gender plays a part in my work. However, I believe that because I am female, and because I do think in certain ways, that, yes, it does. I never consciously make decisions based on those things, but I'm sure that it's influencing me the entire time." While she does not deny the possibility of gender influence, Zelda Fichandler speaks in broader terms about how the work reveals the person behind it, with gender being only one of the elements involved. She also believes this influence to be one that is not conscious and thus difficult to define:

> I think that the persona of a human being is revealed in the directorial work that they do, deeply revealed. I know that when I look at my work, I really know who I am. In the moment-to-moment process of the work, I don't know that's happening, but the choices that I make for how characters behave, the physical life of the actors, the intensity of the relationships, and the way I incline to show the cultural surround of the play infects every moment of living and every detail of the production. All of this shows me what I'm interested in, how I think relationships are affected, what I consider to be important in living out situations and making choices and dealing with either the success of the choices or the failure. It's very revelatory.

Although very aware of the various theoretical positionalities, Liz Diamond agrees that the influence of gender during the work itself is not conscious, saying, "I don't think about gender when I'm directing a show—there's too much to do." Michelle Blackmon reflects on the same issue by using the example of a recent directing project with an all-male cast in a play about experiences in the army. As a black woman, she was selected for the job because of her race (and, presumably, her skills), not her gender. She insists that gender considerations played very little part in her work process during rehearsals, although she did find herself wondering about potential effects prior to beginning the rehearsals:

> While I'm in the middle of the process, gender is not something that's on my mind at all. I don't deal with the process of directing a piece by thinking, "Oh, I'm a woman and how does that affect the piece?" But that's not to say that I don't ever think about it. When I was going into *Soldier's Play*, I thought, "Gee, I wonder how these guys are going to deal with me?" But once we got into the process, I totally put that away. I just said, "This is a piece like any other I've directed and we're going to jump in there and do it." In any of the work that I do, I don't think about it in terms of being a woman. Everything you do influences you and being a woman, I act in certain ways, I move in certain ways, I communicate in certain ways, so I know that it's a factor. But I don't deal with it in the sense that, "Okay, I'm a woman so I'm going to be different than if a man were directing you."

Although most of these women don't think about gender when working, they do generally acknowledge it as a potentially significant factor in their working process. There are some women I talked to, however, who for the most part did not seem to want to acknowledge gender as a significant artistic influence at all, even if they did occasionally admit to certain ways they thought being a woman might make parts of their process different. In her desire to eliminate gender considerations from the directing process altogether, Fontaine Syer exemplifies the liberal feminist position that more radical theorists and practitioners find dangerous to feminism. Syer knows just where she stands with these feminists: "I think the best thing for anybody to do is to do good work and for all of us to stop thinking of ourselves as women directors because I guarantee you men don't think of themselves as men directors. We just need to do our work well and get on with it. This is why I was never what you would call a bright light in the women's movement. I believe if you put your mind on something, you'll accomplish what you want. It doesn't always work but it's a starting point."

Barbara Ann Teer is adamant that gender is not a factor in her work. She identifies creative work as "feminine" in nature, however, so she seems to presume that the kind of work she does is already gendered in its essence. Although she does not identify herself as a feminist, this belief places her in agreement with the position of radical or cultural feminism:

> I don't contemplate gender ever. It's a luxury question, in my opinion. It's an intellectual process that I would go through to get to some kind of answer, so I'm not inclined to have an answer for how gender affects or doesn't affect my work. I would speculate that since the creative field is feminine in its energy, it would affect it in that way. Since the creative process comes through

a more feminine—or the right brain, or whatever one wants to call it—since it comes through that side, the context of everything I do is feminine and creative. So I am grateful that I'm feminine gendered or female, whatever that means. It affects my work spiritually.

Both of these women see identifying with gender issues as a limiting and potentially damaging factor in their careers and wish to avoid its influence whenever possible. They are clearly not alone in this feeling, but in their desire actively to reject gender as a consideration, they are the most outspoken.

Making Art versus Making a Career

Like Syer and Teer in their different ways, Maria Irene Fornes also believes gender should not be a significant influence while working. She seems to connect an awarenesses of gender and power dynamics with commercial and business success in the theatre, whereas she sees the artistic process itself as completely different. She does, however, like several of the women cited earlier, acknowledge the possibilty of an awareness of gender issues after the fact, contrasting this retrospective awareness with the creative impulse of the moment, an impulse which she sees as obliterating all other considerations: "There are two kinds of awareness. There is awareness as I'm working, and awareness if you ask me and I can think of it. I'm aware when the question comes up, although I don't think about it at the time. When I work, when I'm directing, not only am I not aware of my gender, I'm not even aware of myself. I'm so concentrated on what's happening onstage." This kind of complete concentration on the work gives Fornes a sense of enormous power, but a power she doesn't give much thought to because it comes to her as naturally as breathing:

> MIF: I don't see directing a play as a job, you see? I think if it were a job, I'd feel, "Oh, I'm now the boss and I'd better maintain my position as a boss." I don't see it as a job, but I see it as a position of my own right. I don't see directing theatre as a career. If I did, I think maybe I would have some problems because in positions of authority I am a coward. I'm not at all strong.
>
> RD: From what I've seen of your work, in the position of authority as director, you certainly don't seem to be a coward.
>
> MIF: The difference is that I think writing a play or directing a play is like a dream you are having, a fantasy you are having. I don't see myself as having a power in my fantasies or in my dreams because the power is so total, so assumed. I have no power because I have total power.

Fornes goes on to deliver a strong critique of artists who play at power politics in order to get ahead in their careers rather than concentrating on the artistic work at hand:

The sooner that a writer or a theatre director can give up the idea of career, the faster they will be able to have a career. As long as you do your work, but you relate your work with getting in there—to convincing people that it should be done, or acting in a manner that will make them think, "Oh, this sounds like a good play," because of the way you are—you are not an artist. Even if it works once, it doesn't work all the time, you know? It is totally a waste of time. You have to concentrate on the work and the pleasure of the work. You do one play, then you get down to another play and enjoy the work. Your relationship has to be with the work, and the rest, if it's good, will follow. If the work isn't good, what does it matter whether you wore the right outfit and you spoke in the right manner, whether it got done in one theatre? It's not going to get you through life. Don't waste the time on it. I see theatre as an art, you know, but if you want to be a professional then, of course, you know better than me what you have to do—what clothes to wear, how to appear, how to turn your mind around so that you can sound right. But I would say if you want that, why get into theatre? Theatre is not a good business, you know? It fails all the time. If you want to be a business person, go into business. If you want to be an artist, then you should listen to me.

The differentiation Fornes makes between the business of theatre and the creative work of theatre and the possible existence of gender issues within those two concerns is not uncommon among the respondents. Melia Bensussen is quite specific about her views on this issue:

There's making art versus making a career, and whereas in the making of art I'm not sure what a gender choice is, in the making of a career it's viciously apparent to me. There were all these given assumptions that I began with as to what kind of director I am and what kind of work I do. I think a lot of those were gender-based. I find the longer I spend doing what I do, the more it becomes about changing those things, adapting, growing and shedding my preconceptions. As I shed the preconceptions, I feel like I am freer to use my gender, which is to say myself, as an artist and as a director. I think where the gender differences affect us most now are less in the building of the art and more in the building of a career.

Like Fornes and Bensussen, many women I spoke with see the two elements of business and creativity as strongly connected throughout the directing process, which often combines both the business and artistic functions on a single production. In fact, the majority of them are clearly quite conscious of many issues of gender in the business aspects of theatre, but are not nearly so aware of gender in terms of their artistic work.

Summary

As the reader can see, the directors' initial perceptions of gender's influence on their artistic work are varied and complex, encompassing a continuum of responses from a constant, conscious awareness to no influence at all; hence the perception of gender as both everything and nothing in relation to the role of the director. The majority clearly see some gender influences, although they often wish they did not have to acknowledge their existence because those influences seem to imply various kinds of limitations. They simply want to be good directors, not good "women" directors.

4. LEADERSHIP QUALITIES IN A GOOD DIRECTOR

While the degree of emphasis differs, most theorists, educators, and practitioners consider leadership to be an integral part of the directing process, and the most often acknowledged quality of a good director is leadership ability. It is referred to directly or indirectly in almost everything that is written about the field, and in the early twentieth century, directors were particularly strong in their advocacy of artistic leadership and power because the profession was in the process of defining itself with vehemence and vigor. References to leadership ability are prominent in the interview responses, but it seems many women directors are trying to redefine the ways in which they assume artistic leadership as well as how others receive them in that position. Before we explore what effects the women directors perceive gender to have on their exercise of artistic authority, a brief look at what leadership means in the directing process is in order.

THE IMPORTANCE OF GOOD LEADERSHIP

Early Theorists Set the Framework

The influential early theorists sometimes had different ways of articulating their ideas on leadership, but taken together, these ideas created a clear and cohesive picture of an authoritarian leader who controlled and guided the artistic vision—a leader who was always referred to as male. Vladimir Nemirovich-Danchenko referred to the director as an all-powerful organizer who is "the real dominator of the production."[1] While situating the director's function as secondary to the dramatist in terms of interpretation, André Antoine clearly advocated the authority and leadership of the director.[2] This position was commonly held by most of the early directors, including Jacques

Copeau, whose work had an incredibly powerful influence on the succeeding generation of directors. His vision of the director was that of a man embodying both artistic and moral authority.[3] Alexander Tairov advocated the voluntary subjugation of the actor to the director and employed the stereotypically masculine metaphor of the director as "the helmsman of the theatre [who] pilots the ship of the theatrical production, avoiding shoals and reefs, surmounting unexpected obstacles, wrestling with storms and gales, unfurling and trimming the sails, and all the time guiding the ship toward predetermined creative goals."[4] Gordon Craig seems to have taken the notion to its furthest extreme with his passionate identification of the director as the supreme artist of the theatre, stressing complete obedience to his will and vision and relegating the actor to little more than the director's puppet. To further emphasize the image of authority, Craig also used the metaphor of the theatre as a ship and the director as its captain.[5] As directors began to claim a strong authorial function in their work, this kind of directors' theatre ultimately resulted in the creative contribution and authority of the director being seen as equivalent to or greater than that of the author. Hence the notion of the all-powerful auteur director developed.

Contemporary Directing Texts
Emphasize Leadership Qualities

In contemporary teaching texts about directing, the imagery of the power and authority of the director continues. Thankfully, the imagery is now starting to be presented occasionally with the feminine pronoun or gender-neutral language. Robert Cohen puts a strong emphasis on the power and leadership abilities of a director. He begins his text by stating: "the most important single directorial quality is leadership. The director must initiate, must organize, must arbitrate, and should be able, as well, to command, induce and inspire. These are the absolute minimal demands of directing."[6] Robert Benedetti, though not as direct and emphatic as Cohen, seems to take for granted the authoritative role, referring in his text to the director's "executive capacity."[7] This guidance of the process consists of structuring the ensemble and focusing the production team through the use of priorities, goals, and explorations. These activities all lead to a production concept by aligning the efforts of the team so that all individual work contributes to the group purpose. It involves editing and adjusting the individual efforts to produce a single whole with its own integrity through what Benedetti calls "quiet authority," which he defines as a special blend of openness and firmness.[8]

Like Benedetti, R. H. O'Neill and N. M. Boretz presume the importance of the leadership role by devoting two chapters to the function of director as manager and administrator. They emphasize that the director must lead by example, using high standards and discipline coupled with enthusiasm and effective communication. They introduce their section on the qualities of a good manager with the words of Zelda Fichandler:

> There has to be one leading perception in the creating of a production. And in the modern age that perception has commonly fallen to the person called a "director." It's a case of subtle recognition by all that the director has the roadmap. And that only works if the director convinces her team. The director does this by a kind of proselytizing, by artistic leadership, by exciting people by her belief or insight that this is a thrilling route to go. Then everybody's creativity, instead of being squashed, will be released to enliven and enrich the journey. There is creative interchange, but someone has to be the guide so that a seamless experience occurs for the audience where everything fits together as if by some law of inevitability.[9]

Francis Hodge puts more emphasis on communication than executive or managerial qualities but refers to the director as the communicator-leader as well as master craftsman and total designer of a production. Hodge believes a good director should be a strong leader but cautions against the misuse of leadership and authority even while advocating them as necessary to the directing function:

> A director communicates when he is a natural leader who knows how to work with, and not at, other human beings. ... Appropriately used, strength is not dictatorship but an honest expression of opinion that can be supported and opened to discussion without generating fear and insecurity. The dictator-director is the director who is very unsure of his ground, which actors will quickly detect, and though as people they may try to be very cooperative, they will find his leadership hard to accept. There must always be a certain amount of the salesman in the director because he must get across his ideas; yet, it is the soft sell, not the hard one, that will keep him on top of a situation.[10]

Alexander Dean and Lawrence Carra seem to place the least direct emphasis on issues of leadership, concentrating their text primarily on the pragmatic elements of composition and physical staging. Their approach to the use of these elements acknowledges, however, the authority of the director and the need for leadership in the process of stage composition. "[F]rom all the opinions and evidence presented, including those of the playwright, directors must make up their individual minds and take a stand. ... [T]he creative process cannot work on indecisiveness. Somehow, right or wrong, a stand must be taken."[11] While putting varying degrees of emphasis on the importance of leadership in their own work, the women directors interviewed often raised their experiences with issues of leadership and how they believe gender might be an influence on their directing process as a part of their initial response to the open-ended question, clearly indicating that it was prominent in their minds as an issue strongly related to gender.

THE POWER OF THE DIRECTOR

Directing as a Means to More Artistic Control

In a lecture delivered to college theatre students in Portland, Oregon, in 1992, JoAnne Akalaitis, then artistic director of the Public Theater in New York and one of the most well-known directors of either gender in the United States, talked about her reasons for becoming a director. "As an actor I felt humiliated by the directors. I didn't have enough power and I felt like I was not being treated like an artist. So I became a director, and as soon as I became a director I realized that there was simply nothing like it, that what I had been heading for all these years was I wanted the power. I wanted the power and I wanted the responsibility." When asked on the phone to expand this thought to include her perceptions of the influence of gender on this position of power, Akalaitis explains: "I feel very comfortable with power, and I find that women in power feel comfortable with power. I see it. I don't see them being uncomfortable with it at all. I'm glad I'm a woman. The burden of being a man is so much more taxing. In a way, women are a lot freer. They've never had power, so they can be very uncensored in their behavior, in how they use it, if they're smart." She goes on to impart how she had initially been told when taking over the Public Theater that the board of directors would probably never come to the theatre for meetings because it was too complicated. It made more sense to her, however, that they should come to the place where the artistic work was done. "It may have been womanly of me, but I said they should come to where we work. And they did. It was because I didn't know any better that I could say they should come here." Akalaitis has since been removed as the head of that theatre and replaced by a man so it is possible to speculate that this uncensored power behavior might have had something to do with that dismissal. In fact, in a magazine interview some months after her dismissal, Akalaitis said as much by explaining that she believed her experience had been "disturbing and demoralizing to the theatre community in general. It sent a signal about what happens to women who assume too much power."[12].

Like Akalaitis, several other women went into directing because of dissatisfaction with the treatment or quality of direction they were getting as actors. Alana Byington is very aware of a need for more power in her decision to move from acting into the more satisfying work of directing. She cautiously identifies a possible gender behavior in that situation: "I think one of the reasons I became a director is because I don't like that feeling of having so little power over my life. To me, that would be my masculine side, and I always have to qualify that by saying those are very arbitrary distinctions that we've made between masculine and feminine."

Although she does not refer directly to any dissatisfaction as an actor, Susan Finque identifies leadership and power as socially valorized attributes of masculine behavior, once again referring to the arbitrary nature of the definition:

> SF: My masculine energy comes in handy when I'm at a production meeting, when I'm trying to deal with schedule, when I'm trying to get what I want, when I'm trying to deal with someone who's telling me "No." By that I mean masculine energy is equivalent to assertiveness, aggressiveness, invasiveness, being demanding, taking up a lot of space. I don't necessarily think that those are masculine attributes, but we have to do something, to say yin and yang somewhere.
>
> RD: And we are socialized to accept those as so-called male behaviors, masculine behaviors?
>
> SF: That's right. In that respect that stuff comes in handy when I want to get money, when I want people to listen to me, when I want to get what I want, when I want to create a spirit of leadership. I do find that it has been important in my work to take leadership.

Although the women directors often express dissatisfaction with these artbitrary distinctions between masculine and feminine behavior, the accepted dualities still seem to provide many women the easiest, most useful framework for their discussion of leadership issues.

Shared Power and Getting the Job Done

While Finque and Byington identify their power as a more masculine attribute, Julianne Boyd believes women have their own way of wielding power during the rehearsal process that is quite different from the images usually associated with masculine power: "I think, perhaps, power plays aren't as important as getting the job done. You don't come in and claim your turf. You come in and say, 'There's a job to do, let's get it done.' I think women often search for the answer. Men often state who they are and what they hope to accomplish before they think about the answer. Women come in a little more open." Even with her sense of openness, Boyd always comes into her rehearsals knowing what she wants to accomplish. This gives her the ability to exercise more authority if she deems it necessary.

Patricia Blem holds a similar belief. She brings up the familiar metaphor of the ship and its captain to describe her feeling about the power of the director, but with a different slant from Tairov or Craig. She puts more emphasis on the shared power of the group than on her autonomous authority, but she shows no ambivalence about using that authority if the group process isn't taking the show in the direction she believes it should go. She does, however, identify this use of power as a learned behavior:

> It's like I'm at the helm of a ship and everybody has their input. I'm only steer-
> ing it, but everybody else is the ship, and so everybody's strength is some-
> where in that place, and I just decide what course we will take. However, I
> am very strong, and when I feel that somebody is definitely misguided and
> going in a direction that I don't think is right for the play, I will steer them
> back. Then, if it gets to the point where they don't respond to subtle guid-
> ance, I'll use my power. I'll say, "Just do it. You have to do it." I've learned to
> do that. As I've grown as a director, I've become more confident in doing so.
> I guess that's the stronger in me saying, "It's time to do what I say. It is my
> way. I am the director."

Many of the women have learned to utilize their power as directors, but
like Boyd, they don't believe they accord power the same importance a man
might. In a recent article about women directors who have worked on Broadway, the author notes that these women hold the common belief that "they
are perceived as less power-hungry, competitive, egotistical, and manipulative than their male counterparts."[13] This sense of using one's power differently
will be addressed more fully as the women talk about their ways of collaborating in Part Three.

Embracing the Power

Liz Diamond is definitely one of the directors who cheerfully and easily embraces the role of leader, emphasizing its importance in directing. She
also embraces the idea of sharing responsibility as another equally important
aspect of good directing, although she does not attribute it solely to gender:

> I love the leadership of directing. I think directors are, by definition, control
> freaks, power mongers. It is a kind of Wagnerian impulse that causes one to
> direct. Because after all, you're responsible for this totality. I completely
> embrace that. I want to see my ideas, my visions up on stage. I want to test
> my reading of a text against that of my collaborators. I really want that pas-
> sionate debate, that aesthetic and intellectual bout. I would be loathe to assert
> that my collaborative style—which is open—is linked to gender. I am not pre-
> pared to do that because I think that it's anecdotal and totally historically con-
> tingent. So the fact that I love getting in a room with a bunch of actors and
> engaging them so much in the process that they feel a shared responsibility
> for the whole creation, I think that's good directing. I cannot believe that male
> directors cannot do the same thing. Strong leadership is essential, and actors
> must know that you are prepared to say "Yes" or to say "No" at any given point,
> so they know that there's someone who is prepared to take final responsibil-
> ity for the work.

In spite of never feeling competitive or power hungry, Penny Metropulos believes: "Women who go into directing are probably very strong willed.
It's a trait you have to have. I think you have to believe enough in what you
want to say that you're not going to be thrown up against the wall too often."

Like Metropulos, several of the women who seem quite comfortable in the exercise of their personal power credit their privileged and supportive background. For them, being a woman was never perceived to be an obstacle in getting an education or making career choices. Their first encounter with gender resistance had been after leaving the confines of the family and after their personalities had been strongly formed. Occasionally women might refer to being a tomboy or being given a boy's treatment and privilege when young, but more often they would refer to parents with strong humanist values. One good example is Timothy Near, who although she was given a boy's name, was treated like a princess throughout her childhood, but a princess who was also given a strong sense of social responsibility and egalitarian values:

> TN: I was treated like a girl, with romance and dresses and curls. So I'm not quite sure how I got here, because I think that to move into this kind of position of power you have to have had more things going for you than what typical 1950s girls were given.
>
> RD: It takes an awareness of your own power to run a theatre.
>
> TN: Yes, and a kind of courage so that even when some of your decisions could take everybody right down the hill with you, you make them anyway because you must follow your heart. Somewhere that came. I think it probably came from my parents' belief that people are people. My parents gave great respect to human beings, and people were people, of all races and cultures and sexes.

Maria Irene Fornes views the director as an all-powerful figure with an objective eye who provides artistic leadership for the entire production, although some might see the viewpoint of a director who is often the playwright as hardly an objective one. Fornes uses the metaphor of a boxer and his trainer to illuminate her point, explaining that although it is the boxer who will fight, the trainer is deeply involved with the boxer's performance, watching from an outside point of view to be able to give hints on strategy, and thus becoming indispensable to the boxer's success. Fornes clearly sees no difficulty in assuming power in her own artistic process, and when asked about the perceptions of others regarding her personal presentation of this power, she doesn't seem to care how they receive a woman in authority:

> I don't care very much. I mean, it isn't that I think about it, and then I think, "Oh, I don't care." I simply don't think about it very much in my work. I want to stress that because I think the main way a person can become liberated from other people's prejudices and preconceptions is not to take on certain attitudes that can be damaging to the individual. It may work, but I think it's very damaging. The way you can become powerful and not have damage is to have such a direct relationship to what you are doing that you are really oblivious to people seeing you one way or another. In a way, if you're obsessed, and the work is good, it doesn't matter. I don't think that people see me as a woman, or as anything, until they do. When it happens, I'm able to say, "Oh,

he expects me to be wrong about this because he doesn't think that women usually can do this." As much as you see me in rehearsal behaving in a manner of total authority, I am sure, although I am not conscious of it, but I am sure that there is not one gesture, one moment when a person could identify my authority. Let's say if a person were looking at a video tape, and there's no sound, and you would say, "Who here is the director?" They would look and say, "I don't think the director has come in yet." Because I would be like this [demonstrates a closed posture, very withdrawn into herself]. It isn't that I am watching how I behave, but I know the way I dress, the way I act, I know that I'm totally careless; I don't care. I don't think it's important.

My own observation of Fornes in rehearsal is somewhat contradictory to her belief that unless people can hear her talking, they will not perceive her authority. Perhaps it is because the actors already understood and acknowledged her authority and position, but I believe a careful observer would be able to tell who was the director. It was made especially obvious by the way actors waited with their focus on her throughout long periods of silence or inaction while she was evaluating or working through a script change. In a discussion where she was explaining a change or giving a note to an actor, even when many were participating in the discussion, she had a strong, animated presentation of leadership, and actors responded directly to it. What is occasionally true is that her conversation is circular, not always direct, and there are sometimes long pauses while she works something out in her head. Listening to an audio tape of the rehearsal one might, in fact, think she is not communicating authoritatively. Furthermore, her physical appearance is quite unassuming, especially when she is not focused on the work. I believe, however, that Fornes presents much more authority than she gives herself credit for. Perhaps this is because of her sense of having total power without thinking at all about power. She definitely takes it for granted when she is focused on her work.

Personal Presentation and Power Issues

A number of the directors believe that the theatre is a privileged place, a rarified atmosphere where artists are more flexible, more liberal in their thinking, especially in their ability to keep gender-based expectations to a minimum. Whatever resistance might be met, Liz Diamond believes it is significantly less than one might encounter in, say, an accounting firm. At the opposite viewpoint is Pamela Hendrick, whose experiences have left her to conclude that some business firms, especially those working with newer styles of management and conflict resolution, are actually more progressive regarding gender expectations than some theatres she has worked in: "More and more, men and women are turning in the theatre to the collaborative model, as they are in business. In fact, sometimes it surprises me because I think the business world at its most progressive, even though it's set up as this paradigm of masculinity, is much further ahead in terms of embracing the collaborative models than the theatre world is."

As an artistic director, Timothy Near is aware of the power interaction with her board of directors and brings physical appearance more specifically into the dynamic, comparing it to appearances in the rehearsal hall:

> TN: When I'm in the rehearsal hall, I wear the most comfortable clothes I have. When I'm meeting with the board I try to dress more like them. Most of my board are business executives—men and women. I find that uniformity of dress is helpful for communication. If I were a man, I don't think I would worry about this, but being a woman and an artist can lead the board members to feel protective of me and that is nice, but not necessarily good. So I do what they do—wear "business attire" so we can talk business and it works.
>
> RD: It sounds like you're aware of playing a much more gendered role in that process than in the artistic process.
>
> TN: I don't feel clothes matter in the rehearsal hall. If there is gender awareness there, it has less to do with appearance and more to do with past experience.

Although appearance is a large part of personal presentation, there are other factors in operation as well, including the manner in which a woman assumes her power. While being one of those who believe that artistic creativity is a genderless process, Sharon Ott sees gender as having an enormous impact on certain more external elements of the directing process. First, she discusses the way gender can have an impact in the area of personal presentation and issues of sexuality and power in appearance: "It's especially hard for a woman such as myself, a woman who actually has what would be classified as a conventionally good-looking presentation that perhaps is more overtly sexual than Margaret Thatcher. I think the only women who often have made it to those positions get de-sexualized. A sexually attractive woman in power is not something that society is comfortable with yet." Ott goes on to explore the expectations involved with how others conceive of women in positions of authority: "Unlike the fact I don't think gender plays much of a role in internal choices, I think it plays a huge role in external events, on every level. I do think that there is still an issue of how to conceive of women in authority positions. In a traditional director relationship, there's often a patriarchal feeling of 'Oh, Daddy, am I doing it right?' But it's different with a woman. The whole basis changes, and the only kind of authority figure that people can readily ascribe is mother, and that's a different set of issues."

As our discussion continues, Ott also alludes to problems that might be encountered by women who are more soft, subdued, and feminine in their personal presentation than she is, having grown up as an extroverted and "bossy" kid, who was a tomboy before blossoming into a prom queen. When

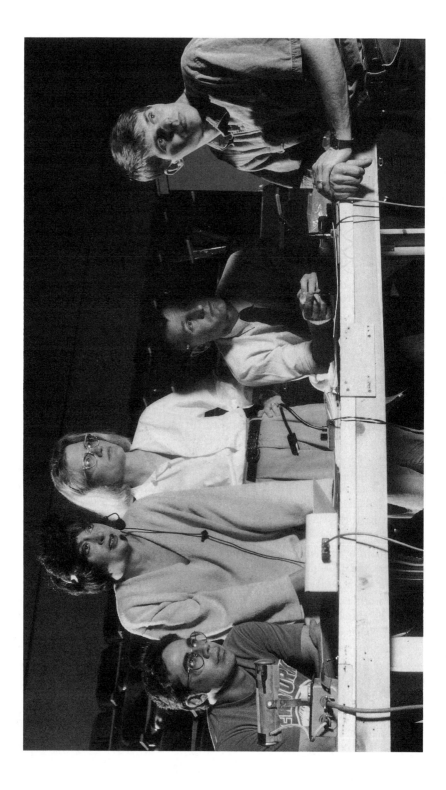

asked how she thought others perceived her as a leader, Ott astutely evaluates her image as well as her own learning process while discovering the uses of power, emphasizing that this is something she was not encouraged to think about while growing up:

> I think part of me learning to be in a position of power and authority has been me learning how to deal with something that I was not trained to deal with. I'm certain that I've come some distance. If you asked people for their impression of me five years ago, it might be different than now. I think some of that is based on the fact that I've learned things, that it really was new to me. I still make mistakes, but probably I made more as I was beginning to be in a position of authority. I know some of them were because I didn't understand the nature of authority; it wasn't something I was brought up to understand. I didn't think it existed, and my first impulse was, "I'm not your boss, I'm your friend." It took me a while to understand that I had to be the boss. There are certain things you can and can't do. Familiar, easy behavior is possible, but you have a responsibility. I actually know this from some other women in similar positions, that sometimes what's perceived as cruel behavior from women is because of that lack of awareness. It's not because women are being cruel or offhand, it's because they're not really aware enough of authority, because they're not accustomed to it. I've had to become astute to the nature of having some sort of power over other people's lives because I really was not brought up that way. I was brought up as this prom queen and never assumed I would have power over anybody's life.

As Ott struggled with understanding and accepting her power, it definitely influenced the ways others perceived her authority. In fact, in a recent magazine profile, Ott's unwillingness to match up to the usual kinds of gender stereotypes was identified as a factor that made her unpopular in some quarters when she first took over Berkeley Rep in the early 1980s.[14] It has been the experience of others besides Ott that the assumption of power, combined with a refusal to operate within the bounds of traditional gender expectations regarding personal presentation, can often lead to some kind of resistance, at least until a woman has been in a position of authority for some time, allowing others to get used to her particular style of leadership.

Regardless of the background that brought them to positions of artistic leadership and authority, a majority of the directors seem at ease with that power. They are quite aware, however, that others are not always as comfortable as they are. The reception by others of a woman in authority is a significant issue for almost all of the women interviewed. It is in the reception of their authority by others that most of the women feel the issues of power and gender manifest themselves.

Opposite: **Sharon Ott (second from left) with (from left) Anthony Taccone, associate artistic director, Kate Edmunds, scenic designer, and Michael Suenkel, stage manager, at a technical rehearsal for Noel Coward's** *Private Lives* **at the Berkeley Repertory Theatre (1993). Photo by Ken Friedman.**

RECEPTION OF WOMEN IN POSITIONS OF AUTHORITY

Perceptions of Others About Women in Power

Until women gain more experience in the leadership role, the perceptions of others often seem to be a more powerful influence than any internal factors. Melia Bensussen sees the way others perceive her as a woman to be a very strong influence in her reception as a director, even stronger in her case than ethnic identity because she believes it shapes and controls all other influences: "I am described more quickly as a woman director than I am as a Jewish director or a Hispanic director, I think. What I've noticed in my career is that if a white woman turns down the job, I'm offered it. I'm on what I would call a 'nice white girl director' list. Obviously that's a characteristic of mine that is compelling, so that when directors are replaced, or when I pass up a job and they go to someone, they usually go to a white woman. It's that network of people who are offered a similar pool of work, and I think gender is what connects us."

When asked to expand on how these gender expectations might play out in her work, surprisingly Bensussen answers from a position of insecurity regarding her style as a leader. She also contrasts male and female styles and expectations regarding the exercise of these styles as she understands them:

> Where my insecurity screams is that they're not going to take me as seriously. I feel like the women who are taken seriously, women who are succeeding more in mainstream theatre, have adopted—or it comes naturally to them—but I feel like they have adopted more male mannerisms. I guess there's a toughness, there's a bit of a coldness, a lack of emphasis on interpersonal relations. Those are not necessarily traits that come naturally to me in terms of how I live and how I work. I'm afraid it means that I'm not always taken seriously. An agent once said to me that he never trusted a director whom actors loved because if actors loved the director that meant that the director let them get away with too much. I don't think the agent's comment was gender specific at all, and yet I see that I quite value my collaborative relationships with actors and designers, and I value that people feel like they do their best and that they're collaborating with me. I think that gets interpreted in this male world as lack of leadership. I think these same things hurt male directors, too. So if you're a man or a woman director, but you go against this notion of what it is to be the leader, I think you suffer.

Susan Finque also implies problems she has experienced in a position of leadership, making a negative comparison between the reception of her own behavior and the reception of a man's exercise of the same power:

> They see me as a bitch. I think that to a great extent people find me forward, rude, demanding, loud, and there are other people who find me refreshingly honest, candid, immediate, Jewish, New York, a breath of fresh air in an otherwise

polite world. I don't make enemies. I'm a diplomat and a communicator, but I do think that I intimidate people, and I don't mean to. But unless there is some predefined relationship going on where we are finding out about each other—such as a collective work—I am going to go about the business of what I'm here to do on this planet. I have a way of going assertively about what it is I need to do and sometimes making people afraid of me. If I were a man, I'd probably be a big star on campus. Definitely. Because nothing can stop me. Basically I'm committed to the art, and I have great ideas and love to do it and will bend over backwards. But obviously, my femaleness, my lesbianness, my outspokenness are too much for people.

Finque also briefly refers to how people seemed to erase her artistic partnership with the other director at Alice B. Theatre, a gay male. While they shared decisions equally, she believes there was definitely a difference in the way the public saw them, generally relegating her to little more than his assistant by ignoring her. It clearly annoys her, but Finque refuses to be subverted from her purpose by worrying about it: "People always write letters to him; the press always refers to him. Whether it's because he's the male and I'm the female, or whether it's because he founded the theatre and I came on board eighteen months later, whether it's because we gave him the title founding artistic director and me associate artistic director, rather than co-artistic directors, I don't know. But obviously, at the root of it all is sexism. And, frankly, I don't have the time to be affected by other people's stupidity. I don't have interest in investing my time and energy into victimizing myself because somebody else is an idiot."

Tori Haring-Smith defines how her power is perceived as did Finque, by using the all-too familiar stereotypical language: "I think I'm perceived as a tough broad, in large part because procedural issues make me crazy, so I get very tough on designers being on time and schedules being adhered to. I have a very strong sense of compartmentalized roles even as I collaborate. I think you can collaborate from a clear sense of 'You do this and I do that,' and that makes me seem tougher than some people, male or female. I'm certainly perceived as a feminist—that crazy feminist director doing her thing again."

Michelle Blackmon also makes a comparison between male and female ways of being received when exercising one's power, especially where direct criticism is concerned:

I think I may approach things a little more male-oriented in that I don't shy away from anything, whether it be criticism or whatever. I have, on more than one occasion, had the misfortune of dealing with things that were difficult and I felt, "Well, I have to tell the truth. I have to let people know." It mostly comes out when people want to know what you thought about something— your criticism, your critique of their work. In this business it's very difficult. No one really ever wants to hear the truth. They want to hear what they want to hear, and being a woman, my sense of forthrightness isn't always appreciated. That's why I say I have a much more masculine approach. If I were a man saying those things, I don't think they would question it, not in the same way.

Unfortunately, this inevitable comparison between male and female exercise of power seems all too common among the women directors interviewed. It is heartening to note, however, that most of the women here, while having experienced this double standard at one time or another, seem to feel they have found strategies for overcoming these expectations or have simply been around long enough not to worry about them, to have outlasted the negative perceptions of a woman in power. The place where these resistances are seen to linger, however, is in the area of the commercial theatre or in some major regional theatres with much larger budgets.

Power, Gender, and Economics

The dynamics of power and gender are often perceived in the reactions to women in positions of authority, especially in relationship to a board of directors or when fundraising or other business and administrative concerns enter the process. Julianne Boyd sees the reception of women in authority as less of a behavioral issue and more of an economic one, especially in the commercial theatre or when big money is involved in a production: "Producers still worry, 'Should we invest all that money in a play directed by a woman?' That still exists and until producers can make money from women directors, women will still be second class." She did, however, insist that if you have a proven product, one that a producer wants (as she did with *Eubie!* in 1978 on Broadway), gender will have nothing to do with it. She once encountered a producer who believed that she might have problems as a woman handling the male stagehands, but the anticipated problem never materialized. In fact, in her ongoing awareness of gender reception and issues of leadership, one thing Boyd notes is that "Actors, particularly males, have come up to me during and after the rehearsal period and have gone out of their way to comment on what a good experience they had with a woman director. This happened much more often five years ago than now as more actors are working with women directors."

This dynamic between power and economics is also relevant for women who have been artistic directors at one time or another, which includes over half of the women interviewed. In the early 1970s, Zelda Fichandler told Fontaine Syer as the latter was starting her career that one way for a woman to get work as a director was to start her own theatre, but she added somewhat facetiously that she "wouldn't recommend that to a dog." When asked to elaborate on her advice to Syer, Fichandler makes it clear that her original motivation for starting a theatre was not to find work in the commercial theatre—although she knows some women in the same era who did—citing instead the desire and need to create a viable artistic home for herself. A number of the women interviewed here have done just that, including Syer herself, who describes the positive as well as the negative aspects of being a woman in the position of running a theatre:

> One of the reasons I no longer run a theatre in St. Louis is that as a community, the people who control the real power and the real money are not fond of bright women. They're threatened by them. I'm aware that in some ways, in the administrative work with boards of directors, fund raising, public relations, that it is very much to my advantage to be a woman, to be tall. I'm very often going to be the only woman at this presentation, which gives me more focus. It makes me stand out. But whether it helps in the long run is a different question. In general, I think it doesn't help. I think that if I had been a man running a theatre in St. Louis, we would have had our building long before we did.

Fichandler herself tells of a visit by some Broadway producers to her theatre in the early days of its existence. She describes their responses to a woman in the position of authority, indicating that she believes things would be different if that same visit took place today: "They came down to the Arena to see a new play. I had them in my office for coffee, and they said, 'Who runs this place?' I said, 'Well, I guess I do.' And they said, 'But I mean who *really* runs it, who makes the financial decisions and heads the institution and makes policy decisions and so forth?' And I said, 'Well, I guess I do!' They were a little bit nonplussed because it's a big building, because I was quiet and not particularly outrageous or dominant seeming, or whatever. But that was some twenty years ago. I don't think they'd feel that way now."

Brenda Hubbard expresses the problems she has experienced in being a woman in authority, especially as they relate to dealing with producers or a board of directors, primarily in the regional theatres. She also makes a comparison to how the same behavior would be perceived coming from a male in a similar position and similarly connects powerful behavior with masculine behavior. While her comments focus on the business side of theatre, these perceptions have a strong impact on Hubbard's sense of herself as an artistic figure of authority and on the loneliness she experiences as a result:

> I take myself and put myself into a kind of a hard-core business mode when I'm dealing with producers. Having been an artistic director in the position of being a producer, but also having dealt with producers when I was in that position, I would say that I tend to be more male in the way that I deal with money issues, and hiring issues, and things like that. I'm less diplomatic in those situations. I think that a lot of times because I'm a woman being very male in the way that I deal with those issues, I am perceived as being a ballbreaker, or difficult, or aggressive, unpleasant. While all of those things, those kinds of quality judgments, may have an element of truth in them, I think that when I watch men do the same things in the way they're negotiating and communicating and dealing with things, they don't have those value judgments

labeled on them. They are much more apt to be considered a real go-getter, someone who knows what he wants. When a man is aggressive, they say he's assertive. When a woman is aggressive, they say she's *aggressive* [and much more]. As a result, people have dealt mostly with men in positions of authority. I think when they deal with me in a businesslike way, there's a different kind of intimidation that goes on. I'm aware of it, and sometimes it's upsetting to me because it's not my intention to intimidate people. Other times, I very deliberately use it as a leverage tool because I know that if I come on mild-mannered and soft-spoken and feminine and polite, I'm not going to get what I want. I think the thing that happens as a result is that, having to be more male or masculine in the way that I communicate to get what I want, I then am going to have to suffer a certain amount of alienation from people as a result, which creates a certain level of loneliness in your work process, you know? When you first deal with that, it's sad and it's unpleasant and it makes you feel bad. I think over time, if you stick in the business, it's just one of those things you have to learn to accept. There are a lot of learned behaviors that women haven't learned yet about directing, and there are a lot of learned behaviors that society has not learned yet about accepting women in positions of authority. We don't have a whole lot of background to draw upon.

The ability to modulate her authoritative behavioral style according to the needs of the situation is another way a woman director plays out her complex role, and Hubbard has clearly identified the performative nature of the directing function as well as of gender. She was also one of the directors to assert clearly that it's not just women who need to learn new behaviors if women are going to be accepted in positions of power and authority.

Different Kinds of Challenges to a Woman's Leadership

Although many women in the study think they have no difficulty assuming the leadership role, some sense of challenge or resistance has been experienced by almost all of them at some point in their careers. Even some of those who have never experienced overt resistance cannot really be sure they haven't been the victim of more covert resistance, and several thought they might have been. Julie Taymor seems to be unique in regard to this question, however. She is the only one to insist that she believes it to be an advantage to be a strong woman working in a male-dominated field. Although she feels unclear about how gender works in her artistic vision, she is quite sure of how it plays out in the working dynamic. "I feel that being a strong woman has many attributes when working with men because there's no competition then between the men and there's no butting heads up against each other. There's no feeling that one male is going to overpower the other. There's no ego thing involved. If you're a strong woman, there's instant respect you get from the men." Others interviewed clearly feel that a strong woman, far from getting respect, is more likely to be seen as a threat.

Emily Mann finds her reception as a female artistic director has generally been very positive, but like the women cited in Chapter Three, she touches on the possibility that she may simply be ignoring the sources of any problems to do with gender:

> I'm very lucky and blessed here. I have an amazing, supportive board, staff, and audience. I think probably I was being tested quite hard in the beginning, but I don't know whether that has to do with gender. That's a tricky question because I probably in some ways do know, but I made a choice early on that I was not going to let that enter into my thinking. So in a way there is a kind of conscious denial going on. I decided early on that's their problem, and if I dealt with their problems, I would probably be so angry I couldn't work. For me, anger is a very crippling state to live in, and I start making decisions that I don't like out of anger. I actually don't want to know about it. If there were antifemale letters coming in, for example, the staff knows not to show them to me. It gets me too angry. I don't need to read every crank, crackpot, sexist, racist, conservative to reactionary letter that comes through here.

In the same article on women directors where Sharon Ott was featured, Mann brought up the point that a woman in a leadership position needs to be careful about her behavior in order not to threaten anyone. A woman artistic director will "have a harder transition to power, have to prove [her]self more, and [she] can't make as many mistakes."[15] This seems rather disheartening for those who aspire to more than simply leadership in a single production, but it was not an unfamiliar predicament among the women. Mann explores the differences between managing a production and managing a theatre. While reiterating some of Julie Boyd's points, she describes her general sense of comfort in the leadership role, along with the small ways she sees herself needing to modulate her style with producers or boards of directors, but not with artists:

> I've never had any problem with gender that I know of, in terms of actors, designers, or any of the artists that I've worked with and collaborated with. I have sensed it from producers where I have to be better at showing that I'm good at budget, good at taking control, making decisions. I think they worry about women being able to handle all that. I think it stands in the way of getting a job. I think it can stand in the way of being trusted with a [certain] size of show. That's been proven over and over again in my experience. But I haven't found that from the artists. If you're good, they listen. If you're giving them what they need to do their work at the top level, they listen, they're there.

Although Mann seems to have had no trouble, a number of the women shared their experiences of feeling that male designers sometimes talk down to women directors, presuming a lack of knowledge or experience in technical areas. The women who experienced this problem generally responded by getting through the difficult situation however they could. Then they often began requesting more cooperative designers in the future, and occasionally they developed a strong preference for working with female collaborators. This issue will be explored in more detail in Chapter Ten. Bea Kiyohara artic- ulates her perception of the way in which she believes woman are challenged at every level, but especially when it comes to the technical aspects of the- atre, and how she sometimes responds to that challenge:

> BK: If you're not on the same wave length, sometimes the communication drives people crazy because men are much more specific; "What do you mean, that feel?" So if you can't articulate the visual through the emotional impact that you want to create, then I think that's hard. A hindrance, I think, is over-articulating something. I think sometimes we get a little defensive because in our directing we're always having to justify and explain why. I personally find myself getting defensive sometimes when I maybe don't need to do that.
>
> RD: Do you think that is because women are conditioned not to feel com- fortable about being assertive?
>
> BK: Absolutely. We're not used to it. Men make decisions and choices, and they don't have to explain. That's a creative choice; I mean, it's just under- stood. But I think women get challenged a lot more, at every level.

A number of women pointed out that as a director their relationship to the issues of leadership and resistances to it is constantly adjusting and chang- ing for a variety of reasons. Gloria Muzio discusses the changes she has expe- rienced through the years, indicating that she would have thought quite differently about this issue ten or fifteen years earlier:

> I think that's probably the single most thing that's changed about me in the last fifteen years I've been working. As a woman at the beginning of my career, I felt that the leadership was what was crucial. That was something I had to be clear about, that this was my production. Things felt different than they do to me now. That's partly because of how I've changed and partly because of how the business has changed. But I do remember feeling that I had to be a leader, I had to be strong, I had to be tough. And yet, as the years went by and I became more comfortable in my work, I also didn't want to lose what- ever it means to me to be a woman, to be feminine, to be "not a man." Except for very early in my career, I never felt compelled to do it the way the men do it, whatever our woman's perception is of what that means. I think I began feeling a little defensive about it. I was very young when I started, which had as much to do with it as being a woman. I felt I had a double whammy, of being a young woman, that I had to have a facade of not being a young woman, "I'm a little tougher than that, and you'll be surprised," that sort of thing. But as the years go by and as you become more comfortable, things are different.

Because most of the women I spoke with have had significant careers in directing prior to our conversations, they seem quite comfortable in the exer- cise of their creative power and executive authority, whether it has been learned or has come naturally to them. It would be interesting to talk to women directors early in their careers to see if this comfort and acceptance comes strictly from longevity or if women are being accepted more comfortably in the artistic leadership role in the 1990s. But no matter how comfortable one gets with one's own sense of leadership, as many of the women point out, there can still be problems in how others perceive and respond to that authority.

Summary

To this point, we have primarily discussed some of the ways a woman thinks she responds to being the leader of an artistic process, along with some of the ways others perceive her, including some subtle, covert forms of resistance or challenge. Five issues have been introduced in this discussion. The first is a general acknowledgement that leadership and authority are important to a director, but that women may sometimes approach these issues differently. Second, the personal presentation of a woman in a position of power can have an effect on how her authority is received. Third, although theatre is generally perceived by these directors to be more flexible in its gender expectations than some other fields, others still presume certain sometimes stereotypical and derogatory things about a woman in power, such as a presumed inability to take control when large budgets are at stake, or they respond negatively to a woman who can take control, especially when she uses behaviors that are recognized as expected and exemplary in a male authority figure. A fourth issue encompasses the different kinds of tests and challenges to a woman's authority that emerge, sometimes leading to conscious behavior modification on the part of the woman. Finally, it was acknowledged that as careers progress, these issues become less prominent. Although most believe there could have been a gender influence in their initial reception as leaders in the directing process, their reception is also presumed to have as much to do with early career suppositions and limitations as anything else. It is clear that fewer women have had the career longevity to overcome these resistances.

5. PROBLEMS WITH POWER

No matter how comfortable a woman becomes with her own sense of leadership or how she learns to modify her behavior to deal with subtle, covert forms of resistance, there can often be problems in how others receive her authority. Most of the problems come from situations where women feel a sense of challenge or discomfort because of gender expectations from others with whom they are working. Several point out that even in a profession where sexual stereotyping and overt discrimination are usually less prominent, one is still apt to hear people (generally, but not necessarily, males) occasionally wondering whether a woman is powerful enough to do the job of the director.

RESISTANCE TO WOMEN IN AUTHORITY

Lack of Familiarity with Women Directors

Some of the resistance to a woman in power may simply arise from a lack of familiarity with women in the director's position. Roberta Levitow believes that actors respond differently to women directors and that gender often becomes an issue to be discussed even if there is no overt resistance involved: "Actors will talk to me about it and say, 'You're the first, or the twelfth—no, seldom the twelfth—woman I've worked with.' They know the number of women they've worked with, and they have an opinion about it. 'I guess I have trouble working with women directors,' or 'I love working with women directors; this is my favorite, I prefer it.' But it's something we end up discussing at a certain point, which I find interesting."

Penny Metropulos recounts her experience with a similar situation in a theatre company with whom she had recently worked:

> There were several young apprentices in the company, playing supporting roles and taking master classes from the older actors. One of these classes was

a seminar on gender. I was asked to participate, as it seemed I was the first female director most of these young actors had ever worked with. I was interested to see if the men had preconceptions on hearing that a woman was going to direct a [Shakespeare] history. They were very honest, and their responses were varied, though each of them had, indeed, considered the prospect of working with a woman. Their responses included fearing a woman would not be tough enough to handle the political aspects of the play, being eager to work with a woman as their experiences with male directors had been so unsatisfactory, and believing that a woman could create a better balance (i.e., more humane) between the political and poetic aspects of the play. Almost all of them felt that my process-oriented approach was due to my being a woman. I tried to explain that this was a matter of personal style and that, although it may come from our feminine nature, it was not unique to women.

Although it can obviously be irritating to be constantly reminded of your gender while simply trying to do good work, if this kind of discussion is a director's most frequent experience of gender issues in the directing process, she should consider herself lucky. Unfortunately, most of the women I interviewed could describe vivid and sometimes frequent experiences of resistance.

Constantly Proving Herself

A number of the women, most especially those who are in the early years of their directing careers, believe they are constantly being put in the position of having to prove again and again that they can handle the job. It seems that it is not always easy for those in the hiring positions—producers and artistic directors—to trust women directors. Julianne Boyd concurs that in her experience there is still an unfortunate tendency to blame any problems with a particular director's work on her gender regardless of other factors involved, thereby eliminating future opportunities for other women because the producer might fear similar problems: "It's an old story and certainly what I found when I did a study on women directors for the Women's Project and League of Professional Theatre Women in the mid 1980s. One woman's failure is a failure for all women, and one woman's success is her own success until more women succeed." Although she was referring to a 1980s study, our conversation took place in the early 1990s. While she admits there has been some measure of progress, Boyd clearly believes this is still an issue for women in the theatre today.

Although it can be difficult to know for sure, several women thought they could identify at least one circumstance in which they did not get a directing assignment because of being a woman, perhaps because of a similar kind of resistance. These problems tend to diminish as the women get older or more established in their reputations. They can still be a large obstacle, however, especially for women directors who are looking for opportunities early in their careers. Seret Scott insists that her biggest gender issues always have to do with getting the job in the first place: "I have been turned down because the artistic director has said, 'Well, I really like what you have to say about the play, but I think a man should do this.'"

The issue of not being forgiven, of having to overcome the limited or negative expectations of others and also of having to constantly prove and re-prove yourself, seems to go double for women of color. Scott continues to explain:

> Most anything I'm dealing with is going to come initially through an ethnic place, before gender. Any of the battles I'm fighting seem to be more geared toward ethnicity. A lot of that has to do with the fact that more women are directing now, being allowed into the inner circle. Now the big problem for me is, "But you're black, so what do you know about anything *at all*, being a black female?" Double whammy. They seem to think I'm totally stupid, I have no creative vision, and what would I know about anything? The perception is that I'm lucky to be where I am, that I don't know very much, and I don't know anything about other ethnic groups. That's what I encounter. It's always there. But it goes away the more I work. People start to say, "I think you need to consider Seret for such and such a project" because I have proven myself in so many areas. Everybody feels like they're always proving themselves. Not just me.

Penny Metropulos agrees that testing of a director is inevitable. She does not believe, however, women are the only ones tested: "I have found that occasionally there are those who have not respected me initially, but their attitudes generally change when they realize that I am capable and cooperative, but strong-willed. These kinds of 'tests' exist for men or women." It may be, however, that it takes women longer to pass these tests.

In defiance of this perceived lack of faith in women, Julia Miles, artistic director of the Women's Project and Productions in New York City, offers this advice for women directors: "You have to be daring and courageous and go for it. That seems harder for women to do than for men, but that is the answer. Be bolder and not afraid of it. You can make a mistake, and I know that women directors aren't forgiven the way men are, but you must not let that stand in your way. You've just got to have a lot of courage and act on your courage, and be very well prepared."[1]

Physical Appearance and Resistance

Physical appearance can also have an impact on the way others view women in authority. Fontaine Syer is certain that she has lost at least one job because she was taller than the male artistic director doing the hiring. Conversely, Penny Metropulos initially believed that physical appearance could play a large part in resistance to women directors and was convinced that as a small woman she was often perceived as weaker and less authoritative than other women. As her career progresses, however, she no longer feels her size to be a problem. Liz Diamond, also a very small woman, explores the contradictions she finds in her physical image of being a leader:

> How I am perceived as a director is hugely influenced by gender, particularly how I am perceived by older men. I think that as the younger generations of male actors come up—young men who have been raised by women who've worked all their lives and are fully assertive, independent, strong individuals—I think that's changing. But I could almost say for men over forty it's more of a challenge to win their confidence, to win their trust. I'm amused at times at the relationship of size to leadership. The fact that I'm small is really amusing. It's very funny to stand in front of an actor like Ben Halley, whom I adore, and to come up to his waistband, and to be telling him what to do. But then, I figure Napoleon did it, so I'm not going to worry about that too much. I find that in a strange sort of way as I gain confidence as an artist, as I gain confidence as a leader and go into rehearsal armed with that confidence, with clear and strongly articulated ideas about the project on which we're about to embark, that in a strange way, to the extent that my size and femininity, my gender, my sex, is a factor, it may be disarming because there's less to get past. There's less of a perception of an obstacle, there's less of a perception of dad. I'm not dad, and I'm never going to be dad. I think that can actually be a plus. And there's also the occasional erotic charge. That, too, can be a plus.

Julie Taymor is also very aware that appearance, especially if it heightens sexual attraction or awareness, can play a big part in how a woman is received as a director, creating a climate for possible resistance with the wrong wardrobe choices: "I like the sexual dynamic between men and women when I work. I like that there might be an attraction, but I'm very conscious that you shouldn't look too attractive when you're working. A lot of women know that if you dress nicely or if you pay attention to your appearance, then people think that you must be lacking in talent and intelligence. It's always interesting to watch how much makeup or how much grooming a woman is allowed to do in the workplace, in any field."

Melia Bensussen also shares an example, not of direct resistance, but of expectations and misunderstandings she experienced early in her career based on appearances: "At one of my first regional gigs, someone from the staff of the theatre came in and asked me where a prop was. I looked up and said, 'Excuse me?' They said, 'Aren't you the new props person?' I didn't look like what a director was supposed to look like to this guy. I was in jeans, I don't wear makeup, I was in flat shoes, sneakers. I still looked like a grad student, for better or for worse."

Although she is a very small woman, Patricia Blem found more resistance from actors to her youth than to her size: "As a young female director, they tend to not hear you. With their years of experience, they are sure they know what they're doing and you have to fight that, and say, 'Let's try it like this,' or 'I want it this way.' They still tend not to hear you until you work with them a while, not letting them get off the hook. The schools of acting they've grown up in approach the work quite differently than I do, so finding the key to communication is the challenge. I've found older men more resistant to my direction than women of the same generation."

Resistance from Male Actors

The most consistent resistance to women in authority encountered by these women seems to come from older male actors. In her speech, JoAnne Akalaitis remarks on the resistance she has felt from some middle-aged male character actors: "I have to say that the process of theatre is refreshingly non-sexist. However, I notice some middle-aged male actors have a very hard time working with women directors." Many others agree with her assessment. Seret Scott recounts an instance of resistance she experienced early in her career, after getting the job and before starting work on a show: "On one of my first jobs I was asked as a woman whether or not I thought I would be able to deal with the cast. It was a ten-character cast, six of the ten were men, and of those six, all of them except for one was over the age of 60. I was asked whether I thought I would be able to handle it from the perspective of age—because they were thinking I was so much younger—and also from the perspective of me being a woman and dealing with these older men. I said that I felt like if there was going to be a problem about my being a woman, it was going to be a problem that the actor already had. It wouldn't have a lot to do with me."

Mary Robinson remembers some encounters with a similar kind of resistance to her leadership when she was younger, but believes the situation is changing for her as she gains more experience:

> I often felt rather defensive about being young, tried not to be defensive about being a woman. I can remember walking into a rehearsal when I was twenty two years old, directing a play, a Shakespeare play, and having an actor say to me, "Well, that's the way a woman would think, but this is a scene with men." Or having somebody say to me early when I was directing *Of Mice and Men*, which is a very male play, "You're going to learn a lot about men in this process." You know, comments like that. They wouldn't say that to a man. I remember once walking into rehearsal and a man whom I had cast [on the basis of seeing him in another show], but had not met face to face said, "My god, you're young enough to be my daughter." I bet he wouldn't have said, "You're young enough to be my son." When I was under thirty, I had a lot of experiences with actors with whom I was working. Now I'm forty years old, and I think I'm probably older than most of the people in the cast. I'm more confident, and I think these issues are just not there anymore, for the most part.

Even if they do not believe gender to be a part of the actual creative process, almost all of the women are able to identify certain instances where they have experienced a sense of being challenged or questioned because of being a woman. Even Zelda Fichandler, who initially insisted she had never experienced discrimination in the theatre, suddenly remembered a past incident:

> It isn't that I'm free from discrimination, but in my profession I haven't experienced it. I just haven't had a moment of it. [pause] Oh, I had an actor—I had to take over a show from a director who was flubbing it, and this well-known classical actor said to me, "I can't work with you. I have to tell you right now, I can't work with a woman director." I said, "Well, we're just going to have to work it through because we've got ten days to open the show. You're going to have to get used to it and fast because the show has to open. I'll do my best to make this comfortable and pleasant for you, but I'm the director and this is how it's going to be. Do you want to quit?" He decided not to quit. He wasn't hostile to me, he was just miserable. We got through it and he was brilliant.

Fichandler believes the actor-director relationship can lend itself to very powerful connections. Because of the intimate nature of the work and the fact that the director has control over the actor in so many ways, there can even be psychological projections which occasionally provoke temporary resistance. She believes, however, that gender is only a small part of this dynamic: "I've had actors who have projected onto me sexual fantasies, dreamt about me, hated or loved me out of proportion to what our relationship actually was in fact. I've had someone come in and say, 'I hate you.' Then I say, 'Okay, why do you hate me?' 'I hate you because you control me, you can decide what parts I get to play. I just hate you.' So I say, 'Well, maybe you'll like me better tomorrow,' and they do. People always project on people who are in authority roles. That's common." She then speculates that, although this kind of projection may go on regardless of the gender of the director, perhaps women directors hear about it more often: "Maybe because men don't want to hear about that stuff. But this thing of being hated or loved is just really being a central figure in a universe, whether it's the family or something larger. Their hating and loving has nothing to do with you, really."

Roberta Levitow explores other psychological territory in her discussion of potential resistance from actors:

> There's all sorts of seduction and mesmerization besides just honest and open communication that directors participate in. I don't think I'm somehow immune to such technique. It's necessary sometimes. You end up finding yourself trying to seduce someone into giving you a good performance, or love them into it somehow, or conjure them, or cajole them, or sometimes just talk to them straightforwardly, but not often. You've got to use what you've got as an artist striving to see something that means so much to you completed, this feeling, idea, or intuition that needs to be actuated. I'll do almost anything,

anything I'm capable of figuring out how to do, to make sure I get it there. It's not something I necessarily adore about myself, but I find myself doing it. And that starts bringing up gender issues because it depends on who you're dealing with, and what their response is hearing that or feeling that from a female person versus a male person.

Timothy Near agrees with Levitow about being willing to use whatever devices she can to get the best results, which can definitely set gender expectations into play. She also identifies a kind of "gender phobia" and shares a story about a particularly difficult actor who was actually able to shut out her influence to such a great degree that several weeks after the production he did not even recognize her when they met in the street. She reflects on why that might have happened:

> There have been times, especially with older men, where I feel that there's a questioning, a fear of letting me get close, a fear that maybe I'll do something to them, and so I see all kinds of juggling for position where vulnerability won't happen, from hostile, to calling me honey, to sexual, to patriarchal, to literally not remembering me! You know, a director plays all these roles: you can be the shrink, you can be the nurturer, you can be the adviser, there can be a sexual excitement. There's a lot of things going on. Just as actresses can have that with a male director, men have that also with a woman director. Everybody uses what they can use to get to the best work, and I don't mind any of them as long as they're not destructive or cruel. I think we all get into that room, and we want to do the play. It's so personal that you do call on gender relationships with everybody who's there. And that includes the director.

Susana Tubert adds another twist in the experience of male resistance to her authority:

> When I first went into directing I had no role models, and every once in a while I'd run into difficulty with a male actor. Eventually I figured out the subtext to the scene that was being acted out in the actor's mind in rehearsal. If he decided that I was attractive in a way that made him want to play a kind of sexual power game with me and if I decided not to play along by his rules of the game, the repercussions of my disinterest would take an interesting turn. The actor would transfer into his work his impotence at not being able to get my attention, to "seduce" me, and the energy would get released by not taking my direction. Because he could not confront me directly as his director, a kind of passive-aggressive resistance allowed him to feel somewhat in control. I always found it a childish and embarrassing behavior that eventually showed the performer how self-defeating he was being. Now that I've become more relaxed and centered in my role as a director, these issues don't come up. Perhaps my boundaries are more clear to the people I work with, or perhaps I'm too busy to notice anymore.

Although these examples of male resistance are fairly common among the directors, many of the examples came from their past. Most of the women report that although they still experience these kinds of incidents occasionally, they do not do so with any regularity as their careers progress.

Resistance from Other Women

Although most of the resistance was perceived to come from men, occasionally a woman would identify an experience with another woman as one of the most unpleasant examples of resistance she has ever encountered. Sharon Ott, although she didn't give a specific example, has obviously had some kind of trouble with female performers: "Often the people who have the most trouble with women directors are older women, because they've grown up in a theatre where most of the directors were men and they've really become accustomed to the paternalistic kind of thing. There's no way another woman, especially a younger woman, can provide that, so they feel unsupported and at sea, and it has nothing to do with the way that the director is trying to talk to them. It has to do with what they're assuming is a necessary component of dialogue." Opposing a noncritical preference for women collaborators simply because of their gender, Fontaine Syer cautions against simply trusting other women without knowing the individuals concerned. She thinks that not all women are as supportive of other women as they would have us believe, and although she refrains from giving details, she has clearly had some kind of negative experience in this regard. Julianne Boyd has also had one of her most difficult experiences with a woman artistic director, but she was quick to say she also had some of her best experiences with female producers.

Challenges to Authority

Diana Marré takes a slightly different angle on resistance as she addresses the issue of younger actors, seeing this kind of testing and challenging as an inevitable part of her pseudoparental role as a theatre educator. She identifies the resistance as coming more often from male students and believes it definitely affects her more than it does her male colleagues in the university because she becomes a kind of mother substitute:

> DM: They have me confused with their mother anyway. They expect me somehow to be nurturing anyway. If I'm the slightest bit nice, or if I take to using positive reinforcement a little too often, the male students will roll over me like a boulder. When that happens, I always have to crack the whip. I always have to be Machiavellian and turn it around, make them fear me, and chew them out in front of the whole cast, or do something real butch to get their attention again. I hate that. I really feel stung by that. I don't find that to be nearly such a problem in the profession. That's one reason I was drawn to theatre, because the men in this profession don't take those roles for granted

in the same way. We're too used to having to deal with dubious, sketchy, and ill-defined sexual parameters in this profession all the time anyway. With student actors in particular, you've got to tailor your style of communication to something they're going to take seriously. I think I get more of those kinds of issues and expectations. I don't think my male counterpart gets that, and I really don't think it's any difference in our demeanor. They just assume I'm going to be nurturing.

RD: Do you see that as being part of the directorial function?

DM: Well, I do mother my actors to a certain extent. I protect them to a certain extent. But I did that when I coached softball, you know? I just have a protective feeling about my team, but I'm not going to give them a break. I think I can push them harder because I do give them the feeling that I like them. I get more out of them that way. Really, it's just behavior control that we're talking about, and that's more my style than to demand or threaten or ride them too hard. I like to treat them well until they push me and I can't. Discipline is really important, and they can't get the feeling that I'm not concerned about discipline. I don't cut them any slack that way, and I expect the best from them. They all know that, but eventually it'll happen every time. Some male student will try to push me or try to get special treatment. It happens nearly every show, and I've just come to dread it. I can't seem to forestall it. I just think it's part of their gender expectations. The women don't do it, that's the other interesting thing. I never have that kind of trouble from the women. They understand where I'm coming from with the positive reinforcement thing, and they don't really try to take advantage of that in the same way.

Marré seems to believe she must respond with discipline in order to maintain her authority, and she speaks of cracking the whip to reestablish authority. Others use similar imagery of power struggles. Maria Irene Fornes also identifies this resistance as the one place in her process where she becomes aware of gender as a specific influence, and she speaks of the need to go into battle to maintain her authority: "I am aware of my gender when there are times when men—it has happened very few times but it has happened—that I'm directing a man and I find a kind of resistance. At first, I think it's just that the person is proud, or in some way not liking my style, or something. Then I realize that it's because I'm a woman. It has to do with authority. They don't want to give up authority. They don't want a woman to tell them what to do. This type of man would probably struggle with a male director, too, but less. I've had a couple of times it has happened that I have had to get into battle and prove that I know what I'm doing."

During the rehearsals I observed, there was a challenge to Fornes' authority. The rehearsal was almost finished for the day and she was attempting to complete a few short notes when the female stage manager cut her off abruptly, saying it was time for rehearsal to be over. Fornes wanted to go on because she had only a few short comments, but the stage manager insisted that the rehearsal was to begin and end by her watch. Fornes then became quite angry at this sudden concern with time when rehearsals had been beginning late for several days with no attempt at discipline of the actors from the stage manager. A brief verbal flare-up ensued, and Fornes summarily dismissed everyone with an admonition that rehearsals should begin on time if she was going to be held to such a precise ending time. After the incident, Fornes confided that she was definitely not thinking about gender during the altercation, but that she felt her reactions of frustration and anger once it was over were very feminine. She did not elaborate further, however, and when questioned in the formal interview about the incident, she said that gender might have played a part in the conflict, but then she quickly tried to downplay its significance by finding other reasons for the challenge:

> I think it has to do more with not being used to being in a situation that's creative, more than it's a question of being a woman director. I think if she were used to a director who is working with the elements they have [rather than always rewriting the script], whether it was a woman or a man—what I'm saying is, she probably objected to my going over time because she thinks I'm sloppy, generally. That's what my assumption is, that she believes I don't know what I'm doing. I think if I was doing everything according to her idea of a person who knows what they're doing, I don't think she would have interrupted, man or woman. I think if someone described to her that incident the way it was, she would say, "That's not how it happened. I said to her it was time, and she said she wanted to continue, and then she asked 'Why are actors late?'" So, she probably interprets from this whole thing that I object to the actors being late.

According to the existing texts, an exacting nature and an insistence on continuing to work and change details until they are exactly the way she wants them should be considered decisive, authoritative, and strong leadership, all admirable qualities in a director. When a woman does behave in a decisive, authoritative manner, however, and doesn't back down when her tolerances and boundaries are tested, she is often considered, as Fornes was, to be "difficult."

Negative Images of a Strong Woman

For a woman director, being decisive and authoritative can sometimes lead to a very stereotypical negative image—being known as a "dragon lady" or "bitch," an epithet that is not unfamiliar to a number of the women interviewed. Tisa Chang discusses her experiences with this stereotype:

> At first people will test. I have to say that the tests came from white males; they tested me more. I think Asian males—there's a kind of buying into my cultural kind of propaganda, so to speak—could relate more. I also found it in the producing organizations in the regions. In one place I was invited to direct, I found the whole male design team, the people who work there, were

Tisa Chang (right) at a gala benefit for Pan Asian Rep after receiving matching funds for an NEA challenge grant from the CCNY Chinese alumni president, Kathy Ding (center), with master of ceremonies, TV reporter Ti-Hua Chang (left) (1995). Photo by Corky Lee.

very resistant. Of course, this was 1976, so I felt that you got a lot of testing then. The whole concept of a woman director, and a Chinese American woman director, was very different. I think if I had been less anxiety-ridden, I would have probably been a little bit more diplomatic. But what happened was that in order to be listened to in getting what I needed for the production, I had to come down hard on some people. So I have a reputation for being a dragon lady, or overly strong. I don't particularly have a big sense of humor, but I realize now that humor would certainly have diffused the situation a lot. I think also being an attractive woman makes things a little more complex, given the preconceived notions. I'm very careful about keeping the ground level.

The idea of wanting to level the field to maintain a sense of control or leadership is an interesting one, and several others made similar comments about feeling a need to establish their leadership very strongly at first in order to forestall any potential resistance or perceptions of weakness, imagined or real. Roberta Levitow on the other hand, seems ambivalent about her dragon lady designation. She seems willing to embrace it, even with humor at times, but is also frustrated that it has to be any part of her experience at all:

RL: I feel like I've had a lot of leadership experiences through most of my life. I'm the oldest child, I was head of the scholarship society in high school, and there were a lot of activities before I entered the theatre where being leader was something I would leap to take the opportunity to do. But I do find that I'm challenged by resistance. The larger the setting, the more demanding the setting, any resistance that I get, all these things really call into question how far I'll go, whether I'll be willing to be seen as a dragon lady. It's taken me a long time to get a good sense of humor about that. Now I just say it. "I'm nice now, but hold on. Check me out in about three weeks, I'll be a dragon lady. I know that's what you'll think, 'She's a dragon lady.' But I know it too. It's coming. There'll be a time where I get very firm about what I want. I'm going to expect you to do it, and I'm not gonna want to talk about that." It's definitely been a progression of my own development to feel that I can do that without sacrificing something that is precious to me.

RD: A number of the women I've talked to have brought up similar issues in a slightly different context, talking about needing to be better behaved because as women they don't feel they have the freedom to be the dragon lady, as you say, without taking some intense resistance for it because of the gender issues.

RL: I think that's true. I remember talking to a woman artistic director, who's a great supporter, and when we were working on a play at her theatre, one of her technical staff people was frustrated with some things that were going on, things that I was taking a firm stand on. I remember calling her up on the phone and saying, "Don't do this to me. Don't let me become the dragon lady. Don't let me become the bitch at your theatre. See what's happening. All I'm doing is saying I need this done. Is this unreasonable? No, it's not." I actually had to appeal to her because it was evolving that way. There were some issues I felt I had to be very firm about, and it wasn't pleasant for anybody, but I think it was right. That situation was beginning to define a persona that I think was definitely related to a woman speaking like that.

RD: So if a man had asked for those same things, you don't think there would have been any resistance?

RL: I really don't think so. It would have been within expectation and probably a sign of some kind of strength of character and vision.

In our discussion of a woman's expression of power, Sharon Ott was reminded of the social cliché about angry women, articulating through her own experience that the cliché is still in operation and a woman must nevertheless learn how to express her strength: "When a woman gets mad, it's perceived in a different way. I mean, really truly, if a woman gets angry it's often that she's being bitchy; when a man gets angry, it's not usually given that sort of adjective. It's the crucial issue. If you can't exert strength, how can you be in a powerful position? You have to be able to do that. You have to be able to be angry and not be afraid of it. When people hear women get mad, they say that's being bitchy, but it's not being any different than when a male gets angry. However, it really is received differently." This awareness of a double standard in operation has led many of the women to feel the need to modify their personal behavior in response to expectations regarding a woman in authority.

Issues of Behavior

Intolerance for Certain Behaviors in Women

As a result of experiencing resistance and challenge, one belief held in common by most of the women interviewed is that in order to escape negative stereotyping, women directors must be better behaved, especially when expressing anger or dissatisfaction. In her speech, JoAnne Akalaitis relays an anecdote which reveals this belief and the seemingly inevitable and stereotypical comparison to comparable male behavior: "I know that a woman director has to be better behaved than a man director. If a man director runs to the prop person and shouts, 'How can you? It's insane. You're insane to give me this cup. Only an insane person would bring this to me!' They say, 'Oh, you know that man, he's so interesting. He's really temperamental.' If a woman director does the same thing, she is a bitch. She's a bitch, or worse." Akalaitis reemphasized this idea during our phone interview, attributing the problem to a general difficulty in perceiving women in authority positions, and she implied that punitive action might be taken against certain behaviors in women, whereas the same behaviors might go unremarked in a male director: "In general, there is intolerance for impatience, or a woman's losing her temper, or being emotional, not just in rehearsal, but in the world of boards of directors and power structures in theatre."

Julia Miles of the Women's Project, using Akalaitis herself as example, points out that often, if a woman is seen as demanding or aggressive, she is dealt with quite summarily, especially by the media: "Last season, we went through the firing of Joanne Akalaitis at the Public Theater in New York, and I don't think, if she had been a man, the press would have been so harsh on her. They didn't say anything about her great achievements, her unique vision, her influence on younger artists. Somehow people feel that either women are so strong that they can take it better than men, or they don't care and they just feel they can get away with not being as well mannered towards women as they are towards men."[2]

Anne Bogart definitely agrees with Akalaitis, especially about the world of boards of directors. In fact, she believes that this same kind of intolerance for behavior that is outside normal expectations was a significant factor in her own dismissal from Trinity Repertory Theatre:

> I think that the board trusted me less than they would a man. I think they
> freaked out when I was there because they were used to a man coming in and

wielding power in a particular way. I came in and wielded power in a very different way, which has to do with nurturing, inclusiveness, associative working as opposed to linear working. These methods terrified the board because it was so different, because it was not as clear cut. So I would say, on a level of career, I think I'm definitely affected by gender, by being a woman in the field in that way. I keep finding that I am part of a group of women who have had that experience.

In a magazine profile of her assumption of power at Trinity Rep, Bogart emphasized these same qualities which led to the difficulties the staff and board had with her style of leadership, particularly following in the footsteps of her highly authoritative predecessor. She insisted she simply could not be an autocrat and that she wanted "more sense of common participation."[3] Like Akalaitis, Bogart describes a kind of director who fits the rather temperamental genius model. It's interesting to note that she also automatically identifies this director as male: "There are some really good directors who are assholes, who are complete Napoleons, but still their work is really good. They're not accommodating or nurturing, or even collaborative, but they're connected to their necessity, and people follow them or do what they ask them to do because they sense that the guy is on an adventure, that he's going somewhere with it." Julie Taymor points out that the autocratic genius identity is one regularly denied to women, regardless of the merit of their work: "This is something I've wondered about—why an 'enfant terrible' is a male-dominated sort of identity. When women do extraordinary works—Peter Sellars has been an 'enfant terrible' for twenty years—but when a woman has that kind of temperament it's usually said she's a bitch as a director. It's very acceptable for men to have the kind of personalities where it doesn't matter if you like them as directors. They're such geniuses, they're so brilliant that people do what they say because of the prestige of being in this man's production."

Gloria Muzio concurs but suggests that this kind of director puts an ego stamp on a production that she believes does not belong there. She thinks that this aspect of women's conditioning as well as expectations about their behavior might actually best serve a production:

> I was brought up very traditionally so I still have a lot of those what I now consider to be hangups about what it is to be a woman—that I can't shine the light too strongly upon myself. That's not good. But in a way that happens to help my work because I believe that a play really should look as though it hasn't been directed at all. That's always my ideal, for it to seem like it just happened that way, that it was not self-conscious in any way. I'm more willing to let go of a personal thumb print on a production because that's not what it's about for me. That may be gender related, I don't know. Or it may be just good directing. I know that other directors, men directors, have said that same sort of thing. Who knows where it comes from? It might be that I have that little key to something because I'm a woman. It might be that a man

director has that same key because of some experience he had with his third grade teacher.

Although many women realize that the temperamental or autocratic image is often much more negative for them than for a male counterpart, like Muzio, most of the women who brought up this notion don't really want to be able to be an "enfant terrible."

A Moderate Style of Leadership Can Be Advantageous

Emily Mann talks about how, at an early point in her career, this double standard regarding temperament and expression of anger was made quite clear to her by one of her male mentors. Mann sees this as a positive influence and clearly believes that the demanding and temperamental director is not a good role model for directors of either gender:

> Women who are where they are learn that early. I remember when I was at Harvard, there was a professional male director who was having a tantrum in the theatre because he didn't get what he wanted. One of my mentors said to me, "You know, a woman could never do that. You must know you can never lose your temper, you can never have a tantrum. As a woman, it will destroy your career." I'm actually quite glad he told me that. On the one hand, I probably had different stress illnesses because I didn't let it out. But on the other hand, one usually does better work when you don't fly off the handle and have tantrums. You try to solve problems. Because of what we as women couldn't do, I think we had to get better at problem solving, working with people, and getting the job done. We weren't allowed temperament. I don't think that's necessarily bad. For example, I think I have a very happy theatre because I don't like people who throw tantrums. I like living in an environment where people are proud of the work they do. You don't just fly off the handle and say ugly things. If you want something better, you sit down like a human being and you talk about it. I don't like tantrums in children, I don't like tantrums in adults. It doesn't help the work, it doesn't help the environment, it doesn't help the institution, it doesn't help the artists you're working with, or the artisans you're working with, or the technicians you're working with. It helps no one. So we weren't allowed that luxury of telling people off and having tantrums. I think that's okay.

Many other directors also speak of their awareness of the need to moderate their expression of anger or otherwise alter behavior in their working style because of gender expectations. Alana Byington believes she modifies her behavior from time to time in response to someone's reaction or potential reaction, but like Mann, she finds a moderate style of leadership suits her personality:

> I believe very strongly in being a partner of the people I work with rather than a dictator. I honestly believe that's a difference between a good director

and a bad director, but I do think it may serve me better as a woman. I'll get away with being gentle and careful of egos. I personally think if you put people on their guard, you get less of their inspiration. But I do believe that there are a lot more male directors who get away with it anyway. They direct by force of personality. I think there are more people who will take that from a man. But since I'm not interested in directing that way, I guess it's okay. I am conscious that, as a woman, I occasionally have to be careful of a fragile male ego. Recognizing that situation and proceeding delicately is the same as recognizing any other aspect of an actor's personality and incorporating that information in how one proceeds with that actor to help them achieve their best work.

Liz Diamond also feels a moderate style of leadership is more to her liking, although she does subscribe to the notion that you don't have to be liked to do good work. Furthermore, she links the ability to lose one's temper without consequence more to the point in one's career than to the gender of the director:

> LD: I don't love conflict. I'm not a fiery temperamental person. I don't like loud voices. I'm much more interested in creating consensus and cooperation than I am in creating tension. However, I think a certain competitive edge in a room can be exciting. So when I feel that some actors are really committing and some aren't, I'll call the ones who aren't on it. I think that being willing to not be loved is very important in a director, remembering that it doesn't matter on opening night if they think you're a total ass or if they hate your guts or if they love you, provided the work is really beautiful and strong. I don't see loss of temper as a tool to be used. I don't believe in it. I think it is a manifestation of a loss of leadership and a loss of control in the process and in the rehearsal room. I think it is to be avoided at all costs. There are times when you must put your foot down, when you may have to raise your voice to get what you want, particularly if you're dealing with someone who has lost control, who has lost his or her temper. It's like throwing cold water on a fire. But I think that the few times that I have lost my temper—which was when I was younger and starting out—were bad moments, moments that I would not repeat, moments I'm not proud of.
>
> RD: Do you think these moments were received differently because you were a woman?
>
> LD: No, I don't think so. Let's put it this way, an older, experienced, more well-known director of either sex has more money in the bank and engenders more fear, as it were, in staff, in crew. That person thereby has more chips to call on in those moments when he or she loses it. It's less costly. When you are inexperienced—male or female—when you're young, when you're working with people for the first time, you have less power to draw on, and it is going to affect the way that eruption is received. I think that's true for a male, and I think it's true for a female.

Melia Bensussen agrees that women must use anger cautiously, although she, like Tisa Chang with her desire to level the ground on which the interactions take place, believes it to be an occasional necessity, at least until the image of leader can encompass other attributes besides simply the power to demand results: "I think as a woman director you have to be very careful about how you get angry. At the same time, I think if you don't ever get angry as a director, you're not taken seriously, either. I think this all goes back to these really old ideas of what power and leadership are, and a sort of pater familias image, which I'm really not into. I look forward to the day when I have enough work behind me, when being apparently casual is not misunderstood as being lax. I see that as happening only after a body of work is behind me."

Rita Giomi is also aware of this form of intolerance. In addition, she tells of the difficulty she has expressing anger or frustration without tears, and her awareness that as a woman in the position she's in, she must guard against any kind of emotionally demonstrative behavior:

> I think we are put in situations as women that we have to be more careful about what happens because it's still too easy to write us off as hysterical women. I hate to say this, but I think it's true. I think it's still easy for a lot of men in particular, but women do it as well to other women, to dismiss what's being said by a woman in anger as hysteria or bitchiness or uncontrolled behavior, when that same behavior coming from a man is strength. I am, at times, a little more conscious of making sure that I'm level-headed. On the whole, I'm a pretty level-headed person, so it's not like that's a big problem for me, but I do check myself some times. Some of it is because personally, as a woman—and I think a lot of us are dealing with this—I find it very difficult to be righteously angry without weeping. When I'm really pissed off, that's just the response that comes from me. It doesn't weaken the response in my mind, it's just the way I respond to it. But you certainly can't do that, even in a situation where you have the right to be angry, when you feel like you've been mistreated or whatever. It's not like I get mistreated a lot either, but I think you are on guard.

The sense of needing to be on guard or to modify behavior in some way because certain behaviors are often perceived by others as unacceptable from a woman is something many of the directors have experienced throughout their careers. Most of them do not feel this modification to be a truly negative consequence, however. In fact, some of them see it as a benefit for the director, but moderation, too, can cause certain kinds of resistance.

Love of Collaboration Can Create a Different Kind of Resistance

It seems that when a woman is too strong there is often resistance, but the reverse can also be true. If she is seen as a weak leader for any reason, negative criticism can surface quickly. Susana Tubert identifies this different kind of resistance as she describes how she sometimes feels challenged because of the nature of how the collaborative process works for her:

I love to collaborate. I also love to think out loud through my ideas. I don't protect myself when I'm working. I'm willing to be vulnerable, to not know all the answers, and I see theatre as kind of a dance sometimes, sometimes a battle between the material and me. The challenge is to see how we are going to achieve this perfect harmony, dancing this tango of ours. During my collaboration with designers, I will hear myself saying, "Well, what if we did this?" "What would happen if we did that?" It's my way of working through things, much in the way that an actor works through a scene in a rehearsal process. It's not surprising anymore to hear back, most often from male designers, "Well, you're the director. You know what you want, right?" which subtextually means, "*Do* you know what you want? You're the one who has to decide. Why are you asking this of me?" This mostly happens when I'm on the road, working under pressure with designers I may have just met. It's a kind of testing period which goes on at the beginning of the rehearsal process until it's clear that I know what I'm doing, that I'm in control. To *them*. It's always clear to *me*. I mean, there's no question that I'm going to do what I want to do. I just don't like to have it all figured out ahead of time. I like to keep myself open to what may evolve with everyone. It's now funny to me when that kind of misinterpretation takes place. I smile and calmly answer, "Yes, and you're the designer, so we're going to collaborate."

Tubert is by no means the only one to identify that the willingness and desire to collaborate is sometimes received as a lack of decisiveness, some kind of problem with exercising power or even not knowing what to do. Interestingly, although she initially responded to this perception of the problem by turning it inward, she no longer feels the need to wonder if she should change something about her own process or the presentation of it in order to allow others to be more comfortable with her in the leadership role.

Alana Byington feels confident in her abilities as a director but does believe that if she becomes unsure, other people may attribute that lack of confidence to gender: "If I feel competent, then the people I'm working with tend to believe that I am, and I think that that's one of those things that, if you let somebody see you're unsure, then they're going to start doubting you, and they may say one of the reasons is because you're a woman. But I think we must have the right to say, 'I don't know' or 'I'm not sure,' and I've often found if you say, 'I don't know, what do you think?' with confidence, people may be startled but won't necessarily doubt you."

Melia Bensussen relates an incident she recently read about when the desire to collaborate resulted in a woman film director being removed from her position of leadership and replaced by a more autocratic male director. Bensussen relates this to the trepidation she sometimes experiences regarding her own process. She clearly believes, however, that this kind of collaborative working is the essence of good directing:

Where I see gender most affecting my work as a director in the most obvious fashion is on my conception of leadership and what the room feels like with a person in charge and what that person in charge is like. I recently read an article about a woman film director being fired off a set. A man had been hired to replace her, and one of the crew members had said how it was good to have a captain of the ship now because there hadn't been a captain before. A woman's not the captain of the ship somehow. When he was asked why he hadn't felt like there was leadership, he said how this woman obviously didn't know what she was doing because she kept turning to other people for their opinions. That struck me because I know that when I direct, I feel very much in charge and very much in control. I know that I'm the one who's setting the aesthetic and the interpretation. But I also know that when I'm working, I am constantly looking for input, constantly sharing my opinions. I'm not saying that men don't do that. I think that's the essence of good directing.

Although most of these women view collaboration as an important part of the directing process, they also realize that their leadership style needs somehow to be made clear, even as they collaborate. This leads some women to expose collaboration consciously as part of their overall plan (in the design phase or as rehearsals begin), thereby avoiding the perception that they are weak or unsure when they ask for opinions or responses from other artists. This tends to reinforce their position of leadership.

INTERNAL RESISTANCE AND SELF-DOUBT

Lack of a Sense of Entitlement to Power

During our conversations, most of the women identified various kinds of problem situations reflecting how they were received by others in positions of authority, but only a few really explored any problems that wielding power created within themselves. A certain discomfort arising from lack of experience with power or the expectations of others has been mentioned in some of the previous responses, as has the perceived need to modify behavior which seems to be received by others as inappropriate or uncomfortable. Only a few, however, reflected on what might be happening at a deeper level.

One clear expression of gender expectations and the subconscious problems that can exist for a woman director came to me in a letter from a friend, fellow director Diane Olson Dieter, an educator and free-lance director/actor in Portland, Oregon. Dieter believes that it is not overt discrimination that has punished her, but rather the way that, as a woman who was expected to get married and give her life over to a husband, she was raised to believe she had no individual rights. Therefore, her creativity in the theatre became an "unnatural act" because it involved claiming something for herself. This sense of inferiority "introjected into [her] consciousness" presents her with constant internal challenges to being able to exercise her authority: "Being inculcated with the belief that personal boundaries were the province of the male, I had no sense of reasonable boundaries for myself. Therefore I would become easily

Anne Bogart (center) directs unidentified acting students in her viewpoint technique during the Saratoga International Theatre Institute's summer workshop at Skidmore College (1994). Photo by Mark McCarty.

frustrated because I had no clear sense of entitlement. As a director, I find it difficult to insist on things because I don't know that it is my 'right.' On the other hand, I don't feel comfortable giving people leeway, and I wonder whether I can retain their respect in the creative process."[4]

Similarly, Anne Bogart identifies the issue of lack of confidence or sense of entitlement as one of the most significant ways gender influences her artistic process. She speaks insightfully about how her social conditioning thoroughly permeates her working style and how she has difficulty, even today, shaking this sense of self-doubt and sometimes even embarrassment at her own considerable success:

> I find more and more that a deeper psychological problem in my own conditioning is that I don't say things terribly directly. I feel because I am a woman that I insinuate myself on a process, rather than direct a process. I think the wielding of power is very different. Because I'm a woman, I deal with more self-doubt as a director because directing is a power relationship. Because directing is a position of being responsible for the finished product, how I carry out that responsibility is much more full of doubt than [it is for] most men. I guess it's also a positive thing, too, because doubting is actually very healthy. But I find it very difficult to assume power. I can use it, and I'm very conscious of using it. It never is an assumed thing. I always ask, "Why should I know this better than anybody else? Why should I have the right to demand something?" I think it's harder for me to go to a regional theatre and demand

a higher budget, my own designers, actors of my choice. I find that men are forgiven more for throwing tantrums and making demands. This is not an original thought by any means, but the minute a woman makes a demand, which directors tend to do, they're seen as temperamental. So I'm very self-effacing, and I think that has to do with conditioning. Any obstacle that is in front of you is a challenge and is a positive thing. So in a sense, the gender issue is both very negative and very positive in that I've had to prove myself and work harder than most men to do what I do. But I keep sabotaging it because I am more self-effacing. Maybe I'm changing because I'm more aware of it now, but it took me a long time to be aware of how indirect I've been, and how embarrassed by success or accomplishments.

Tori Haring-Smith mentions how this same kind of response to her conditioning and the sense of not having the right to make demands often leads her to apologize when she needs to assert her desires for something special, particularly in the area of technical details: "As a female, I've been trained to apologize when I ask for something. Especially when I'm talking with designers, my impulse is always to ask, 'Can we do this?' I usually work with male designers, and I always accept their statement that we can't do something, rather than saying, 'Well, we must do it,' which I have seen many male directors do. My position is, if they tell me they can't do it, I have to accomodate them and solve the problem some other way."

Victoria Parker also identifies this sense of lack of entitlement as a major issue: "An important influence is personal power and the social training men have beyond women, the training to use personal power freely. I certainly haven't felt the freedom that I see a lot of men having in using creative power, the freedom to make creative mistakes. I always feel a little bit like I'm on roller skates all the time, and if something goes wrong, I really have to bust ass to show the cast I know how to handle it. I think there's a general command that a male might have that I also have, which he has more freedom to express." When asked how others perceive her in positions of authority, Parker seems uncomfortable with claiming power for herself:

> I think it's really interesting because I've heard from a number of people that they think that I'm powerful, that I have power when I work, which is a lot of times the opposite of what I feel. I feel like what I do is open the dam and let the water go. I think what gives artists the feeling that I'm doing something is that I have let them free. I think they perceive me as a very congenial partner. I think they see me as a collaborator because I'm collaborating and am congenial with them. I'm powerful, but I think they see me doing things that I don't really do. It always puzzles me that people have the picture that I manipulate things in this powerful way because really, the only thing I do is give power to them. If the reins were completely in my hands, I think they'd have another picture of me.

Furthermore, when Parker perceives others having problems with her in a power position, she withdraws her overt power as a result. In what could be seen as a particularly feminine move, she has also developed an aversion for obvious exercise of power and avoids any situation that seems to be what she calls "power-tripping":

> I tend to work on the premise that the best leader is the invisible leader, and so I don't generate power that makes people respond to demand right away. I withdraw my power a little bit. I have a feeling there are a lot of male directors who don't consider power a problem. I don't know, but my guess is that they just tell a person what they want and assume people will jump and run. I have a tendency to believe that I won't get the same reaction because I'm female. Because I think arbitrary manipulation is incredibly destructive, what I tend to do is to really organize myself behind the scenes and put out dribs and drabs of what I need way ahead of time. I have a tendency to want to give the other people full rein, so that they don't feel that they're being pushed on or pressured by me. I'm very aware of that all the time. I don't want people to think I'm power-tripping them.

Reflecting her own insecurity with power, Parker says that when she works with females in other positions of artistic authority, such as designers, she is careful not to challenge them: "I do feel sometimes that women are new enough to being in command of their own art that it's necessary to let them do it and not give them too much aggravation. I protect women more than I do men." In an interesting contrast to several other women who clearly believe that many men are threatened by women with power, Parker says she believes that men are more comfortable exercising their power and do not feel as threatened by challenges to it as she believes women might. She then makes, however, an intriguing reversal regarding the need of some men to prove themselves in positions of power, although she simply raises a provocative question and does not explore it further:

> As an actor, I've rarely worked with a male director who lets you go, or who says, "It's up to you. Show me what you think this play is about." I think there's that self-protection thing—I see it more openly in males—to protect the power that they already have. And with some I wonder why they "exhibit" this power when all they have to do is walk into a room—the voice is lower, the body is bigger, the history of male dominance, everything tells me that you're in control here. So an exhibition, a demonstration of that power, always confuses me. As an actor, I only really listen to a director who doesn't do that. I can't listen to a director who doggedly does the control thing, whether it's male or female.

Parker is obviously not alone in her ambivalence about power and the need to prove it to others. Brenda Hubbard is aware of sometimes feeling uncomfortable or insecure in her power and admits to looking for actors who will not challenge her authority too much. Interestingly, she believes she is more able to deal with challenge from a man than a woman:

> When I'm casting women, I'm casting women who will not challenge me too much or threaten me too much. I do the same with men, but it's a little bit different. Because I'm accustomed to men challenging my direction more than women, I'm probably more comfortable being challenged by men than by women. The women that I tend to cast—this is a generalization but I think there's a lot of truth to it—tend to be very hard-working, somewhat insecure, somewhat needy, and will put me in the position of being the counselor, the guidance person, and the authority. I tend to cast men who I think will be more fun to be around in the rehearsal process, who have a good sense of humor, and who can accept my authority without becoming too threatened. That is a major issue as a woman director, people being threatened by you in a position of authority and leadership because you are a woman. That is the one issue I think I deal with every time I direct a play in some fashion or another, although sometimes it's very hidden, and other times it's very open.

Getting used to the challenges to her authority, whether they are internal or external, is a very important issue for the woman director. It is an issue that seems to change over time, however.

Initial Discomfort with Taking Control

Some women speak of an initial discomfort with power, taking charge and asserting leadership, which has since been overcome through experience and career longevity. They are not always sure whether this has more to do with age and experience than with gender. Zelda Fichandler, however, is quite sure gender had a significant effect on her development and describes how she came to leadership with a lot of effort. She does, however, believe it to be generational and thinks young women entering the field today might not have the same experience:

> ZF: I think directing must attract people who don't mind taking charge, though it took me years to be comfortable with that. It took me years, endless years, of having that gnawing in the pit of my stomach that I was being bossy, that I was enforcing my point of view when there were a dozen other points of view that needed to come forth. I came to a sense of comfort with presenting the central vision and then through collaboration fulfilling it, late and with difficulty.
>
> As I look back, I was pretty much indoctrinated with what it meant to be female by my parents not paying for my college and thinking it was unnecessary, and setting the goal for me of a good Jewish husband, raising children, and finding that I was very difficult to raise, a maverick, and they didn't like my politics.
>
> RD: If you had been a son, this would not have been a problem?
>
> ZF: Not ever a problem. I went into all kinds of bizarre things, premed to become a psychiatrist, Russian language and literature, contemporary Soviet civilization, union organizing. The form of political radicalism that was there at the time absolutely did them in. So these things have their time. It's much

easier now for a woman to take charge. You don't have so much internalized negativity about yourself as a person of authority.

I had and have a strong desire to be perceived as feminine in the conventional way. But when I'm directing, I actually lose all these things. I become lost in the task, lost in the material, and do honestly need the input of the other people. I'm not working collaboratively in some abstract way. I need it. I want it in order to do my work. But people of my generation—at least for me, I can't generalize—I'm sure there's some who came to it easier, but I came to it hard. I came to leadership with a lot of labor.

Mary Robinson, who is younger than Fichandler, also believes that asserting leadership and control does not come as naturally to her as do other parts of the directing process. She attributes this more to internal conditioning than external resistance but insists she can assert her authority whenever needed. She stops short of attributing this to gender conditioning, saying simply, "Everybody's more comfortable with some aspects of what they do than others, but leadership does not come as naturally to me as the other parts of the process."

When Roberta Levitow discussses her own personal issues with the acceptance of leadership and authority, she connects it particularly with issues of design, an area where she feels less secure than in her dealings with actors, hence her need for what she calls "internal overcompensation":

> RL: I'm either appropriately prepared, or perhaps unnecessarily prepared, to deal with issues of authority in both my dealings with the design process and the design implementation. I feel more comfortable in the rehearsal room where you create a kind of familial feeling. But as far as the authority to implement a design and make sure it happens on time and make authoritative decisions about this choice or that choice, I'd find myself in a design conference feeling like I really had to take a firm stance in order to see on stage what I felt was right to be seen on stage. I personally take responsibility all along the process to clarify the authority issues. I expect that other people are going to have more difficulty with it, and I find myself caretaking their experience. "I'm going to lead you through how this will be, so that you will understand my idea of authority." I feel that's because I'm female. We wouldn't have to debate this, or even explicate it, if I was male.
>
> RD: Do you feel that it comes from external resistance to you in the position of authority, or is it internal self-doubt?
>
> RL: Sometimes there is external resistance, frankly. But I don't generally get overtly challenged, and sometimes I wonder if it isn't internal overcompensation. I feel that I need to be very, very clear because I don't get to be as soft-spoken as a man can be and have my will be done. I sit through a lot of other directors' work because I dramaturg a lot, and the men speak softer than the women. I've noticed it in myself, and then I see it manifested in other people's behavior. The women I watch tend to be more adamant at certain points. The men can whisper a command and it will be done. I think it's an assumption of authority, I really do. I think that if it's soft-spoken by women, sometimes it's thought to be not meaningfully meant, not to be taken so seriously. We tend

to speak more forcefully to make sure it's communicated that we take this seriously and intend to have it implemented. To me, this is politics and social
behavior, it's not necessarily the artistic process.

Levitow also talks about the next generation of women directors, the students she meets through teaching directing at UCLA. She notices that in
their working process they do not seem to follow through or take even aesthetic choices as far as she believes they need to go. The female students do
not seem to be willing to take that leadership, to risk being seen as forceful,
difficult, or demanding. Although she has no idea to what causes to attribute
this trend and clearly tries to counter it through her work as an educator, it
definitely gives her cause for concern.

Pamela Hendrick talks about her initial self-consciousness when she
started directing, explaining it as a mixture of external resistance to her size
and to her gender and self-doubt and insecurity based on her social conditioning as a woman. She has countered both of these factors by discovering
a collaborative, nonhierarchical model of leadership in which, under her guidance, an entire group can together focus on creative, collaborative problem-
solving and common goal setting:

> I think that gender has an impact on almost every facet of my working process
> in some ways; partly because I'm hyperaware, through my studies, of the way
> in which gender is performed in everyday life and how inherent it is in the
> texts that we use in theatre, how inherent it is in the vocal patterns we use,
> the body language we use, and the choices that young actors make, all actors
> make. I think they're all very gender-influenced. I think that the most obvi-
> ous way that gender manifests itself in my directing process is probably in the
> way in which the dynamic of the rehearsal process is set, the way in which
> my leadership role as a director is set up, and the way in which my actors inter-
> act with me, with each other, with the text and with the whole process. I think
> that gender very much comes into play there. I'm very comfortable with my
> gender as a leader now, but I haven't always been that way. When I started
> out as a director, I was much more self-conscious about my leadership role as
> a director. As a small woman, I felt often that my leadership was challenged
> as a director. When I first expressed an interest in directing as an under-
> graduate, my professors were, I think, amused and sort of metaphorically pat-
> ted me on the head because I was this petite woman, or "girl," as we were
> called back then. I think that I carried a lot of insecurity with my early deci-
> sions to pursue directing. I knew I wanted to do it. I was very interested in
> it, but I did feel quite insecure about my ability to command the kind of lead-
> ership that I thought was required then because—I know this is stereotyping
> to a certain extent—but it was a very paternalistic role. I came out of the
> school that really looked at the director as the benign dictator, the stern but
> loving father who would make you suffer but it would be for your own good.
> When I stepped into that role myself, I think I was feeling that I had to be
> more dictatorial, less pliable than men. It was a defensive posture. If I don't
> do this, if I don't behave more like a man than a man, then they will walk all
> over me. But I found that model very uncomfortable. Then I went in the

opposite direction and thought that what I could probably do is be almost a nondirector, it could all be very process-oriented and we could all share the power. That simply blurred everything because there were no clearly delineated roles. Therefore, there was no way to effectively solve problems when they arose. I constantly would have actors, usually women, telling me that I was just too nice and I had to be more of a hard-ass. It really wasn't until I started investigating the processes of conflict resolution that I came up with the model that really fit me comfortably as a director. My process has evolved to the point where I set up my rehearsal process as a collaborative, nonauthoritarian model that I'm very comfortable with, that I can get my actors to become very comfortable with, where rather than focusing on power and leadership issues, we can focus on creative, collaborative problem-solving, and common goal setting. In retrospect, I think my discomfort was mostly internal. It was a model that just wasn't me. I was trying to behave in an authoritarian fashion that was pretty much foreign to my way of communicating. It wasn't the way I related to my friends, to my family, to my colleagues when I was a performer, or as a teacher to my students. But for some reason, I felt that when I stepped into that role as director, I needed to mimic that benign dictator behavior for fear of being challenged by my actors. I think some of it was external, too. I think that my actors were used to that role as well and in fact did challenge me when I didn't effectively try to operate that way.

Liz Diamond shares this same experience of gaining confidence as her career progresses but is reluctant to attribute those early experiences solely to gender: "Over the years, I've gotten stronger because I've gotten more confident. Whether my initial lack of self-confidence about coming into a room and bossing people around, what that had to do with me as a woman versus what that had to do with me as a neophyte, I really don't know. I don't know what the determining factors are." All the women were given a chance to make a final statement at the end of the interview about gender and its influence, and Susan Finque seized the opportunity to reemphasize the acceptance of power as an issue of key importance for women in the theatre:

> I think the constant struggle for women is that in almost any organization you walk into, there's a man signing the checks, and you walk into the backstage and women are doing everything. We need to grab some privilege. We need to ask ourselves what we want in our craft and in the work and go after that—not what's good for people, not what we should be doing, not what we owe someone, but what we want. And though that may sound egocentric, I think that it ultimately will serve us as artists and as community workers because you are a better person to the people you are working with if you yourself are clear about who you are, what you want, what you need.

Summary

Whether the problems are external or internal, the ability to exercise authority and leadership has been clearly identified as a major gender issue.

Although some of these women directors came to leadership and an acceptance of their own power with difficulty while others assumed it easily, they all agree that it is definitely an essential aspect of being a director. The need for women directors to feel comfortable exercising their authority in a leadership position is equaled in importance by the need for others to also feel comfortable receiving that authority. In contrast to the few women who admitted to personal and internal discomfort with taking leadership, most women focused on their experiences of eternal resistance to a woman in power and how they learned to deal with them. Several issues became evident as the directors explored the various kinds of resistances they have experienced from others. A lack of familiarity with women in positions of authority can sometimes lead to responses ranging from curiosity to trepidation to outright resistance in varying degrees from actors or designers. Women directors often think they have to prove themselves repeatedly in order to establish their authority over the creative process. Direct challenges are most often experienced from older male actors or male designers, but some directors also experience similar resistance from other women. There is definitely a perceived intolerance for certain behaviors from a woman, such as forceful expressions of anger or power. This intolerance can lead to regular behavior modification on the part of the director, resulting in a more moderate style of leadership, a style many of the women equate with good directing regardless of gender. In fact, many of the women seem to have chosen to sidestep issues of power by concentrating on developing another aspect of the director's function, one for which they feel they have more affinity—collaboration.

Part Three • Collaboration Issues for Women Directors

6. COLLABORATIVE QUALITIES IN A GOOD DIRECTOR

If leadership and authority are fundamental qualities of a good director, so too is the ability to collaborate, to be inclusive of and sensitive to the creative input of others and to create an open and encouraging environment where artistic interaction can thrive and prosper. Even the most autocratic of directors must acknowledge the creative contributions of other artists. Therein lies the paradox of the director—to be the visionary orchestrator of all expressive elements and individuals in the production, and yet not simply treat them as raw materials to be used but rather allow them to contribute to the life of the piece through their own creative work as well. It is in their discussion of collaboration that the women interviewed express a sense of their greatest strengths as directors.

THE IMPORTANCE OF SUCCESSFUL COLLABORATION

The Early Theorists Again

The notion of successful collaboration obviously does not preclude the existence of leadership and, in fact, often results in an ideal of the director's authority being subtle or quiet rather than overt or confining. For a moment let us return to some of the same director-theorists cited earlier in the discussion of leadership qualities in a good director for what they have to say about the complementary quality of collaboration. In one way or another, all of the early directors and theorists stressed the importance of collaboration and identified theatre as a collaborative art. Ironically, collaboration was the greatest problem faced by Gordon Craig, one of the strongest advocates for total control by a single visionary artist, who discussed actors as if they were nothing more than puppets for his creative use. In spite of his conviction that this controlling vision was the most important factor for the successful director, practical artistic success eluded him, perhaps because he neglected the other side of the directing coin, collaboration.

Alexander Tairov describes the intrinsic role of the director as coordination and harmonization of individual creativity to the collective creativity.[1] Jacques Copeau speaks of exerting influence through sympathetic understanding and believes that the process of directing a play is most productive when it adapts to and accommodates every one of the diverse interests and creative individuals involved so that the needed unity evolves from these collaborators and is not imposed on them.[2] Tyrone Guthrie presents the same idea through his notion that the function of the director "is to be at rehearsal a highly receptive, highly concentrated, highly critical sounding board for the performance, an audience of one. He is not the drill sergeant, not the school master ... he is simply receiving the thing, transmuting it, and giving it back. ... His process is one of psychic evocation, and it is performed almost entirely unconsciously."[3]

Contemporary Directing Texts Explore Collaboration

In one way or another all the major directing texts explore the issue of collaboration, sometimes in conjunction with a specific step of the process, sometimes as a concept modifying all the diverse functions of director from start to finish. Often the notion is stated overtly, other times it is implied, but it is always present in some form or another. In addition, the exploration of the nature of theatrical collaboration almost always invokes such ideas as letting collaborators work *with*, not *for*, the director, learning to trust feelings and intuitions, being sensitive to individual emotions as well as the dynamics of group interaction, and nurturing the other artists by creating a positive environment of emotional support in order to make it safe to risk spontaneous creative ideas that are new and untried. Encouraging and stimulating the creative participation of the other artists should then lead to a larger, more exciting result than any director alone may conceive.

In preparation for his text on directing, Robert Benedetti sent a comprehensive survey to many prominent contemporary directors asking about their theatrical values, and repeatedly his respondents stressed the importance of collaboration to a director. He writes, "The most striking similarity among the responses I received is the repeated use of certain active words and phrases such as 'sharing,' 'collaboration,' 'commitment,' 'creative energy,' and 'flow.' The recurrent images express a kind of energy that is uninhibited and unselfish, flowing outward from the self to others—to fellow workers, to the audience, and finally, to the world at large."[4] Among others, Benedetti cites Zelda Fichandler, who emphasizes that theatre is "a collaborative form.

There's too much for any one person to bite off, and the most illustrious directors in history have always had people they share their work with. ... 'Collaborator' is really a wonderful word; it means 'to labor with.'"[5]

During a later interview with Arthur Bartow, Fichandler presented another insightful image of the art of collaboration and advocated its importance for any director: "We have to teach ourselves and each other the art of collaboration, 'co-laboring' in order to express a collective consciousness—the fundamental act of making theatre. In the rehearsal process, in the heat of opposing viewpoints, the right way is found. However, in the end, talking and working together is not enough. It's necessary to do more, to internalize one another's viewpoints, to think as ourselves and also as the others, to permit the perceptions and needs and priorities of the others to mingle with our own while preserving our separateness."[6]

Benedetti uses gardening as a useful metaphor to describe the way the director should support and nurture the collaborative artists, especially actors. What could be more nurturing than creating a fertile environment which allows seeds to grow and flourish? He translates the gardener's process into the progression of rehearsing a play in the following stages: preparing the climate of growth so the ensemble can work together effectively, planting the seed by giving a sense of direction to the group, cultivating through rehearsal exploration of all elements of characters and actions, shaping and pruning by editing input and solidifying connections in the emerging performance, and harvesting by adding visual/technical elements to synthesize all elements into a united performance.[7]

Robert Cohen believes we are currently entering a new period in the director's development that will put an even greater emphasis on collaboration. This transformation is a result of the decline of the authoritative and all-powerful director-manager prominent in the late nineteenth and early twentieth century. This decline has been accompanied by the rise during the last several decades of the free-lance director who has occasion to work with many different companies and situations in the course of a career and, as a result, requires a great deal more flexibility. This new way of working demands more collaborative skills than in the past. The director, rather than being an autocratic artistic leader, is now generally considered "the first among equals [because] the need for collaboration and for artful, effective collaboration, has never been more important than in the present age."[8]

As Cohen has stated, the role of the director does seem to be changing into a more collaborative one, but it is interesting to note that in addition to the increase of free-lance directing, there is a corresponding increase in women directors in the theatre, many of them in the position of director-manager. Perhaps their increased presence in the profession and the defining role of collaboration in their work has as much to do with the changing notion of the director's function as the rise of the free-lance director.

SOCIAL CONDITIONING AND COLLABORATION

Collaboration May Be Easier for a Woman

In one way or another, all of the women interviewed address the issue of collaboration, with most expressing the belief that collaboration is extremely important to their directing process; in fact, it often seems to define their work even more clearly than the notion of artistic leadership. A number of the directors interviewed believe the ability to collaborate comes more easily to women, especially because of their social conditioning as a mediator in the home and family environment. They believe this history allows them to embrace collaboration more fully than their male counterparts. Some even go so far as to say that women may be better trained for this aspect of directing because, as Rita Giomi puts it, "No matter how much we think society has changed, we as women are really trained from early days to watch people, to be sensitive to their emotions, to be ready and available to people, to take care, to nurture, and to develop all those qualities that I think are what make good directors."

Giomi elaborates on her beliefs regarding women's unique suitability for directing, referring to a conversation she had with another woman director on this very subject: "Emily Mann once told me that on the whole she thought women made better directors because we are trained from birth to observe. So much of directing is observation applied to specific situations. I'd never really heard it put that way, but I think she's really right. I would agree with it because I do think so much of directing is observation and attention to detail, and I think we are trained to do that from the beginning." Giomi is, however, reluctant to ascribe the ability to collaborate simply to gender differences, identifying that conclusion as an oversimplification of a very complex issue:

> What is great about theatre is the ability to take men and women and put them into a collaborative process. You're not just working with your own influences. You're working with your particular vision of the piece, but funneled through the influence of others as well. I'm not a high concept director, I'm not a director that walks in with a completed concept in advance. That's not the way I function. I rely a lot on designers and actors in terms of that collaborative process. One of the things I enjoy the most is channeling all that combined creative energy into a single vision of what the piece needs to say, what needs to be illuminated about the work. I don't think that is simply because I'm a woman. It's because of all I am and the way I work, and yes, of course it's colored by the fact that I'm a woman in this particular society, working in this particular business, with the particular influences I had growing up.

Others also referred to Emily Mann, long before I was able to interview her myself. At conferences and in print, Mann has been quite vocal about women's ability to collaborate making them ideally suited for the function of director, especially within the regional theatre environment, saying, "I think women are uniquely suited to work this way. Theatre is about collaboration, about people working together, and that involves real nurturance. What you're doing in a resident theatre is making artistic homes for people and enhancing the quality of life in a community. And that's long been a female job."[9] When I was finally able to meet with Mann herself, naturally I asked her to elaborate about her beliefs, and she was happy to comply, reiterating her often quoted belief in women's unique suitability for directing:

> If you're talking about what makes people tick and about the human condition and the emotional life and soul of character and story, then in fact you're talking about skills that have been traditionally thought of as female skills. It's actually quite subversive to say, but how women have been acculturated is a natural for directing. I cannot tell you how many men have said to me, "All my life I have never been able to open up to men. The people who know me emotionally are women." So, to have a woman director, and often it's the first time they've had one, is liberating for them because they're emotionally free. It's just a natural part of our culture that men show their feelings to women, not to other men. So if they're doing any kind of very scary or brave emotional work, many of them feel much more comfortable in a room run by a female. This is all talking in very broad general strokes, but it is so interesting when I look at the things that are asked of a good director, which is detail in emotion, detail in dress, detail in the decor of a home or a room, materials and things that often men don't think about twice. Also, I think when you're dealing with difficult relationship pieces, this is something that women were uniquely trained for, traditionally in our culture. It's supposed to be the woman's job to take care of relationship, to take care of people. That kind of training is very useful for the theatre. It may not be good for an equal relationship at home, but it's very good for the theatre. So there's all that going on, that kind of observation, knowing what's going on under the surface of something, under the words, watching behavior and sensing people's needs, both in terms of how they work and then in terms of what the text requires. There's all that stuff that is, in fact, the old-fashioned female skills.

Barbara Ann Teer also believes that as a woman she is uniquely suited to her work, particularly because of a deep sense that her creative work has a strong element of caring for others: "My grounding is in the culture of people of African descent. Culture comes from a Latin word that means 'to care for.' So when one is committed to taking care for and of other people, it appears that as a woman I may do a little more of that, whatever that means. I may be a little deeper into my caring mode, my heart chakra may be more open, because mothers historically take care of children. So from that point of view, I would say perhaps that is a natural gift of a woman to be able to care for, because we have children and we know what it's like to take care."

Although she initially thought of her way of working as being defined more by her background as an actor, Roberta Levitow also believes women are thoroughly socialized to stand in support of the work of others, making them ideal collaborators. She goes on to describe her own process of collaboration:

> I tend not to give an external description of the behavior or the choice. I tend to try to lead someone into it in a much more collaborative way, with them taking a lot of leadership in the character development. I leave more to an actor's own devising. I used to think that's because I was an actor, and because of that I came slowly towards expressing my desire for a performance from an external point of view. I didn't see it from the outside. I saw it from the actor's process, and the actor's process was more important to me than anything else. When I ask myself if that was because I was a woman, I think that one would have to acknowledge that a great majority of women in our culture and globally are better prepared, or prepared by instinct, or prepared by socialization, to stand in support of another person's effort, to feel satisfied when another person is making progress, and to get very involved in the process of the relationship. All of those things are, in a positive sense, part of being a collaborative worker—to be in support of someone else's progress as well as your own, to be involved in the nature of the process in getting that work done, and to stand by someone as they do their good work, while you do your good work. I'm sure that certain affects of my persona were part of that—meaning how I walked into the room, where I sat at the table, how loudly I spoke when I spoke up—all those things that are the affects of my personality, that are definitely "female-ish." That's why other people might have said, "Of course I was working for a woman, I would never mistake that process for a man's process." But I don't remember thinking of it that way.

Not only does Tori Haring-Smith agree with the others that collaboration comes easier to her as a woman, she believes it is a profound influence that goes beyond her directing work, becoming almost an unconscious part of her world view: "So much of the work I do is collaborative that I hardly see it as an influence now. It's something that spreads beyond the theatre for me. It's not just an artistic process, it's a way of seeing the world."

Collaboration Can Be Learned

Adele Prandini is another who believes that women have a background more conducive to the exchange of ideas, a conditioning that leaves them particularly receptive to being able to collaborate. Cautioning against value judgments or generalizations, however, she points out that it is a behavior men can also learn if it becomes important enough to them:

> It's hard to say that all women make better directors than all men. I don't think we can make that kind of sweeping generalization. What we can say is that women are trained and have a better understanding of being open and accepting other people's experience and respecting that. This is something men have to first get conscious of and then learn how to do. Women have been learning how to do this all along. It's very dangerous to make generalizations about

gender behavior these days, but at the same time you don't want to sweep the differences under the rug. How this relates to the battle of the sexes is the whole relationship of power. I think that good theatre is not based on a traditionally patriarchal, hierarchical structure; that structure works against art. I think collaboration among equals is a far more open process, and for that reason it's more creative. It's a marvelous, wonderful, powerful thing, that creativity, and if you can get five or six people at a rehearsal having a good day together, the power is magnified. It's an incredible thing. It has marvelous results.

Zelda Fichandler also talks about differences in gender conditioning and sees women's side of the equation, which she identifies as the receiving impulses, as much more relevant to collaborative efforts: "I think the art of the theatre is rooted in the art of paying attention, hearing, listening. That may be something that women are more accustomed to doing than men, who tend to be cast in the role of giving out rather than receiving, announcing rather than questioning, knowing rather than being curious, more active modes of behavior than women are accustomed to. If that hypothesis is true, it could be that women are favorably positioned to lead collaborative efforts toward the discovery of the deepest truth." She further emphasizes that the end product can be so much more complex and rich if it involves the best, most creative work of many individuals working together, truly exchanging and expanding their ideas in the process:

> I don't do collaboration in any sort of manipulative way. I really need it. I relish it. It makes your authorship—which is where the word authority comes from, authority means you "wrote it"—it makes what you write so much fuller and bigger if you can really incorporate the expertise of a lot of other people. Actors are living inside the moment, and if they're good actors, they can tell you what they find there. Designers bring a whole awareness of how space and space broken by objects can provide an emotional resonance or allow for choreographic movement in a way that you might not know as well as they do. The process is so much more thrilling when a group finds a collective truth. When there's a collective consciousness in a group, the process is exhilarating. If your vision can be shared and contributed to by others, that can only strengthen the vision. It can't hurt the vision, it can't deplete it. It can only add to it and make it more vertical, more complicated.

Fichandler goes on to talk about her beliefs regarding the teaching of collaboration in directing: "To teach this is better than to teach a hierarchical system where the director does this, the designer does this, the actor does that, the stage manager does that, to compartmentalize all this so that there's no interchange." In her own teaching, she has used the idea of "role reversal" to explore this interchange of ideas with her students and to prepare them better for future collaborations: "I would have a small group—the director, the designer, the dramaturg, and a small pool of actors was available as needed. I'd give them the opposite function to perform. I'd give the director the design for the project; the designer, the dramaturgical part; the dramaturg, the directing role.

And they'd rotate so they'd begin to empathize with what the other person's role was." This was an attempt to break down the tendency to compartmentalize functions and to give all the artists a broader perspective on collaboration and the production process.

Alana Byington believes that women are sometimes uniquely suited to the collaborative elements of directing, but she shares an interesting anecdote about collaboration and perceptions of gender differences:

> I would have to say, if I was going to use very general principles of feminine and masculine, that a woman is more suited to directing because the things that we consider feminine traits are things directors need. I absolutely do believe that. Now whether that goes along with believing only women can have those traits, of course I don't go along with that. One of the best stories I ever heard about a director was about a male director who was so good at making actors believe that something was their own idea that the actors in the show were saying, "He didn't do anything. We had to come up with everything!" Whereas my friend, who had watched him in rehearsal, saw with what art he pushed someone in a direction he thought they needed to go in such a way that they ultimately found the answers themselves. That's brilliant. That's not something that's easy to carry off, but I think that's the height of good directing.

Byington identifies this particular male director as gay, which brings up the question of where gay and lesbian artists might fall along the spectrum of masculine and feminine attributes. She has no ready answer for the question, however, nor did the interviews identify sexual preference as anything other than an additional influence on certain artists who brought up the issue on their own. Byington also discusses how the need for ego gratification can interfere with one's ability to collaborate well, implying that although the behavior can be learned, women's cultural ability to suppress ego might make them better prepared for collaboration:

> I really think you have to leave ego out of it as much of you can. Keep the part of it that allows you to work, that pushes you forward, but keep it out of the process. It's not about me, it's about the work. Perhaps women have been forced to put ego aside so often that I don't know if it's nature or nurture, but they're better trained for that. On the other hand, I don't know that I'm that well trained for it. I've never had children. I've never had to cater to a husband. I never had to cater to a father. I had a father with a lot of "feminine" traits. I was always encouraged to be smart and to pursue whatever goals I wanted. So, if I have a predisposition to suppress ego, it's not nurture, it's nature. I do know that the artists, designers, and actors I've worked with who share this view (work before ego) are the ones I've had the most fruitful collaborations with, and there are equal numbers of men and women.

Like several others interviewed, Byington is willing to admit the possibility that women might be better suited to collaboration, but few are eager to make a definitive statement to that effect.

There Are Always Exceptions

Gloria Muzio is cautious as she begins her discussion of collaboration, saying, "I don't know what it feels like to direct a play as a man, but it seems to me that it's harder for a lot of men to be true collaborators. I'm being very careful because I've got a lot of good friends who are men. In fact, I know women who are very tough and not interested in feelings and I know men who are soft directors and not that interested in leadership." Acknowledging that she dislikes generalities about gender and can almost always find an exception to any pronouncement that can be made, Muzio goes on to describe her own sense of why she can collaborate so easily:

> GM: What has been very important to me is establishing those collabora-tive relationships over periods of time so that I always prefer, as I'm sure most directors do, to work with designers I have relationships with. Therefore, this whole leadership issue isn't an issue at all because you're working with peo-ple who trust you and whom you trust and collaborate with. Ultimately, the final decisions are yours and the world of the play is in your head somewhere, or your heart, but you are truly collaborating. You're using the best of every-body around you.
>
> RD: Do you think that comes to you easier because you're a woman?
>
> GM: I think it takes pushing your ego down. I can't make a judgment about men having bigger egos because there are women who do as well, but it comes to me fairly easily because the show is never about my ego. It is about subli-mating a lot of my needs and my ego for a higher purpose, which I think women are very good at. That really is a lot of what directing is, finding what the higher purpose is and pushing down whether I want to do this today or not. It's not about that. It's about what I need to do in order to get that higher purpose. I was brought up in a very traditional family and was brainwashed that my needs were not as important as [those of] the boys around me. That message was very clear, and I fought against that, rebelled against that terri-bly, violently. Yet that still was a message I learned as a kid. I think that as an adult, I'm always wrestling with that and find that I can use that now in a way that's helpful.

Mary Robinson puts a different twist on the gender question by talking about what she believes is a changing stereotype as well as the general ten-dency she sees in all directors toward a more collaborative approach: "You can't say women are better directors because they're motherly, because the whole definition of fathers has changed. Fathers are not the stern task mas-ters they were once purported to be. Fathers are much more motherly and vice versa, so that distinction has blurred, and I think the fathers are more nurturing. Perhaps men directors have changed over the years as well."

Melia Bensussen also talks about her ability to suppress her ego and adds her awareness of a cultural influence on the kind of gender condition-ing she experienced while growing up:

MB: There's a way of doing it, a language of collaboration that I feel as a woman comes very naturally to me. The more sophisticated I get, in some ways I move away from some of that, but the essence I would hope I would always retain. There is not a need to be, as it were, the big dog on the set, the big dog in the theatre. I take it as a given that I'm in charge, and there's a lot of room for other people to create as well. I don't need anyone to think that it's all coming from me, even if it is. I'd rather it feel like a collaborative process.

RD: And you see that coming easier to you because you are a woman?

MB: I do, but I think part of that comes of being raised in Mexico City. I'm half Mexican; my father's Mexican. I think sometimes it's hard to separate gender from gender in a context because I was raised with the idea that pushy women are the worst thing in the world. To be a loud aggressive woman, to be a woman who tells men specifically what to do, is really to be unattractive in all senses of the word. I don't mean simply physically, it's just to be an ugly person. So, I think the collaborative instinct could be interpreted as manipulative to some extent, but it comes from a life of wanting to share, an apparent sharing of authority. I don't mean to say that it's simply a manipulative tool and that the cooperation and collaboration are not useful, that it's simply a way of being in charge. I think it really leads to a collaborative spirit.

Pamela Hendrick believes that the increasing number of women becoming directors and women's propensities for collaboration are going to have a very positive effect on the state of contemporary theatre:

I feel optimistic in many ways that as more and more women move into the role of director, they will be changing the model under which theatre is produced and that it is going to become more collaborative. It already is becoming more collaborative. I really think the main reason is that a collaborative model takes the focus off individual personalities and power struggles and puts it on serving the play. I think theatre is such a complex art form and it takes so much energy that any model that can get rid of the negative energy and concentrate on the positive energy, that can set up and work for common goals, is going to be a more efficient way of putting theatre up. I think its time has come.

In contrast to those who believe women are better suited to directing, Timothy Near wonders whether gender differences really have anything at all to do with the directing process. She calls attention to the already blurred gender boundaries in the theatre, previously alluded to by several others:

TN: If you take the names off, or just put us all in capes or something so nobody knows, I wonder how much you'd be able to tell. Of course, a male director has got a lot of female in him. When you go into the arts, the genders start to blend because we're artists.

RD: Don't you think there are a lot of things about the directorial function that we might associate with gender behavior, but which are also things we associate with good directing?

TN: I agree with that, but I think that it can be very confusing at times to actors. I think women are more collaborative, but I also think a good woman director ultimately puts a very strong hand on what her piece is. That moment where the hand starts to move in and make those decisions can be confusing to people who either want it black or white. It's either all collaborative, or it's all dictatorial and patriarchal. I think that's why some women directors are confusing to actors. One week we want collaboration, and the next week we are dictators. We're not just happy to go with however the whole crowd votes. The way that we work is to try to have everybody put forth their ideas. We know that what we're moving towards is going to be richer if there's more diverse opinion and input. But ultimately a good director has a vision.

The ability to respond to diverse opinions and input is certainly not unique to women, but most directors I spoke with believe the emphasis on the importance of being truly open to contributions from other artists is more common among women directors. This premise seems to involve an acceptance of a somewhat stereotypical notion that women have more access to their emotions and intuitions than men and that they are more comfortable within a group process. This book cannot avoid reference to these clichés, because they are often part of the responses received, but most of the women are quick to point out that in the theatre they believe sex-role stereotypes are much less distinct than in society at large. Many are also able to cite experiences with highly collaborative and nurturing male directors or, conversely, with women who felt a strong need to control the artistic process in an oppressive way, thereby undermining any sense of true collaboration. For every stereotype there always seem to be exceptions, yet certain stereotypical descriptions persist in the comments of those who are hoping to break them. It seems difficult for them to find a way to discuss issues of gender and collaboration without first referring to the clichés, then trying to disclaim them.

A DIFFERENT APPROACH TO COLLABORATION

Women's Ways of Collaborating

Collaboration has long been important in writing about the directing process, but many of the women interviewed seem to believe that their approach to collaboration is different from what they have experienced or heard about the approaches of many male directors. This point of view is especially prominent among women who had careers as actors before going into directing. Many believe that while men have tended to acknowledge the need for collaboration, they have often seemed reluctant to truly give over much of their control to the group process. This need to stay in control seems to make their process less conducive to true collaboration. Anne Bogart tries to elaborate on the differences she sees in her approach to collaboration:

Liz Huddle (standing) at a design conference for a forthcoming production of Shakespeare's *A Midsummer Night's Dream* at Portland Center Stage (1995). She is working with (from left) scenic designer Karen Gjelsteen, lighting designer Meg Fox, and trapezist/choreographer Robert Davidson, who will help her to make the fairy kingdom airborne. Photo by Michael Holcombe.

AB: I'm going to say the ultimate stereotypical thing. They say there's two ways to make a sculpture. One is you have an image in your head and you have a stone, and you bang away at that stone until you have the thing that's in your head. The other way is to know that inside the stone there's a sculpture, and your process is to find the thing that's already there. I very naturally belong in the second category. I come in having done a great deal of research and work and thinking about a production, but I don't come in with the finished product in my head. I find that is a way a lot of the people aren't used to working. I say, "In any actor there is a perfect actor. How do I find that perfect thing?" instead of trying to bang that person into my image of what they should be.

RD: Do you think that's because of being a woman, or do you think that's just being a good director?

AB: I think it's because of being a woman. I actually do. Because that's what happens to us biologically. There is a baby in us and it comes out.

Liz Huddle identifies herself as only recently more aware of the influence of gender in her work as a collaborator, but is able to make a clear distinction between what she believes is the masculine side of her work and the more feminine, collaborative side:

I'm very aware of it now, in terms of the process that I utilize, which is a nurturing process—trying to wed the needs of the play and playwright with the individual creative instincts of artists, actors, designers, etc., and to bring those together into a cohesive, complementary whole that grows together—rather than dictating what happens. I find that most directors come from a very masculine place. The instinct is very masculine; it's dictatorial, it's intellectual, for the most part it's a place of control, and it can be a place of manipulation. As I've watched the process that I use, I distrusted it at first. I thought it was not working. It really does, but it takes tremendous faith and confidence that the methodology you are using will indeed bear fruit and to maintain enough control of it, to maintain the objectivity to a degree that you are able to bring it to fruition. I'm not an auteur. I don't begin with conceptual vision of a play. I'm not a concept director. I begin with, "What is the play? What does the play want to say?" and then work very collaboratively with a group of artists, actors, designers, and develop the play from there. I usually begin with the actor and with the language of the piece and develop from there. I really deal from the internals of the play. I'm much more interested in what a group of actors and performers bring to a piece than them realizing a preconceived vision that I bring in, and I love working that way.

The collaborative process as described by Huddle is used similarly by Sharon Ott, another woman with a strong sense of her tendencies toward what would be considered masculine behavior in conjunction with her desire to also be open and receptive to collaboration. In our conversation, Ott is articulate in her ability to define the differences in approach she perceives between men and women. She had recently been reading Carol Gilligan's *In a Different*

Voice, which explores gender differences in psychological and moral develop-ment, and she invokes imagery similar to Gilligan's hierarchy and web[10] to explain the differences she perceives in women's ability to collaborate:

> Women really are a little more apt to be collaborative in their general notion of how things should be done than men. I don't know why that is, but I do believe it's true. Responsibility is shared laterally. Women are particularly comfortable with that, and not as likely to want to assume a hierarchical order with them at the top but rather a more lateral order that, if they're the leader, has them at the center. It's a circle radiating out from something as opposed to a line going from bottom to top. Sometimes that can be problematic because I think that society still is based on a hierarchical behavior model or orga-nizing principle. It's more obvious to me from the women film directors I know. The film industry in America is so male, and it's so much based on this notion of the director as a kind of fascistic major domo. Almost all the women film directors I know get into trouble because they do things like ask the cin-ematographer what he thinks of this or that idea, and the producer will say, "No, you can't do that." It creates chaos on the set because it's perceived as not being authoritative, whereas really it's being collaborative. It's seeing your-self as the leader, but in a different way, like at the center of a wheel as opposed to the top of a column. I do think that affects artistic choices and also gen-eral organizational things.

In observing Ott's rehearsal process, I could definitely see the openness to input as well as her position at the center of the work. The playwright and actors were constantly asked for their opinions and impressions. Ott often used the phrases "Your ideas are my ideas," "Let's see how this feels," "Let's explore that idea for a while," or "Feel free to move if an impulse happens," when experimenting with staging or interpretation in the early rehearsals. The playwright, Heather McDonald, voiced her appreciation of Ott's openness to me, noting that she had worked with some directors who had never asked her for her opinion. McDonald was quick to point out, however, that this open versus closed attitude did not necessarily manifest along gender lines in her experience. Although the openness was clearly part of Ott's process, it was also equally clear that she was in control, at the center of all this experi-menting. On one occasion, when too many ideas were flying fast and furi-ously, she cut off the input and tried to simplify what was happening in order to clear the air and, perhaps, to bring the process back around to something closer to her own emerging vision.

In her discussion of collaboration, Cynthia White cites gender differences in communication as described by Deborah Tannen in *You Just Don't Under-stand*. Tannen, a linguist, takes care to remind her readers that generaliza-tions tend to capture similarities and obscure differences, but she believes that ignoring differences is riskier than any danger in naming them. One of the points in Tannen's book which has a strong influence on White's think-ing is that differences in communication between men and women often come from their differing emphasis on intimacy and connectedness versus independence and autonomy. White believes this difference creates a distinctly female approach to collaboration and is part of what makes her more comfortable with group process: "I think there is one typical male/female difference in that I'm much more inclined to direct and lead by group consent. Men are less inclined to say, 'Well, what shall we do?' As a director, you know what you want to do and you want the group to get there. A more male approach would be more to tell them what to do. I think I do tend to mold the group through group process."

This sense of connectedness and comfort that White feels with the group process is echoed by many of the women. Mary Robinson is also fascinated by Tannen's work and draws it into her conclusions about women's ways of, and ease with, collaborating:

> MR: I think the big generalization one might draw, and I think it's a simplistic one, is that perhaps women tend to be more oriented towards collaboration. I'm an actor's director, as opposed to what might be known as a conceptual director. This is not to say that I can't do that kind of work and don't enjoy it, but the work I most enjoy as a director is the kind of one on one, one on two, one on three work in rehearsal where we're really getting at the psychological meaning of the text. To make a big generalization, I think that's maybe a female characteristic, whereas I think men at times can be more interested in painting with broad brush strokes. I like the littler ones.

> RD: In terms of the process itself, are there any particular points at which you see gender to have a more significant influence?

> MR: All the way through, but then we're getting into generalizations because collaboration is one of the main things I love about directing. When you direct, you can touch all the various aspects of the process. I think what I love about it is trying to bring out the best in everybody, myself included, and coming to consensual choices which one wouldn't arrive at on one's own. I sometimes find it actually rather hard to arrive at a choice when I have to make it on my own. That could be seen to be female. I read that Deborah Tannen book which I thought was fascinating. It talks about women's management styles as much more consensual, that a woman might know what she wants but wants it to be something that the people who are working for and with her arrive at themselves. Men sometimes find this manipulative, but that's exactly the way I direct. Even if I know exactly what I want, I think it's much better if it can be arrived at by the actor because then it is the actor's choice and it is much more organic and informed and personal. I might know what I want, but I won't tell the actor because I want to know if the actor will arrive at the same choice in a different way and bring different colors to it and maybe show me something I didn't know. If all we're dealing with is my imagination, then it's going to be a very limited result. Whereas if it's mine plus all the various other people I'm collaborating with, then it will be that much richer and more exciting. I think that's probably the way most directors, male or female work, but that is, in the Deborah Tannen book, pointed out as a particularly female way of working. I can't ignore the fact that that's the way I work. If that's perceived to be female, then I direct like a woman, I guess.

As we heard in a previous chapter, the so-called compliment of being told you "direct like a man" is usually received with ambivalence. While there is occasionally similar ambivalence in thinking about whether they "direct like women," in relationship to our discussions of collaboration, this designation is much more easily accepted, and in some cases even embraced.

Collaboration Leads to Shared Success

An assumption made by all the directors seems to be that in the theatre production process, the whole is definitely greater than the sum of its parts, that is, if collaboration is working effectively. Seret Scott clearly agrees that whether or not it may have any relationship to gender, collaboration is an invaluable part of her process: "When you tell someone what you want without the process of them finding it, they feel aborted in expression. Then you don't get either performance, the one they could have given or the one you want. You get something in between and a lot of ill-tempered people because you're not allowing them to discover anything."

Adele Prandini emphasizes choosing the creative team as the first step toward a successful group process and articulates her belief that women approach the creating of that team with more openness:

> AP: There are many relationships that create a theatre performance. So then, who is the artistic team that I want to work with? Who are these people? What's important to them? What are their goals? What challenges are they looking for in life? Every aspect of theatre makes a statement, so it's important in choosing those collaborators to ask, "Can we work together? Can you communicate?" The process is very important.
>
> RD: I think that particular part of the process may be the same for all directors. A good director wants to build a good artistic team. Do you see yourself, as a woman, developing that team or nurturing that team in any unique ways?
>
> AP: I think that a good director is wise enough to think in terms of teamwork, but often times that is not what we see. We see one person thinking, "I'm the most important part of this puzzle. I'm the artist and the rest of you are working for me and are insignificant here." That manifests itself sometimes by gender lines, and it's silly. But, if you do have what I feel is a more enlightened understanding of theatre, then choosing that team and working with that team is very important.

Prandini then explains her belief that although both are necessary in the directing process, collaboration is much more important to her than power. She seems to be criticizing a kind of power that she believes is antithetical to collaboration and involves too much control: "We're not here to control art. Our job is to expand. You can't expand something if you've got one person saying, 'I want to control it all.' The director is ultimately responsible.

There are some decisions that you need to make on your own; I mean, you're the bottom line here. However, collaboration is very open, a big exchange process. You need to have the wisdom to know the people you're working with, know their strengths, have an idea of what they do better and take the time to explore them, what their thoughts are, what their ideas are. That's not about control. That's not about 'I know everything and we have to do it my way.'"

Having the wisdom and openness to allow others to explore their own ideas is behavior Prandini clearly advocates in any good director but seems to expect more easily of women. Barbara Ann Teer also says she gives her collaborators "the space to learn from trial and error, as long as it comes from a place in the heart." She, however, attributes this more to her background as an actress:

> The way directors worked with me when I was acting, because I supposedly was very talented as an actress, was that they gave me total space to do whatever I needed to do. I could come up with far more creative things than they could for a character. Once I read the play five or six times, I would know what the character needed to do. I work that way with my people—and it's not just with acting, it's with programs, it's with everything—I give you the space to fall on your face because that's the best way to learn. I'm there to make sure you look good. So if you are gifted, and most people that I know are, I'll let you stretch out and do what you want to do. If it's something that I think doesn't further the purpose of the play or the purpose of the person, I'll never take away anything, but I'll add something to make it look the way everybody will be happy. There is a standard of what works and what doesn't work in theatre. So if you know that standard, then you will guide them so they stay within the context of that standard, so they're not doing something that will embarrass them, or make them look overly dramatic, or like they're underacting, or being phony or pretentious. If it's not gutsy and it doesn't come from the heart and it's not honest and open, then I will guide them so that does happen. As a director, that's my job, but by and large, I think you need to give performers the space to develop on their own.

Letting people make discoveries on their own is also very important to Pamela Hendrick, but she is always very careful to make sure that the process, however open for exploration it may be, is also controlled by the group setting of goals, a positive work environment, and the mutual respect of all collaborators.

> When I go into rehearsal, I tend to do a couple of things. First of all, I try to make sure that we are constantly working for common goals. At the beginning and end of each rehearsal, I review what we have accomplished that we should be proud of, where we need to go next, and what work still needs to be done. In that way, I feel like I'm always building on the success of my artists rather than blaming them for their failures. So I would say that my rehearsal process is very success-based. I also ask for and receive a lot of input from my artists, and I give them a lot of freedom to contribute their own ideas

and their own perceptions. Then I shape those ideas and perceptions to fit my production concept. If I reject an idea, I always try to be very clear with them about why it doesn't fit into the production concept and try to keep the idea of serving the play in the front of everybody's mind. The other thing I do is stress constantly with my company members the need for mutual respect. I very aggressively try to keep turf protecting out of my rehearsal process. I never allow that sort of combative language to enter into the rehearsal process. I always try to stop it immediately. I think that keeping those kind of hierarchical and competitive attitudes out of the rehearsal room is probably more of a female model than a male model.

References to group process, shared success, and a resulting product more rich and full as a result of collaborative input were very common during our discussions. Positive experiences over time have clearly resulted in shared good feelings about the efficacy of collaboration.

Loving the Exploration Process

The women I spoke with were nearly unanimous in their affinity for the collaborative elements of the directing process. In spite of potential challenges to their authority from collaborators who occasionally perceive a love of working things out and asking for input as a lack of decisiveness and vision, many of the women still insist that exploration in rehearsals, even allowing oneself to get lost in the process, is extremely important, even desirable, in their way of working. One director who seeks collaboration and loves exploration is Susana Tubert. She discusses her desire to create a group dynamic in the rehearsal process in which everyone feels encouraged to participate:

> I know that by now the idea that women are perhaps more nurturing is a bit of a cliché, but I wonder if the way in which my gender is most clearly manifested in my directing process is through the dynamics I try to create in the room. Sometimes I jokingly tell everyone to "Try everything so that I can have my final say." But the truth is that, perhaps after too many years in Argentina under countless military regimes and fascism, I am very uncomfortable with playing the authoritarian/parental figure in the rehearsal room. I don't like actors to wait for permission from me to try something. I not only encourage but I expect everyone to bring ideas to the floor. It's liberating to trust your cast and to treat them like adults. Perhaps in my unconscious I'm trying to create a perfect world of respect and openness where people can feel safe enough to fail. Perhaps this is the world I never had but always longed for, and as a director I get to invent it every day.

JoAnne Akalaitis is another who loves the rehearsal process and talks about the sense of getting lost in the exploration. Perhaps this penchant developed from her experience with Mabou Mines, a company that afforded her over twenty years in a very dynamic and creative collaboration of artists. She is clearly looking for collaborators with enormous creativity and experience, artists who will work as equals. Akalaitis also identifies another way in which women might have a certain advantage in an exploratory situation:

> Directing has been for a long time pretty much a man's job, and men are supposed to know what they are doing. In a way, one is luckier to be a woman because you don't have that burden of centuries and centuries of having to be filled with confidence. As a woman director, I think one is also blessed because you can say, "I don't know." I say "I don't know" all the time. "I don't know, what do you think?" When someone says, "This doesn't make sense," I also say, "So what?" It's really great not to know because the most exciting moments are the moments when you don't know. For me, doing theatre is very much about the process. I love rehearsal. I love it because rehearsal is where you get lost. In rehearsal is where you fall into big black holes. You fall into that hole and you're covered with mud and slime, and then you lift your nostrils up to try and breathe, and someone steps on your head, and then you have one finger that's crawling out of the well and someone steps on your hand and it starts to bleed, and then you think you have a bit of a glimmer of an idea, and you fall down and have amnesia. It is very much about struggle, and not knowing, and opening the door and there's another door, and opening that door and there's a brick wall. It's about getting lost, but if you are willing to get lost, you might find a way out. Then again, you might not; there's no guarantee about any of this. It can all be a disaster, but it's very interesting. I think it's a life-enhancing activity. It's a spiritual activity, and it's an activity that perhaps broadens communication. It deepens the understanding of what community is because certainly one of the most powerful aspects of theatre is that it is a communal event. You're never lonely if you're in the theatre. So the process is important to me.

Loving the struggle for illumination and inspiration is common to many of the women with whom I spoke. They do not seem to be afraid of ambiguity or uncertainty during the process. In fact, some, like Akalaitis, seem to welcome it. Julianne Boyd reflects on the ability to say, "I don't know," which she considers integral to the collaborative process: "I think it's really true that women can say 'I don't know' more freely, but I think the best male directors do that, too. I think it's a sign of maturity rather than being male or female. The moment you can say, 'I don't know, what do you think?' you have a collaborative process. It's when the director has all the answers and the actors are trying to fit into this rigid pattern that [it] is not a collaboration."

Julie Taymor agrees, pointing to men's social conditioning as an unfortunate and detrimental factor for them in directing: "Quite often men feel like they can't show when they don't know what they're doing. There's a feeling that they have to remain in that position of strength or they'll lose their power. I don't feel that at all. I feel that I have such a confidence about what I do and what I know that I can tell you when I don't. It doesn't take away from my talent or my position, my authority, my power. I haven't the faintest idea whether that's a feminine thing or not, but I do know that it works very well with actors."

While she did not attribute this tendency specifically to gender, Michelle Blackmon also loves the collaborative experience. She used a recent personal experience to describe her willingness to say she doesn't always know the answers in rehearsal. She, like the others, seems to find freedom in not needing to be an expert, at least not in the early stages of rehearsals:

> Theatre is a very collaborative process, and what I like about it is the collaboration. I enjoy that input from other people and the fact that I need to be open as an artist to allow those other feelings and ideas to come in. I get most excitement out of work when other people have ideas and they bounce them off me and I bounce mine off them, and we can create something better with this multitude of ideas. It's given me a greater appreciation for a lot of things, and much more enjoyment of the process of theatre, as opposed to what I see happening out there now, which is very product oriented. When I went into rehearsals for *Soldier's Play*, the first thing I said to the guys was, "Okay, look: I'm not a man and I'm not going to try to pretend that I know everything there is to know about men. You have not been in World War II, so we all have a lot of research to do. We'll do it together and we'll work together." So, we had a learning process together, and I think they saw that in the whole process we went through in rehearsal, I was willing to say, "We're doing it together." I allowed myself to be open in that sense, to say, "Hey, I'm not the expert here, and I will listen to whoever is."

The image that these women present, by and large, when they are speaking about collaboration, is one of excitement, involvement, and commitment to the process. They clearly see collaboration as an indispensible element in their work as artists. As Ott points out, most of them see themselves at the center of a web of artists and are willing to take control when they believe it to be necessary. Most are reluctant, however, to think of themselves as the only one controlling the ultimate destiny of a production.

A Single Dissenting Voice

As always, just when you might think consensus is about to be reached, there is at least one dissenting voice. In this case, it is Maria Irene Fornes, who insists that she is "not into collaboration." Although she doesn't talk as much or as eagerly about the collaborative process, Fornes does put a strong emphasis on the working process and experimentation within that process. She always focuses her comments on the controlling vision of the director, however. Describing the work as an evolution, Fornes clearly adjusts and changes as she goes through the rehearsal process, but she does not seem to want any help while she does it. She expressed during one rehearsal that she most emphatically did not want input from an assistant director provided for her by the theatre, and she insisted on doing her own choreography for a dance segment of the show. Furthermore, at that same rehearsal she stated that she was against a director giving actors much input because she believes the actors lack an overview. She maintains that the work is hard enough to realize without confusing the process with a multitude of ideas. She had previously worked with the highly collaborative Open Theatre but believes that even in the most seemingly open of collaborations, the director must be the bottom line and exert a strong sense of control.

My perception of her process, based on the four days I observed early in the rehearsal period, was that she does respond to actor input but in a much less open and obvious way than most of the other women describe. Although Fornes does not ask actors directly for their opinions, she clearly utilizes their presence and their activities onstage as an element in an ongoing, but tacit, collaboration. She will observe something that an actor does and incorporate it into her own thinking if it appeals to her or seems to fit what she is trying to accomplish. While Fornes clearly discourages discussion about what the actors think should be happening onstage, she seems to explore and test many different things with them, watching carefully to see what works and what does not. The process is very nonverbal, however; she seems to accept subtle input from actors but simply does not want to open the matter to discussion. An example is her interaction with an actor in the play with whom she had worked several times in the past. This woman intuitively understood that she was free to experiment with physical or vocal embellishment to directions Fornes had given her and to expand the boundaries of the notes she had been given, as long as she didn't need to talk about it. Fornes comes in with very few preconceived notions, and her process involves response to the moment by moment interaction of the actors, which is itself a kind of collaboration, but I am quite certain that she is highly conscious of herself as the sole author of the production. In our interview, she talks about her love for the process of directing:

> If you're a director, you have to be involved in that process. Not just in saying, "Oh, I wish it were already opening night because I know exactly how I want to do it." You have to love the process. If you have already that kind of relish to say, "Oh, here we go to do this thing," you're not giving up anything, you're just entering into something else. I think there aren't many directors who don't love the process. Those who don't love the process love the play, and they love the ideas they have, and they want to see that, exactly that, achieved. So, from the beginning everything is perfectly blocked. There is exactly everything that they want. I'm very strict about blocking, but it has nothing to do with any preconceived idea. It's just that as I see the particular person moving as they do, I begin to get ideas from who they are and what they are doing.

Fornes seems in a way to equate control with the preplanning of the visual/technical aspects of the production rather than recognizing that her own control is almost as complete as those who preplan. It is simply that her control evolves from moment to moment rather than coming in at the beginning as a complete package. Although she is constantly adjusting as she goes, she does control those adjustments quite closely and is rather infamous for miniscule adjustments to physical staging in order to find the perfect picture. These tiny adjustments are part of a greater picture of an artist who does not work with themes because she finds the very idea of doing that "paralyzing." Her way of working in both writing and directing is to start with the little details and work closely with them to "get under the situation." Several of the other women thought this sort of attention to detail, as opposed to concentrating on a supposedly universal theme, to be quintessentially female. This point of view particularly reflects an awareness of women's traditional concern with and control over the details of the household and the daily life of the family. Even Fornes believes this arena is one place where women clearly hold more control and influence.

POSSIBLE NEGATIVES IN COLLABORATION

Process Can Supersede Results

In spite of their positive feelings about collaboration as a way of working, several women also perceive potential pitfalls in the collaborative process. The most prevalent is an awareness that a strong focus on collaboration does not always lead to good artistic results. Victoria Parker feels a lack of certainty about being able to deliver the final product: "As a director, I know that I can make the actors comfortable. I know that I can make a safe territory for them, and I can communicate with them decently. But I don't always know that I'm going to be able to deliver to the audience, who is trained on television and the media, something that both satisfies their typical kind of hunger and also says what I want to say." Nikki Appino is aware that her "feminine focus" on process doesn't always make for good art: "My process attempts to find a more inclusive and less disfunctional way of operating. Whether it succeeds or not, or whether it makes good art or not, is not always certain. Often what I find in my own work is that the process is fairly internal and, I would say, almost more important to me than the art has been at certain times."

Although she believes their position in the family as wives and mothers, their cultural background, and the societal expectations for their behaviors make women excellent collaborators (probably even better than men in our society), Julia Miles of the Women's Project cautions against becoming too conciliatory, saying women's conditioning "may make them a little less aggressively precise or demanding. I think women see life in a rounder context than men. You can see a lot of different sides of the problem, but I think you have to be aware that you can use it too much, and it can trip you up."[11]

Susan Finque also explores this same issue, at the same time making a careful distinction between collaboration and the collective process. After first cautioning that nurturing behavior can sometimes result in the suppression of one's personal needs and goals, she emphasizes the goal of coalition, or bringing together unique and diverse interests, but with a clear definition of leadership and boundaries to avoid the detrimental aspects of collective work:

> Working collectively is actually good as long as you go in there with a clear identity and there's good leadership. The collective process can be very draining if there's not a clear visionary. Coalition is what that's all about. I wouldn't say that I would recommend the collective as a theatre process. It's very different than building an ensemble. The collective is where everyone has equal voice. It's a great learning process, but it's not a great way to make art. An actor should be able to do their work, and a director should be able to do hers. I do think that when people with strong individual identities get together and work, because they have something in common or something they want to make work about, that is very exciting.

When these women directors talk about their emphasis on collaboration, my perception is that they all presume a kind of leadership or organizing function in their role as director, quite a bit like Cohen's "first among equals." Being the first doesn't free the woman director from another potential danger in the collaborative process, however. Brenda Hubbard clearly identifies this problem, one which is very closely related to issues of self-doubt and internal problems with power discussed earlier: "I think I am sometimes talked into things that I wouldn't do. Every time I err, it's because I haven't followed my instincts. I don't follow my instincts, usually, when I am challenged by someone else. It could be a producer, or a designer, sometimes an actor challenging me. I think that's a gender thing because I think women are much more inclined to accept criticism about themselves as being true. I think men are much more inclined to disassociate themselves from it. I'm not very good at detaching. I think that men are trained to be able to detach much more easily."

Although she believes that women collaborate more comfortably than their male counterparts, Tori Haring-Smith identifies external reception of collaboration as a potential negative, saying that in some ways she finds collaboration harder because of gender:

> You're immediately walking into a world defined by expectations that are culturally masculine. The expectation is that the director will make decisions and be strong and give orders and demand and get what they want from the actors by screaming loud enough for it. If that's the expectation and then you walk in and your impulse is to be collaborative, there can be problems. I think collaborative males get accepted better than collaborative females because collaborative males at least have the biological equipment and the deep voice to carry the authority culturally, whereas the female is culturally encoded as not

having as much inherent authority when they walk in. I feel that people expect me to direct like a male, in an authoritarian way, and when I direct collaboratively, people don't know how to deal with the fact that I'm not a strong male, but I'm not a weak female either.

Haring-Smith then describes her early experiences with actors during the discussion of her notes after rehearsal. She would always have very detailed ideas about what she wanted to say to her actors, but she wanted to hear their own self-evaluation before she shaped her specific observations. Her experience has been that the actors saw her as less than authoritative because they read her desire for their input as a need for prompting, that she was somehow relying on them instead of doing her own job. She has since developed an opening speech whenever she works with a company she doesn't know: "When I go in with a new cast, one of my biggest concerns is to tell them ahead of time what it is I'm going to do. I expose the process so that I appear to be an authoritarian and in control of my process, although the process itself is collaborative."

Summary

Although some potential negatives were perceived, collaboration was the issue on which the most women agreed most frequently. One rather interesting issue identified is the idea that through their social conditioning and ability to suppress ego, women may be better suited to directing, at least when it comes to the collaborative part of the process. Many of the women are careful to point out, however, that collaboration skills can be learned, and most of them have worked with or known of at least one highly collaborative male director or highly controlling, autocratic female director, making gender distinctions difficult at best. Many women do think that they have unique ways of collaborating, especially in their willingness to admit they don't always have all the answers and to be truly open to input from others. It is clear that almost all of the women believe very strongly that collaboration leads to shared success, a success more complete and rich because of the whole-hearted contributions of the many different artists in the production process.

7. WOMEN'S WAYS
OF COLLABORATING

Several key elements were identified by the women directors in conjunction with their ability to collaborate. The elements intertwine during the process, and sometimes the directors do not really talk about them as discrete units when they discuss how to create the best environment for collaboration in their work. The first of these elements was a sensitivity and openness to feelings and emotions; the second was the ability to create an environment of trust and intimacy for the ensemble. Inevitably, almost all of the discussions contained a mention of the idea of nurturing artists during the process of collaboration. One other important aspect was the ability to use intuition and to trust instincts during the collaborative process. Although it is sometimes difficult to isolate these elements, a further exploration of each of these ideas in turn will create a more complete picture of how the majority of these women directors view their ways of collaborating.

SENSITIVITY TO FEELINGS AND EMOTIONS

A Vocabulary of Feelings

As described earlier, Sharon Ott often refers to finding out "how things feel" during her early rehearsal process. Many of the other directors also refer to their use of feelings, but only a few are convinced that gender is the primary reason. Patricia Blem and Bea Kiyohara each discuss their use of a vocabulary of feelings and emotions when talking to designers. They refer to a tendency to describe feelings they want to evoke with a production but identify the reason for this type of communication as a lack of technical vocabulary rather than gender behavior. It seems likely however, that admitting to a lack of technical knowledge may be more common among women directors, and they also believe that women might comfortably use that type of emotional imagery more often than men. Melia Bensussen elaborates on how she uses the language of feelings, especially with actors:

> What I do with language is say things like, "Don't take me literally but here's what it feels like." Quite often when I express a thought, what I'm trying to do is get to the essence of a thing. There'll be a stage in the process where a direction is incredibly specific, but early on when I'm trying to get to the heart of a piece, I will throw out a lot of words, all of which are trying to connect with something. I will paint around the thing in hopes that the idea will crystalize itself for the listener and get translated into their own language of feelings. I grew up speaking Spanish and Hebrew and then English, so I tend to see language as one more distraction. I assume that words mean different things to different people. I find myself saying over and over, "Don't take me literally, because what anger [or any other word] means to me is not what anger means to you." I rely, ironically, on a lot of language. "I will throw a lot of language your way in hopes that you will reinterpret towards the essence." I don't know if that's a gender trait, that's a personal trait. I could see someone saying that is a sort of female indirectness, of not wanting to simply dictate reality, but I don't think that's what it is.

Tisa Chang also works with emotional imagery but traces its use to her early beginnings as a dancer: "Movement and music have always played a large part in the pieces I've directed or originated. I like to work with visual images and movement, so I often give them an emotion to go on. This is how I communicate with designers and actors, translating emotions into movement. To talk about it excessively skirts the issue of what we're trying to get at, the energy, the immediacy, the drama, the tension, and what I call 'hitting the peaks' for actors."

Theatre Is an Emotional Medium

Fontaine Syer believes that anyone who chooses theatre as a profession, regardless of gender, is someone who is likely to be more sensitive to feelings and emotions: "Theatre is an emotional medium. It isn't primarily an intellectual experience, it's primarily an emotional experience. I suppose there are people who would say that an interest in emotion is predominantly female, but I think it is more connected to the medium. I think men who are involved in the theatre are interested in emotional interaction and emotional rides, too." Although Syer always seems to be trying to neutralize gender involvement in the theatrical process, some of the other women are more convinced the ability to connect to emotions is more accessible to women in the role of director.

Adele Prandini identifies emotions as traditionally within the realm of women, but she also believes that men are now beginning to learn how to access those feelings: "Emotion has been the realm of women, and I think that's why you see so many women in art. Art is about dealing with emotion, and traditionally that's been our realm, and has, I think, frightened men. But they have emotions too, and now we're on the brink of this wonderful change, of seeing ourselves, men and women, for all that we are—emotional, intellectual, spiritual beings."

Women Get More Involved with Emotions

While Prandini speaks about emotions in general terms, Brenda Hubbard is concerned with how male and female directors respond to the emotions of others. Based on her work as an actor, Hubbard makes a very distinct gender comparison:

> In my experience watching male directors work, I think they tend to be less comfortable on the feeling level. They don't talk as much about feelings. They talk more in terms of action, and they see things much more in terms of action. I think that men tend to choose people to work with where there will be a minimal amount of emotional interaction, emotional problems. I think male directors will want to choose people who are emotionally easy to work with. I think I'm inclined to be more flexible in dealing with people's emotions. I've really noticed that men are less inviting in terms of asking you how you feel about what's going on in the rehearsal process. A lot of men I know, that I've been directed by, don't even really make eye contact with me or any of the women in the cast, so in terms of inviting communication, there isn't that at all.

Hubbard goes on to say that emotions are very important to her in rehearsals and that she chooses actors "who have a certain level of emotional availability. I nurture, encourage and exploit those emotions in order to get what I need, the final product, and my perceptions and intuition are key in what I do."

Because acting is such a subjective experience, sensitivity to feelings can be important, not only in character development, but also regarding the artists' personal lives as they approach their work on a production. Gloria Muzio describes the way she works with actors and how she thinks it is different from the way a man might work:

> Perhaps feelings get involved a little bit more. I don't mean in terms of their performance or the character's feelings. I don't know if this is always a good thing, but I tend to be concerned about how an actor feels that day, whether they're feeling good about themselves, and I try to help them feel good about themselves so their work will be better that day. I think it is true in life, generally, that men aren't as tuned in to the feelings, that the work is perhaps a little more separate. "We're here to do a job; let's do the job. It doesn't matter how you're feeling today, or if you feel up to this today." I think if they're feeling really great about coming to work, they're going to be doing better work, so I tend to get a little more involved. I'm sure there are exceptions, but

> I think as a woman I'm more tuned in to how people feel. I recently had a conversation with a friend, and we share a perception that it isn't that men aren't interested in women's feelings, they just aren't as interested in feelings to begin with. I think perhaps that's true with women directors in rehearsals, perhaps there's a little more nurturing going on, a little more tuning into the person as well as the actor. I'm not sure that's always for the better, but I tend to get a little more involved with the whole package, not just the acting.

Alana Byington does not talk directly about emotions, but they are obviously strongly implied in her discussion of the importance to her work of understanding and exploring relationships. Byington acknowledges the affinity women seem to have for this aspect of life and jokes that there is some measure of reality in the stereotype about women's gossip, something she believes may put her at an occasional advantage when working on certain aspects of human relationships in a play:

> I think that a director needs to be able to understand relationship, how people deal with each other, how people negotiate, and how they get what they want. I think that's something that women have an affinity for because we're the ones that sit around dinner tables and talk about that stuff. In the old days of movies, if there was a man who did really well with that kind of work, he was called a good "woman's director." We think men like that, who understand stuff like that, we think they have a highly developed female side. I think we're making some arbitrary distinctions between what is feminine and what is masculine, and we're also saying, at the same time, we realize that this isn't something that is specific to gender, but it seems there's a tendency. Certainly when I work, my heaviest focus is always on relationship. What I'm interested in is what's going on between people. I don't think being a woman has hurt there because I sit around and talk about that stuff with my friends, too.

Later Byington discusses her interest in ambiguity and complex human relationships, but she is not comfortable in ascribing that tendency entirely to gender. When first discussing this idea, she gave women the edge in their awareness of, and comfort with, situations onstage that have to do with the expression of emotional relationship. Later, however, she reversed her position, saying, "If a director fails in my eyes, it is usually in the area of relationship, and there are simply more male directors." When the numbers of women directors truly equal those of the men, it will be interesting to see if Byington's perception holds true or if women really do have an edge in this understanding.

Gender Assumptions Are Hard to Make

Michelle Blackmon also invokes the use of emotional imagery but believes it to be more of a personality preference than a gender behavior. She also points to the fact that the boundaries between certain gender assumptions are rapidly changing: "Where I try to proceed as a director is getting an actor to understand. Because things touch me. They touch me deeply and emotionally, and the way it touches me, I want them to feel that. That's what I want them to be able to portray to the audience, that same feeling. I approach things more from an emotional level than I do from a cerebral level. I don't think that is necessarily a gender thing. I think it's a personality thing. That is attributed more often to women, but these days women are being taught to be more like men. We're being taught to be more cerebral, so it's very confusing out there."

While Blackmon attributes her emotional approach to personality, others find differing influences. Seret Scott does not agree that women directors are softer or more emotional, saying, "I don't believe that at all!" She has seen a certain quality of work being attributed to the gender of the director when she firmly believes that the director was simply presenting the emotional reading of the play itself. Victoria Parker also takes an opposing viewpoint: "I hear a lot about women's sensitivity and emotional capacity, but I really have worked as an actor with a lot of men who are far more sensitive and who have gotten me deeper into my emotions than women I've worked with. So I don't know that I really think about it that way."

This point of view brings us back once again to the fact that even though there is often agreement about certain aspects of the process, there are always those whose experience or perceptions have been in complete contrast to the majority view. What they can agree on is that a sensitivity to feelings and emotions is important in the process of directing. It does not seem to be the exclusive province of the female director, however.

CREATING AN ENVIRONMENT OF TRUST AND INTIMACY

Making a Safe Place for the Work to Happen

The sensitivity to feelings leads very naturally to another key element of collaboration, the ability to create a safe and supportive working environment. This means creating an environment where artists can be vulnerable, where they can risk and extend themselves in order to discover the most insightful and exciting performances possible, rather than simply making safe and comfortable choices which may result in mediocrity. Although she doesn't like to use the word collaboration because it seems to conjure up an image of artistic anarchy, even Maria Irene Fornes is emphatic that she wants to find ways to help the actors trust her. She believes this is necessary in order to make the working process go more smoothly. Liz Diamond emphasizes that "fostering an atmosphere of trust and open collaboration, making it clear that your ego is not on the line when you make a choice and an actor challenges that choice or proposes an alternative choice, is crucial to the art of directing."

Bea Kiyohara also emphasizes the safe environment, but for somewhat different reasons. She notes that the ability to create this safe environment, along with patience and a willingness to teach, are especially important to productions at the Northwest Asian American Theatre, which she headed for fifteen years. She finds women directors' sensitivity more often suited to the different skill levels and the many cultural differences (Japanese, Chinese, Korean, Filipino, etc.) encompassed by the Asian American theatre experience:

> In the artistic process, I've found that women are much more in the teaching mode when they direct. Specifically, they have a lot more patience, a lot more tolerance, especially in ethnic theatre. When we do a show, there's going to be a wide variety of levels of ability, so what we do generally is use the play process as a teaching tool. That is how I have developed my own directing style. As a producer, I also have a tendency to choose that kind of director, and over the years more than eighty or ninety percent of the plays which we produce have been directed by women. Basically, women can take the time to be much more articulate about characterization and about implications of the way actors deal with each other. They're much more caring about the relationship between actors, not only in the play process but in trying to build the team, trying to build the atmosphere in which there's safety, not a lot of competition, but a comfort level so people can be creative and take risks and bring their best to the part.

Barbara Ann Teer recalls similar concerns, especially in the early days of the National Black Theatre:

> I'm less analytical and I would deal more with images and feelings, and this is perhaps a characteristic of my gender. I think I'm very giving as a director. In earlier years, I think I was so tolerant that very often I spoon fed them. We really worked over characterization, beats, and motivation. I'd be so solicitous, and I'm not sure most directors work this way. Certainly now as all the pressures increase and we're asked to produce more on less and in less time, I'm less tolerant. But in the earlier years when it was purely exploration, collaboration, you didn't have to hit those marks right away because there were no expectations. We were a fledgling and unformed entity, so we had the luxury to do that. It's also because I worked with so many who were new to the field. I had to be a little bit more tolerant, more nurturing, more solicitous, more encouraging; otherwise they would have all just slunk home with their tail between their legs, and that wouldn't do anything for the movement or the production.

Susan Finque stops short of saying that all women are good at creating a safe environment and, as a result of that environment, able to develop a cohesive artistic ensemble. She does, however, make a speculative comparison between her own style and the style of her male former partner at Alice B. Theatre:

> I do believe that I am, of the team, the person who understands how to develop and build an ensemble, and he hears his own voices stronger than anybody

else's. There is to that a kind of self-centered male ego trip, although he is a writer, and I am more of a director and actress. So it's hard to say whether it's the craft or the maleness, or whether you just have to look at the whole picture and say it's a combination of things. I am much better at handling groups. I deal with actors' egos much better than he does. I understand how to build an ensemble. He sometimes has ensemble visions, but getting a group of people—from their different worlds, their different cultures, their different races, their different ages, their different politics and aesthetics—from their beginning point to a finished image is really the creative job. It's not enough to simply have an idea. If you want human beings to get there, the process of getting them to experience it is what makes theatre. So there is a shortfall there, and that may have to do with a male egocentricity.

A big part of the job of creating an ensemble by bringing various individual artists together in a harmonious collaboration is being able to create a sense of trust, intimacy, and connectedness in that safe space.

Creating Intimacy with Physical Touch

Several women expressed the idea that physical touch is an extremely important part of creating a sense of connectedness between the director and the ensemble. Patricia Blem explains how she believes her femininity allows her to use physical touch to create a sense of intimacy with the actors: "This is when I know I use my femininity. I use a lot of physical touch throughout all of my rehearsals. Through touching people, both men and women, I can convey something that I can't do with words alone. I will take people aside, put my arm around them, and talk to them alone. Or when with the whole cast, I will reach out and touch the arm of the person I'm speaking directly to. It's a way of creating a safe intimacy that comes naturally to me, and it can often soften tough situations."

Michelle Blackmon agrees with Blem and adds a brief comparison to male directors who, she believes, keep their distance more often: "I think personal space is another issue here. Men have a tendency to be a little more distant. There's a personal space that everybody has, and I think women can get inside that personal space a little bit easier. I find when working with actors, I can put my arm around somebody and touch someone in getting them to try to do something or loosen up. If a man did that to them, they'd have a hard time with it. I think there's a benefit to being a woman director in that sense. I can get closer to actors and more intimate with them and work more from that gut level. I think that's very helpful, and I try to use that whenever possible."

Melia Bensussen, however, points out that our social conditioning may not allow male directors that same kind of freedom, even if they were inclined to want to use it:

I find I have tremendous freedom as a woman director—my guess is that men don't have as much—and that's a physical freedom to have contact with people. I grab actors; I place them physically. I sometimes simply walk through things; I emote them. I stand and put my hand on someone's stomach and bend them over. I punch, I hug, and I'm not aware that I do it half the time. I just jump on stage and say, "Here's what it feels like, do this with your body." I am aware that if I were a man, I would have to think about who I'm touching. Because I'm viewed as not as powerful in the gender equation, I take many liberties that way. I have, however, started to think that I need to be a little more careful to respect the dignity of the actor. I've started to ask before I touch, "Do you mind if I do this on your body?" I used to make jokes about it to male actors. I'd say, "It's good I'm a woman and you're a guy so this isn't a problem," but really the equation is the same: I'm in power and they're not, and I can act on them physically. It could be uncomfortable for them, and they would not be in a position where they could say so comfortably. I feel like I've become more sensitive to that, but I think I do have more latitude than men.

Brenda Hubbard, while agreeing about her own easy use of physical touch, adds an awareness of the possible sexual overtones if the touching comes from a male director. "I'm very physical with actors. I've been told by actors that I can get away with more things because I am a woman. It gave me permission to be more intimate with people and to take more liberties with their physical person. I can hug an actor or touch an actor, and as long as I'm being respectful of their comfort levels, I can pretty much touch an actor anywhere and not catch any flak for it. If a man did that, of course, they would be harassing that person sexually. But with me, it's much more of a maternal thing. I mean it's accepted." Hubbard's reference to maternal imagery is not the only one that surfaced throughout the interviews.

Images of Home and Family

Adele Prandini and Diana Marré both talk about wanting actors to stop thinking of them as mother, but Brenda Hubbard is more willing to embrace the maternal role, perhaps because she is a mother outside of the theatre:

I look at things more openly, seeing the potential that's there. I think that probably comes from being a nurturer—as a mother, as a wife—and from woman's role in society. I'm more accustomed to seeing the potential that could be created out of some situation or some people. I fall into a maternal relationship with the actors I work with, and I think I subconsciously try to create functional family units when I'm directing. The growth process in the rehearsal is the same process of parenting, and it's the same process of having a child. It's got a cycle to it. Certain things happen at certain times in the process, and you have to deal with certain issues at certain times—separation issues, nurturing issues. The functioning of a cast in the optimum experience really is dependent upon each person in that cast finding a place within that newly created group. Since people bring so much of themselves and their family issues into that environment, I think we do create a sense of family, a family unit.

Several of the women in this book refer, both positively and negatively, to the woman director as a mother figure. The image is obviously not a new one. British director Clare Venables wrote about it over a decade ago, and she was by no means the first to employ the imagery. Venables has an interesting criticism of how the use of the mothering imagery makes it possible for women directors to seem to assume power yet still keeps them a prisoner of old and powerless archetypes. She indicates that in her experience many women directors, both mothers and nonmothers alike, see themselves in a maternal or even a nanny role in the rehearsal process. She thinks the image is a very limiting one because it conforms to stereotypes about women, that they cannot be real leaders. Since women are expected to lead their children, however, it is acceptable for women to be "mother-leaders." Venables further asserts that this makes leadership acceptable for women but continues to define them only in relation to others rather than on their own merits as a leader.[1] Although the maternal role may be confining, it is clearly one that many women have been encouraged to accept and develop throughout the years. As Venables points out, it has been one way that many women have been able to assume at least some semblance of authority and control. It is also an image that allows for the combination of authority and nurturing collaboration that the directing function seems to invoke for women directors.

While not specifically invoking maternal imagery and insisting that men can do these things as easily as women, some women nevertheless use other images of home and family when talking about creating an artistic ensemble. Zelda Fichandler explains that she was not originally motivated to start her own theatre in order to move out into more professional work in the commercial arena: "It was creating a home. It was a very nurturing feeling, creating a family, creating a home." When asked how she brought people together to create that artistic family and whether she saw that as being done differently because she was a woman, Fichandler replies:

ZF: I think not. I'm working with a male acting teacher at NYU, and he works on a deep level of intuition and empathy. We work very much the same way. What actors know me for is to be actor-oriented, and I think that must be true of other directors as well. I'm thinking of male directors with whom I've had long-term relationships, and they all work very intuitively and empathetically with actors. I do trust my judgment and taste about actors very much. I keep hoping that won't go away because that's so deeply tied to your capacity to pay attention. I hope I keep that sense, but I don't know if that's a feminine sense at all. I think it's an artistic sense.

RD: Some of the women I've talked to believe that women are socially more trained to be open to that kind of input.

ZF: I agree with that. Part of it is because you've survived by that. I mean, this thing called women's intuition is really a rapid processing of accumulated knowledge about how to survive because normally, as a woman, you're brought up not to have direct access to your voice. "I want..." "I would prefer..." "My way of doing it is..." "I would appreciate it if you would accept my way while you're in my domain or part of my project." We don't have direct access to those words. I notice that I don't even deal with secretaries the way men would. I hand them things with question marks. I leave sentences open-ended without periods at the end, allowing room for response or disagreement.

RD: Would you use that same kind of communication when you were working with actors?

ZF: Sometimes I do, sometimes I don't. "Do you think that...? Does it seem to you that...?" It's part of a teaching technique I have of trying to lead the actor to the conclusion. "I see it this way," I might say. Or, "It seems to me that what it needs here is..." Or else, "I can't hear you," meaning you're not being specific and I don't understand what you're talking about. So it does tend to be a search which I'm leading instead of conclusions which I'm passing out. A male colleague was the first one to put a bug in my ear that what I was doing was making a family and that was the reason I was so connected to it, fell in love with it. It's just a bigger family than your nuclear family, and this is where you feel nurtured and where you nurture. I think it is an instinct of family; it was for me. So when TCG talks and writes about "the artistic home,"[2] I think, "What else would you be doing but making a home?" So my directing fits into the super-objective of making a home. It isn't something I isolate. Now I am a director, now I am a homemaker. Even when I'm not a director, when I'm the producer and trying to help realize the vision of another director, I'm still making a home for that director to make the home for the play. So maybe that's feminine—female. Maybe it isn't.

The discussion of the issue of artistic home and building community is an ongoing one for all theatre professionals regardless of gender. In fact, the Theatre Communications Group (TCG) has ongoing seminars and conferences to explore issues of home and community for American theatre artists. Fichandler is a vocal and influential member of that constituency, but whether her urges are due to gender could be vigorously debated, and there are also many male members of TCG who find this a significant issue.

NURTURANCE

A Gentler, More Feminine Approach

Webster's New Twentieth Century Dictionary defines the verb nurture as "(1) to feed; to nourish, and (2) to raise or promote the development of; to educate; to bring or train up." These are behaviors that are most often associated with the female in our society. In a recent magazine interview, Zelda Fichandler describes how she is interested in webs of human relationships among people, and is always trying to create and nurture them, but she is not sure whether that is feminine or simply part of the creative principle. She does say, "If nurturing is feminine, I guess my femininity has helped." She is quick to say, however, that the male directors she most admires also have "this gentility of spirit that's supposed to belong to women."[3] It is obviously promoting a cultural stereotype to presume that women directors will automatically be nurturing, yet it is a designation many women directors do embrace.

In the course of my early interviews, I received a letter from Sue Lawless, a professional director from New York with over twenty years of professional credits, including Broadway, Off Broadway, and regional theatre. She sent an article from the program of one of her productions which addresses this issue: "I perceive [myself] as a guide and collaborator rather than leader. Most good actors prefer to find the part themselves. My joy comes from finding the people who have talent and helping them find ways to enhance their own [ideas]. ... As an actress, [I] found many of [my] male directors dictatorial. I had always wondered what it was about that power position that made people act that way. Of course, I found out it wasn't necessary to behave that way at all."[4] In her accompanying letter, Lawless explains that she sees her "gentle approach" to collaboration as defined by society as female: "I cannot explain my process without believing that it is a woman's way as we look at the female's appointed role in today's society. Maybe in a different society men would act more as we are perceived as doing now. I do know, however, that there are men directors who approach directing much the same way I do, that is, through a gentler, more admittedly nurturing process."[5]

Melia Bensussen defines what nurturing means to her and remarks that it can sometimes be more automatic than conscious as a behavior choice for her and perhaps for other women as well: "It used to matter a lot that everybody be happy. It matters less now. I think it mattered so much in part because of gender, and the more I work, the less automatic gender choices become. It starts to become simply working in the art form and, as an individual, breaking through. When I started directing, it was much more a reflection of my own identity and at that point became important."

Agreeing in principle with earlier comments by Bea Kiyohara and Barbara Ann Teer about the need to create a feeling of trust in inexperienced actors, Tisa Chang explains how nurturing behavior and attention to certain kinds of details can be extremely important, especially for alternative or fledgling theatres where the director has little else to offer as compensation other than making the artists feel good while helping them grow and develop:

> As the founder of Pan Asian Repertory Theatre, it was my idea to forge an Asian American artistic movement, independence movement. The actors really bought into it. I think it's because I am very well planned and very organized that they didn't fuss a lot. I would see to their creature comforts. This

could be gender related in that women tend to do that. I'm very detail-oriented, and I try to anticipate people's needs or dissatisfaction and cover those bases. I feel that was the only way that I could seduce these actors to work for whatever we were working for, $50 a week I think it was. I tend to be less analytical but good at getting people to do what I want them to do because I've thought it all through. I give them adequate breaks. I can anticipate someone having work problems, so I don't waste their time. Having been in the theatre for so many years as a dancer and actress, I've seen all different kinds of directors and producing operations, and I swore I would never abuse actors, waste their time, and certainly never disparage their input. There are people who become directors to become little dictators, but I don't think there's any room for that in theatre. Certainly there's room for temperament, but ego, no. I think men very often tend to be a little bit more pontifical. They're more hierarchical, but that's a generality.

Many women seem to presume the presence of nurturing behavior in their discussion of aspects of collaborative behavior, and they are always careful to say that although women might be more familiar with expectations of being nurturing, they have no exclusive lock on the behavior. Almost all of the directors know at least one male director who works in the same way. Furthermore, although some have experienced extreme insensitivity and a lack of nurturing in male directors, others have had the same problem with women.

Cultural Familiarity with the Role of Nurturer

Victoria Parker describes being culturally familiar with the role that nurturing is expected to play in a woman's life and how this awareness allows her to choose where and when she wishes to use that behavior in her artistic process as well as giving her a familiarity with the expectations of others:

> I believe that we all perceive the nurturer to be, on some level, a role that women alone have played for too long. We know the role, whether we want to play it or not, of nurturing, nursing someone along, knowing where they're at, what they want, what they need. I feel extremely fortunate in that I know how to respond to that, so I can choose to use it when I want to. I would never want to give that up. It's something that many men have sought, and a field opened up for them when they fell across it. But for them it is innovative. What I'm saying is that it's very familiar to me. It has always made sense. I don't think that it's exclusive to women. I just think that it comes easily, it's a natural thing for a woman to be doing.

Parker refers briefly to the notion that discovering the ability to nurture could be advantageous to men, but does not pursue it further. Conversely, JoAnne Akalaitis, while not using the word directly, is clearly referring to the dangers of overly nurturing behavior. She also hints that nurturance might serve as a mask for insecurity: "I think women are nicer than men. I often think that as a woman director, I act in ways that I shouldn't be acting. For example, when I have a call Sunday at noon to have a very hard technical rehearsal, I've done things like made breakfast for the entire cast. Maybe I'm not secure, I don't know. Perhaps I think they might not let me walk onstage unless I walk in with breakfast. I don't know if men would be doing that." During our phone conversation, Akalaitis expanded this idea, revealing the personal side of this issue a little further: "I like to cook and do things with food, but I think it's a particularly female way of winning over a cast. But it's also part of my life. It's something I do all the time that I think is quite female, quite gender related. When I want things to be all right, I'll make a meal. It's true in my personal life, that I use that behavior as a tool in some way, but it is also very satisfying to me. I don't think men directors do that, nor should they."

Several women also point out other possible dangers they think exist in the collaborative process if a director is overly nurturing, especially the possibility that women might tend to take fewer risks and rely more heavily on the group process, creating acceptable but perhaps not great works of art as a result. While many of the women see some kind of nurturing behavior as a primarily feminine attribute and view it as an important part of a woman's directing process, they are not as clear in their assumptions about the uses of intuition.

USE OF INSTINCT AND INTUITION

Learning to Trust Your Instincts

Culturally, we are used to thinking in terms of binary opposites such as instinct/reason, intuition/intellect, and irrational/rational. These dichotomies have long been associated with gender differences, but not many women defined intuition as gender specific during the interviews. Most consider it of key importance in the creative process to trust your instincts, regardless of the gender of the artist. While intuition was not always talked about directly in connection with collaboration, many of the previous comments tended to encompass the use of intuition along with sensitivity to feelings or emotions. It seems evident that the use of intuition would be relevant to anyone who is in the position of allowing herself to be open to input from others, especially when it comes in the form of feelings, images or metaphors. Trusting gut instincts makes timely responses possible in rehearsal.

JoAnne Akalaitis definitely believes intuition is of paramount importance to a director, although she does not necessarily perceive it to be gender related. She welcomes its presence in her working process:

> I think it's very important for directors and actors and designers to follow their images. There are these images, and people are afraid of them because they

don't make sense and because they're not logical and because you can't explain them. It took me quite a while to have the courage of my convictions and to say to an actor, "I want you to walk across the stage backwards, and then fall down and get up and pick up a tea cup upstage. Why? I don't know. I dreamt about it last night." The director has to get everyone on her trip. What I want when I am working on a piece is that I want everyone to be dreaming a collective dream. I do feel that when theatre works successfully, there are these moments when someone walks on stage and raises their hand like this, and if it is done beautifully, if it's done perfectly, then there is a Jungian moment when the collective unconscious of the audience connects with the collective unconscious of those people on stage, and that is a transcendent moment. A great performance is a series of those transcendent moments. So it's very important for the director to have confidence in these images and in these irrational thoughts and in these feelings, and get everyone on that trip. I feel that when you're all having nightmares together, it's awfully good because you're doing it. When you're doing it, it's exhausting, and it's sometimes quite unpleasant, but it's important.

Gloria Muzio feels very connected to her instincts, especially in regards to visual elements of a production: "I've been told by designers that I'm extremely visually oriented, and I communicate well about visual elements in the production. I also feel I'm tuned in to my instinctive responses. I tend to think of that as gender related, but I don't know that it is. It would be interesting to ask a man that question."

In contrast to the previous comments about learning to trust your own inner instincts regarding visual imagery, Patricia Blem emphasizes the use of intuition in response to the work of the actors: "I listen to the first impulse, which is not necessarily what they're saying but what I can feel coming from them. I'm using my instincts and my intuition at that point in time. If I get to an impasse where things aren't working no matter what I try, I'll inevitably go back to those first impulses and think, 'Let's start it again from there.' I've found that when I do, a lot of garbage gets tossed because those instincts were right on, and I deviated away from them. So, I definitely use my intuition." Victoria Parker, like Blem, also focuses her comments on an intuitive response to the actors. Neither is comfortable with the idea that access to intuition would be gender specific. Parker admits, however, that it is socially more acceptable for a woman to trust and talk about her intuitions:

> I don't see intuition as a gender issue so much as I thought. I certainly know a lot of men who work intuitively. In fact, most of the directors that I've taken block-busting exercises and my process from are male. I am strongly influenced by writings of Joe Chaiken [a key member of the highly collaborative Open Theatre], and so I don't know that it's necessarily a gender issue. But I would say that because my first choice in directing is to follow intuition and because I have the advantage of a good deal of practice using intuitive power, I assume more women use it than men. A woman may be more practiced in following intuition and so intuits more readily from her cast what her next direction must be.

Pamela Hendrick immediately qualifies her discussion of the use of intuition and reliance on instinct by remarking that she is sure there are men who also use these things extremely effectively. She goes on to describe how this manifests in her own work with actors:

> I often find myself telling my actors to trust their instincts. I tend to work with actors in a variety of models because I believe that individual performers all have their way of getting into the role. I work externally with gesture, with voice, with body language to get from the outside into a role, and I work internally with forms of psychological realism to get from the inside out. But after we do a lot of the background work for building character and building story, I often end up encouraging my actors to simply forget all of that and trust their instincts because I have a lot of faith in actors' instincts. I expect that faith, spontaneity, creativity, and multifaceted nonlinear approaches to the process might tend to be more female traits.

Anne Bogart uses these same kind of approaches in her process, but cautions against making presumptions about the use of intuition based solely on gender distinctions:

> Talking about gender is constantly dangerous in stereotyping gender. My first thoughts when you ask that question about the effects of gender on my directing are about the fact that I work differently than most men do, but the words that come out I find highly stereotypical—words like nurturing, free association in work, working intuitively. I don't like saying those things. Yet I find over and over again that I do work with a nurturing environment and I do work intuitively as much as I can. I work intellectually, but also in the moment, intuitively, and nonlinearly. But there must be some men who work that way. I know there are, so I don't trust saying what I just said.

Adele Prandini seems happy to accept her intuition as feminine and gives credit for her access to intuition to the influence of her mother. She also sees in the acceptance of intuition a larger issue than simply following personal instincts regarding the actors:

> There is something that occurs in art, in theatre, and that's this synchronicity. It just occurs. I don't think that we sit back in isolation and get an idea. I think that things are swirling around us constantly, and every now and then we're lucky enough to open up enough that it comes in. That happens time and again. I don't have a word for that. Maybe at another point in time in our history they called it magic or they called it religion or they called it miracle. I don't know, but I know they're here, and it's synchronistic that you become aware. It's not an individual thing. It sweeps over all of us, and we all respond to it in our individual ways. It's a wonderful thing. There's another element to that, and that's relying on that part of yourself that is not the conscious, everyday part. I guess we refer to that as intuition, and I rely on that a lot throughout all the different aspects of the process. I'm very grateful for having a superstitious mother. She's a dreamer. She taught me to trust myself, my intuition. I rely on my intuition in my work, particularly during auditions. Daydreaming is my most important creative tool.

Adele Prandini (right) with actresses Imani Harrington (left) and Iris Landsberg (center) working on Judy Grahn's *Queen of Swords* at Theatre Rhinoceros (1990). Photo by Pam Peniston.

Barbara Ann Teer talks about following an "intuitive flash" and connects the ease with which she accepts that premise to her cultural background more than to her gender: "People of African descent are born—historically, biologically, every kind of way you look at it—into a spirit culture. If you're in a spiritual culture, you constantly intuit, you're constantly spontaneous, you constantly 'go with the flow,' as they say. I was a dancer from the time I was born, and because the body was constantly in motion, and loving it, you connect with a higher force that guides you all the time." Connecting to this higher force, this synchronicity by way of free association, nonlinear approaches, irrational images, and instinct is definitely important to many of these directors. Whether the impulse is related to gender is not an issue of concern, but some do feel women may have easier access to intuition in our culture.

FINDING A BALANCE

The Yin and Yang of Directing

In one way or another, most of the women discuss the need to find a balance in their process between being authoritative and nurturing, echoing many contemporary directing texts. Patricia Blem invokes the language of Eastern mysticism to describe how she balances the yin and yang of directing: "Being able to keep a vision in mind is using the yang energy, and being able to create a nurturing atmosphere for people to become united by it and give their best is the yin energy. I think it's a balance of using both kinds of energies—the nurturing atmosphere and the clear-sighted vision—that creates the best director. If you limit yourself and don't use both of your energy sources, you don't create as fully." Roberta Levitow describes this balance using the terminology and perspective of Jungian psychology:

> My theory is that we're all a composite of anima and animus, and great male artists have tremendous feminine aspect that's present in their work, and great women artists have tremendous masculine aspect that's present in their work. It's necessary to have masculine aspect in your work. It can't be fully feminized work or it isn't the full spectrum of human expression. There's some kind of totality of expression that I see in great male artists that's obviously feminized. These are men who have feminine attributes that are present in all the aesthetics of their work, so why wouldn't it go back the other way? I think the hardest thing in some ways is to claim the masculine, to feel that as a woman artist you have the right to speak with a masculine vocabulary as well as a feminine vocabulary. It's fearful for people to look at it.

Penny Metropulos discusses this necessary balance, not only as particular to directing, but something of importance for all artists in our contemporary world: "In the social and political climate that we are facing, it is more important than ever for all of us to maintain our artistic objectives. There is an increasing need for our theatres to focus on productivity and goals. These objectives are masculine in nature; they have to do with survival, which is very important. But I think if we do not support and cultivate our feminine need to create, to nourish our vision in the theatre, we will only be saving institutions devoid of dreams. This is not a gender issue; it is the need of all artists to balance our natures." A similar perspective on balance comes from Barbara Ann Teer, who tends to see the influences on balancing the equation as cultural:

> As far as I'm concerned, it's all cultural. That's why the question about gender influence is difficult. Males and females are equally creative if they're born in an environment that supports, perpetuates, encourages creativity. Then we wouldn't have to have these discussions. I would like the day to come when we can be responsible for the culture that now isolates and separates everything. The spiritual and material are totally different realities. People who were born into a spirit culture, or who embrace a spirit culture, are inclined to be creative all the time. People who are born into (or embrace) a materialistic, linear kind of culture—where if you don't see it, it doesn't exist, where reality is based on the physical—find it difficult to be creative, or don't want to be creative, because the power is in the controlling, (the) conquest, and these assessments are money-driven. This philosophy kills everything creative

around you. That's what I would like to see be revealed someday. The women's movement, the feminist movements, just reinforce the same reality of scarcity. I know it's necessary for evolution, but it reinforces the same separation, it highlights the same isolation, so that you've got women over here, men over there. I think it's not about an individual, it's about a collective, and it's about balance. There's no limits to your creative possibility. So that's not feminine or masculine, that's just human. To be human is to be creative. We all have both in us, and we need balance. The men in my theatre run the programs, and the Institute of Action Arts has many programs. The administration of those programs, which I do, requires a very rigorous, detailed, paperwork kind of mentality or personality which artists don't normally have. Since we are committed to building a permanent institution that will last forever so we can pass something on to the next generation and the generation after that, we get to sacrifice our creative side to do the more straight line, linear, paperwork thing. This is not as exciting and fulfilling at all, so I tell my staff, "Never stop doing creative things" because when you stop doing creative things, when you stop doing music, or composing, or writing, or directing, or dancing, or singing, or acting, or visual arts or whatever it is, when you stop doing that, something dies inside you. You get very hard, you get very cold, you get very rigid, and very nonflexible, in my opinion, and that is because the balance is not there. So I invite people to keep that creative thing present, no matter how much they get into the business world. So that could be masculine/feminine, I don't know.

It seems easiest for these women to employ the terminology of opposites to describe the necessary balance they perceive in the directing process. It is not always an easy thing for a director to do, however.

Embracing Both Sides

Because of our cultural conditioning, it is sometimes more difficult for women to embrace both sides of the equation with comfort. Mirroring the earlier comments of several others regarding the male and female aspects within all of us, Barbara Ann Teer describes how for years she resisted her stronger, more authoritative side, what she calls the "warrior" in her because she thought it was too masculine. This internal resistance caused her some problems until she found a way she could finally be comfortable with her strength:

> I would avoid being warriorlike (i.e., demanding, authoritative, penetrating, and hard-line) when it was necessary to be warriorlike. Then a distinction called ruthless compassion was introduced to me. That was a combination of the warrior/masculine side and the mother/feminine side, so that you could have ruthless compassion for somebody or something out of your love for that somebody or that something, but it may look very hard or very cold or unfeeling. It had previously been revealed to me that the acceptance of me as a woman would be lessened if I were the warrior type. The historical discourse in this country is that women should be more feminine and gentle and caring and loving, which meant that if I wanted to be comfortable with the

opposite sex, I would have to give up my ability to be warrior like because it was intimidating, and it would cause men not to like me. It would also cause people to call me words like diva and bitch and things like that many women have had to overcome. So I tried to avoid that whole conversation and would spend hours with people to clear them, particularly when I was directing, so that they would feel taken care of and I could get my show produced. Now if I was a different kind of a person, who was not hungry for the approval of others and had a strong sense of who I was as a human being, probably I would have cut through the crap and hired somebody else and gone on steppin'. But because I am inclined to want to be liked and to be loved, I was spending many hours attempting to have it all. That was before I became a real estate developer and entered into a very male-oriented profession for the purpose of building a permanent institution in this community. When you walk around very knowledgeable, competent, and assertive, and you're not attached to any of it, and you have a strong commitment to build something permanent like I did, you let go of those feelings about looking good and feeling loved. You get totally detached from all that ego stuff. You just say what has to be said, cut through it, and go on about your business. So I can say that I've had the full circle. I do not worry about intimidating people anymore. The rigor that it takes to produce anything requires a very straightforward kind of warrior-like presentation at times, and at times it's not appropriate. I find that people who are very secure with who they are as human beings don't need to have those distinctions, male and female. People are people; you get the job done and that's the bottom line. If you get the job done with dignity and excellence, then you're loved and appreciated because that speaks for itself. So I would say that the balance is showing up for me because I am in a different profession right now. I don't feel the same way I used to feel when I was totally an artist and only concerned myself with things that artists concern themselves with. I probably will go out as a warrior who has no feeling about whether it's a man or a woman. You do what is appropriate and necessary to get the job done because that's the bottom line. In the process of it, some people won't like you, some people will think you're cold, and some people will think that you're intimidating. Maybe you are to them, but it's not going to stop you from getting the job done and loving your mate, your children, and your family at the same time.

Julie Taymor definitely enjoys balancing the two sides of directing and uses the imagery of weaving to talk about how she pulls them together in her work: "I enjoy collaboration, and I enjoy telling people what to do. I like both equally. I like having people be able to carry forward my ideas and have them work and having people get excited about them. It's a very thrilling experience, like weaving. I'm beginning to recognize the way that I work, how I look at material and open it up. So, I have a self-confidence that's nice now. That comes with experience and age. I welcome challenge. If you can challenge me and I can't defend myself, then there's something the matter, or you'll tell me something that I should hear. That appeals to me. I find half of directing is really balancing personalities."

Gloria Muzio has also been able to find this balance in her process and is becoming much more comfortable with it as her career develops:

As the years go by and as I become more comfortable, I now have a whole different theory of how it works, which does have more to do with collaboration and, in terms of leadership, really earning respect. It has to do with doing my job and knowing how to do my job, and having good taste and good judgment and being intelligent about it, and not being so tuned in to what I think it is to be a leader. When I was very young, that was very important to me. As I matured, I really don't think about that at all. I think much more about collaboration. I take for granted now that I am going to be the leader because I'm the director, so the balance is going to come more naturally and more easily.

It seems clear that for most of these women, finding the balance in their work between leadership and collaboration is an ongoing process that becomes easier as time passes.

The Best of Both Worlds

Melia Bensussen sees this balance in the directing process as the ability to use the best from both worlds. Like Muzio, she too is becoming more comfortable as her career progresses:

> I think that one's gender, one's personality, is the starting point for one's work. I find that there were all these given assumptions that I began with as to what kind of director I am and what kind of work I do. I think a lot of those were gender based, and I find the longer I spend doing what I do, the more it becomes about changing those things, adapting, growing, and shedding my preconceptions. As I shed the preconceptions, I feel like I am freer to use my gender—which is to say myself—as an artist and as a director. I think it is a journey towards being able to express more clearly what my vision of the world is, as shaped by all these things, as opposed to my preconceptions of what I was supposed to do. Those preconceptions were very gender based, and as I get better and better at what I do and as I learn more, I'm free to choose from a whole range of behavior. I believe in the notion of creating something that is shared, that can be collaborative and very firmly led all at the same time, where you share the best things of both genders' way of working. As I get older, I feel freer to choose from both of those.

From her perspective as a producer at the Women's Project, Julia Miles shares her belief that finding this balance may be women's strength. She also emphasizes not only the balance but the breadth of knowledge required to be a good director: "Directors, whatever their sex, have to know everything. I don't have much patience with directors who don't know scene design, music, or script, because you need to know all of those things. On top of that, you have to know how to move actors around and how to get performances out of them. It's a delicate balance of guiding them and allowing them to give you a lot, to feel safe enough to do that. That's a strong point with women, creating an atmosphere in the rehearsals so everyone can do their best work."

Adele Prandini clearly agrees with the others but goes farther than simply describing the need for balance, saying, "The one thing I think is significant about all this is to encourage women to be proud of their intuition, their understanding, their compassion, and all of those receiving and opening kind of things. At the same time, I hope that all of us can proudly step forward and be happy about being the decision makers and wield that power a little bit and ask for more of it, be more assertive." Her words are an exhortation to women directors and to directors in general.

Summary

These elements—emotion, trust, nurture, and intuition—are agreed on with varying degrees of emphasis by all the directors as characteristics of a good collaborative environment. In spite of a general reluctance to characterize the ability to collaborate as a female behavior, most of the women put a strong positive emphasis on its prominence in their process. Most feel a decided advantage in being free to express sensitivity to the emotions of others and enjoy an openness to input from others. They also feel strongly about their abilities to create a safe, trusting work environment and their general access to the uses of intuition. The key seems to be finding the balance between allowing the collaboration to flourish and developing the artistic vision that allows the director to control and lead the collaboration into becoming something truly extraordinary.

The awareness of needing to develop qualities that have historically been constructed as either masculine or feminine is very relevant to many of the women who have achieved success as directors. In various ways they see themselves as "performing" the role of director in the same ways they are "performing" gender roles, both male and female. Their search for balance in what are generally perceived as male or female qualities tends to parallel the search for a balance between authority and openness in the directing process. Although most women are loath to define it simply as a gender issue, a majority of the directors are, in fact, actively looking for a balance between a more open collaboration and the need for firm guidance and benevolent leadership throughout the process. The main difference between this point of view and the balance prescribed in directing texts is that these women seem to have an easier time submitting themselves to the collaborative portion of the process. A mix of both is generally considered essential to excellence in directing, however.

8. ISSUES IN SCRIPT SELECTION AND INTERPRETATION

While the dual concerns of leadership and collaboration have an impact on all areas of the directing process, there are also specific functional elements where gender is perceived to have an influence by many of these women. The practical element most often identified by the directors as being the place in their artistic process where they believe their choices are most significantly influenced by gender is script selection. In fact, fully two-thirds of the women interviewed feel gender issues are significant in the script selection process, whether it is in the scripts they are asked or expected to direct or in the way they apply their own personal decision-making process to scripts they read for possible consideration.

FACTORS IN THE SCRIPT SELECTION PROCESS

The Woman's Slot

Many of the women are most often aware of being identified by others as women directors because they are often competing for the "woman's slot" or being offered what they commonly refer to as the "girls' scripts." Liz Diamond identifies it as a form of "subtle sexism having to do with the kinds of material I have been assumed apt for—plays by women, plays dealing with subjects about women. However, I'm not necessarily interested in doing a motorcycle movie, so on some level they're right to send certain kinds of material my way. There's no question about that." In this designation, the directors include plays with an obvious focus on women's issues or characters, heartwarming domestic dramas, or light comedies, rather than the broader range of plays and grittier subject material they believe would be

137

offered to their male counterparts. Most of the women who do free-lance work seem resigned to doing the women's plays when offered, simply to keep their work in the public eye. It is clear, however, that they are also trying to find ways to be considered for a broader range of scripts, even while staying open to issues of concern to women. Seret Scott explains her experience with this situation: "I get offered your basic kitchen dramas, family plays or women in difficult situations. They are not what I'm drawn to. I enjoy it while I'm doing it, but it is not my first choice. I'm attracted to political theatre, attracted to issues that are not necessarily about women. I'm attracted to the darker side of things, so I'm not likely to volunteer for certain types of productions."

Although the majority of these directors work primarily in regional non-profit or educational theatres, a recent article about women directors on Broadway identified the same problem in the commercial theatre. In it, Julianne Boyd, experienced both on and off Broadway and the first woman president of the Society of Stage Directors and Choregraphers, examines the reluctance to hire woman directors for Broadway in terms of script issues: "Many producers feel that if they're going to hire a woman director, she should be directing a play about women. On Broadway, how many plays are about women? How many straight plays are being done at all? The bottom line is that there just aren't that many shows opening on Broadway. That makes it harder and more competitive for everyone, especially women who are not yet bankable."[1]

Other Considerations

There are a number of complicating factors in any evaluation of the relation of gender to script selection, and the context of the selection process definitely influences responses. A number of the women interviewed are free-lance directors and generally have little input into script selection itself; therefore, the selection issue for them becomes one of accepting or rejecting various scripts that might be offered to them by artistic directors or producers at the theatres doing the hiring. For the academic director, student needs or administrative dictates can often take precedence over individual artistic desires. When a woman has the responsibility as artistic director to select the season at her own theatre, the considerations are generally much broader, involving the theatre's primary mission, season balance, budget considerations, and other influencing factors. Since none of the artistic directors interviewed here are currently involved with a theatre whose primary mission is to explore women's issues, the varied missions of their theatres create even more diversity in the selection process. In addition to choosing scripts, a large number of the women are or have been involved in creating new scripts, either their own or in collaboration with a group of artists. Ethnic and social factors also play a significant role in several of the women's choices. Furthermore, the same woman can be in several of these contexts during the course of a year's work and can have different responses according to her immediate circumstances.

Zelda Fichandler, for example, does not believe there is an unduly strong gender influence in how she selects work for her own theatre or for her students, but she does get calls from producers who inquire whether she would be interested in directing particular plays for other theatres. Occasionally, these scripts are ones which she identifies as "women's" scripts. She says she also has been "called by women who say, 'I think this would be a very good play for a woman to direct.' A woman might say that to me, so there is something going on there." Most women like Fichandler who can control their selections in their own theatres, or who feel they now get offers for a broader range of scripts, can usually remember some encounter with this issue earlier in their careers. They face the issue in various ways. Their responses range from embracing the "woman's slot" designation, to grudgingly believing they ought to take the "girl's play" in order to get their work known, to starting or finding jobs managing their own theatres in order to be able to control what scripts they direct, to creating pieces themselves, to rejecting any hint of gender influence in the process.

THEMES RELATED TO WOMEN AND GENDER

Woman as Subject

One of the key issues in feminist theories of representation which seems to be most relevant to the women here in practical if not theoretical terms is the issue of identity and woman as subject. In relation to her ongoing exploration of the nature of subjectivity, feminist theorist Sue-Ellen Case discusses the need for a "new poetics." She identifies the necessity to locate theory within practice by applying social critique to analytical perception as well as to practice. Ways in which this can be achieved include exposing or rejecting the sexualization of women onstage, reversing the omission of women's stories and lack of strong roles for women, lesbians, and women of color, and creating new ways to read and view images of women in the theatre.[2] She also identifies the need to deconstruct dominant cultural codes and traditional systems of representation, especially woman's inherited position as an object of desire. She calls for the creation of a female subject position with centrality of focus and the right to speak for herself rather than as a cultural object. Women have historically been denied agency through their persistent and oppressive positioning as the object of the male gaze. This acknowledgment of the right of women to centrality and subjectivity is a key issue for feminist theory. Although very few of the women directors interviewed cited their concerns in terms of a theoretical position, this same issue was identified by the majority as important in very practical terms, especially in relation to script selection and women's presence onstage, although few of them are as radical as Case would advocate.

A Focus on Women and Gender Issues

Only a small number of the women have chosen to make work by and about women the primary focus of their careers. Roberta Levitow has made the choice in her career to specialize in the work of women playwrights. She explains how this choice evolved: "The primary focus of my work has become new plays by women writers. I don't remember making the choice to do this. I just began to realize that the artists I felt most inspired by were women, and the work I felt most satisfied with was plays by living women playwrights." When asked to elaborate, Levitow explains why she felt drawn to this particular kind of work:

> Carrie Perloff [artistic director, ACT, San Francisco] said to me at one point, "How come you don't do classics? Don't you feel like that could be ours, too? Why should women feel that we can't own that same repertoire?" Her comments stuck with me. I don't get hired to do those big classical repertory pieces. It's not what I started to do as a young artist. I led myself toward new plays. What I wanted to do was original work. Carrie's point was really apt. I didn't feel ownership. I didn't feel that Shakespeare was mine, or the Greeks were mine. It was as if I had grown up somewhere else, not in Western civilization. Western civilization belonged to the guys, and new plays belong to me and my women friends. Contemporary society belonged to me, but I didn't have ownership of the past. In fact, historically, we didn't. Carrie's challenge was, "Why can't you take it on?" and I thought, "That's right, why can't I?" But I haven't. Certainly no one's gonna give you that. That would have to be a demand.

Julia Miles agrees that, except in places like the Women's Project which has an orientation to develop women directors, "Women don't get to direct classics very much. It's just beginning to happen." She has no specific recommendation on how to change that situation other than to hope that as more women enter the field of directing, those restrictions will lessen.

Among the other women interviewed, Nikki Appino shares a focus similar to Levitow's. The idea of particularizing her artistic vision to concentrate on materialist feminist issues was an emerging one for Appino at the time of our interview. After spending a year as a Theatre Communications Group (TCG) directing fellow in mainstream regional theatres around the country, she had come to the realization that a focus on women was how she wanted to define her future work. She is also aware, however, of a certain ambivalence and fear in taking that step: "This desire to create women's theatre frightens me to a degree because I also see it as a wave that's happening in terms of gender and in terms of race and class, this desire to be with one's own kind, with less and less communication outside of those safe realms. It's a big tension for me right now. One of the difficult things is that I know this means even less money, less stability, less security, all of that. But there's just no choice. What's happened in the last year or so has profoundly affected why I do what I do. Limited or not, narrow or not, I've finally come to realize that's it."

Although in her current situation as an educator, Pamela Hendrick has broader concerns in script selection, she had previously been a founder and co-artistic director (with Cynthia White and Betsy Husting) of Theatre Three in Minneapolis, which had set out to be a forum for women artists. She tries to define how that background still influences her script selection:

> Our statement of purpose was not to give a voice to a particular political viewpoint, but rather to give voice to female artists. We selected what seemed to me to be a really broad range of texts. Now when I look back on them I realize they really did have some things in common. I tend to be drawn to texts that aren't particularly linear, that are more relational, that deal with a complex kind of web of interrelationships and emotions. I'm very drawn to scripts that are both presentational and representational. Caryl Churchill is one of my favorites, and I'm very interested in the way that she plays around with both psychological realism and a more presentational style of theatre that steps outside of realism and operates on a very metaphorical and nonrealistical basis. She challenges the audience to look at the play in both of those ways at the same time. It's not purely Brechtian. She's not asking the audience to set their emotions aside and step outside and intellectually analyze what they're seeing; she asks them to intellectually analyze what they're seeing at the same time that she sets up scenes that really do engage the emotions of the audience. I think that's a very female view of the art form.

As lesbian activists, both Susan Finque and Diana Marré are actively concerned with the theatrical exploration of gender roles. Finque says she is always on the lookout for new material that allows her to explore the concept of androgyny and "the fascinating interplay of gender." The analysis of gender as a historical event rather than a natural fact has become critical to current feminist theories of performance. Various methods proposed within theatre practice for achieving this awareness include the rejection of realistic acting and the cultural coding imbedded therein, as well as the use of Brechtian alienation, drag, masquerade, and butch-femme role playing. As an educator, Marré makes her script choices more conventionally because of the needs of her students, but regularly uses these kinds of production concepts and cross-gender casting to explore those issues. Several other women are also interested in the exploration of gender on stage but did not bring it up in connection with script selection. Instead, they discuss it in terms of casting issues or character exploration with actors.

An Awareness of Women's Issues

Finding the Female Point of View

Although only a handful of women interviewed seem to be able to embrace comfortably an exclusive focus on women's plays or overt exploration of gender roles, there are a number of women who see their script selection process as guided by a sensitivity to and awareness of women writers, women's issues, or what they sometimes refer to as feminine themes and values, even though they have broader concerns to consider as well.

Tori Haring-Smith always looks first at plays by women and, regardless of other influences, is always attempting to get women's voice on stage, sometimes in new ways: "I'm really interested in working with a lot of classics and trying to reinterpret the story because I think that the conventional presentation is male. The eyes of the critics, be they literary critics or theater reviewers, and the eyes of the actors have all been trained in a basically male point of view. Seeing the female point of view is really difficult, so to achieve it, I try to contextualize the story a lot." Theorist Jill Dolan, in reference to Laura Mulvey's notion that the cinematic gaze is male and constructed for the male spectator, writes, "If male desire is the underlying principle driving narrative, then to disrupt the cinematic and narrative patterns that rob women of their subjectivity, women's desire must somehow find its place in representation."[3] Haring-Smith, well-educated in the realm of feminist theory, is definitely aware of this need to give women subjectivity. If she cannot control the narrative through script selection, she tries to find other ways to disrupt the gaze in canonical scripts whenever she can. An example comes from a production where she served as production dramaturg and successfully talked the male director into reversing the gaze to equalize subjectivity as much as possible.

> I find that when I work with a male director I am often saying, "Okay, if you do that, this is the story I see." Usually the story I see involves the fact that the female characters have been pushed to the edge of the stage, so I'll just keep mentioning them so that they keep coming back to center stage. For example, working on *Twelfth Night*, in the opening scene the male director staged it so that Orsino ogled several of his female retainers when he was saying, "If music be the food of love, play on." He was basically just goofing off with all of them while talking about Olivia, and he got to eye them quite sexually and dance with them very sexually, and they were very conventionally attractive women. The next day, I said "Okay, you had your scene, I'm going to have mine." So in the next scene, Orsino came up from the beach in a little Speedo bikini, and as he gave his orders, one of his female retainers got to literally manhandle him as she towelled him dry. She got to objectify him. So there were ways in which I was able to balance the images. If the director wanted to sexualize the female as the object, I said, "Well, that's fine, you can sexualize the females, but you've got to sexualize the males too. Because her story is just as important as his."

Along with reversing the gaze, Haring-Smith sometimes reverses gender of characters in her mind to help her understand their development when first reading a script for possible consideration:

> I find when I read a script, the first thing I do is identify with the female characters. When I was doing *Bonjour La Bonjour*, the Tremblay play, I had the hardest time understanding who these characters were because I couldn't identify with the central male figure. The only way I could make sense of it was if I said, "How would I feel in this situation as a female?" Then I could go back and see the difference gender made. That reading strategy seemed to be inherently essentialist to me. I don't know why. There was something about changing the biology of that central character in my head. I do that a lot of times now when I read. It's how I understand where gender impacts on the characters. What would have happened if Konstantin in *The Seagull* had been a woman? How would the story have been different? What makes it necessary that Nina is the female? Asking these questions allows me to see the gender differences more clearly.

While not as comfortable in the realm of theory, Penny Metropulos seems to have similar goals to Haring-Smith. She is very aware that women have often been overlooked or stereotyped in the "humanist" point of view, and she always tries to be sure that women's concerns are no longer slighted as they often have been in the past, especially in the classical scripts she often works on. She also remarks that she has had the good fortune to direct scripts on a wide variety of themes and sees that as "an indication that the 'gender gap' is narrowing, at least in the more sophisticated theatres."

Although she does not focus exclusively on work by or about women, and in contrast to her comment about the sexism in others' assumptions about what a woman should direct, Liz Diamond still identifies script selection as the place in her directing work where gender has the strongest influence: "When I look at a play, I can't help looking at it through the optic of a feminist consciousness. I'm very interested in strong female characters. I'm very interested in writing by women. Women have interesting things to say at this particular time in history because their social roles are in flux, their situations radically unstable. Women have been essentially excluded from the stage as writers until *very* recently. And their stories fascinate me, so I'm inclined to privilege them when I have the opportunity."

Cynthia White, who shared Pamela Hendrick's past focus on women's voices at Theatre Three, is also aware of wanting to give women writers and characters a hearing, although her current selection considerations have to be much broader because of the large mainstream festival theatre with which she is now associated. She also feels drawn to "interesting, strong women characters who are not defined by conventional sexual roles."

Sharon Ott says she tries as often as possible within the mission of her theatre to select plays with themes related to women. She also is drawn to certain kinds of violent, aggressive material, however, and her script choices are often mixed in how they represent women's experiences, both good and bad. The play I observed in rehearsal (*Dream of a Common Language* by Heather McDonald) was an exploration of women's struggle for artistic identity, but the one immediately preceding it in the season, also directed by Ott, had been a harsh and violent piece about San Francisco in the nineteenth century. Ott admits to having a passion for exploring the nineteenth century and its effect on behaviors in contemporary society: "I'm particularly interested in the period from about 1860 to about 1940, when women were conscious of being women, and also men—like Freud, for example—were ascribing ways of thinking that were gender based. Since so many of our norms of behavior now are based in the nineteenth century, it's interesting to me to go back and look at that material, and perhaps interesting to me in a way that would not be interesting to a man." Unlike those who want to comment on gender issues, Ott seems content with simply presenting them for scrutiny, leaving her audiences to draw their own conclusions.

Concern for Feminine Perspectives

Some of the other women identify themselves as concerned with what they call "feminine" issues, but not necessarily feminist ones. In fact, several women were careful to say they were not feminists, seeming to equate feminist directing with an overt polemical intent which they did not want to include in their work. Liz Huddle explains her position: "I'm tremendously concerned with a society that has rejected the feminine from itself, and I look for plays that examine existence from not the female but the feminine perspective. Consequently I'm very interested in eco-feminism and indigenous cultures in relationship to existence and find myself much more interested in the process from that point of view, in the feminine in that way—a feminine philosophy of existence. It permeates my choice of work, my choice of plays that I want to do."

Patricia Blem said she, like Huddle, looks for a "feminine" interpretation of existence, whether it comes from a male or female writer, whether it involves women characters or not. One of the identifying characteristics of Blem's feminine point of view is that she is always looking for plays with a sense of hope or empowerment in their themes, which are characteristics she personally identifies as primarily feminine attributes. This clearly implies a kind of essentialist point of view, yet Blem does not consider herself a radical feminist, nor is she familiar with the vocabulary of feminist theory. Rather she identifies her point of view as a Jungian one, believing male and female attributes are present in both genders.

Sensitivity to Treatment of Women Characters

Almost all the directors, regardless of other concerns, identify a special sensitivity to the way women characters are portrayed in the scripts they consider to direct. A number of the women are quite adamant about not doing plays involving violence toward women. Adele Prandini is particularly emphatic about discouraging the oppression of women in her selection of scripts: "I'm careful about material. I'm not interested in putting something onstage that is sadistic to women. There are plenty of others who are interested in it, and we see so much of it. This is not to say that you shy away from controversy, because controversy is healthy. It's challenge that's healthy for all of us, and those challenges in theatre happen on so many different levels. So you want work that is challenging, but then there is this stuff that's just status quo oppression, and who needs it? Who wants it? I don't. I don't want to see it, and I certainly don't want to work on it. Nor do I want to encourage it."

This sensitivity also plays out in a number of other ways including a desire to find strong, central women characters, active women who are not victims, and most especially to be sure the female characters are balanced—whole human beings rather than stereotypical cardboard cutouts. While this is an important issue in script selection, it will also be addressed as the women talk about working with actors on character development.

Rejection of Stereotypes

This sensitivity to stereotyping seems especially important to the women of color with whom I spoke. Not only do they wish to confront the negative ways women are portrayed onstage, but they are also concerned with how ethnic characters are portrayed, which can lead to another potential career limitation for them in the eyes of others, a limitation similar in character to being stuck in the "woman's slot." Susana Tubert is concerned with ethnic as well as gender issues and has turned down some plays for reasons of ethnic stereotyping. She believes she would definitely reject projects that she found offensive to women, but has so far not been put in that position: "If a theatre is going to ghettoize me, it will do so, not because I'm a woman but because I'm a Latina. I suspect producers go through an automatic selection process, which in my case has yet to become gender specific. It's been more about the Latino experience, which doesn't upset me as long as the plays are good. For seventeen years I was an Argentinian, until I came to New York City and became a 'Latin American,' so directing those plays is great. At the same time, I am dying to direct a classic. How do I explain to these artistic directors what it meant for me to grow up hearing Chekhov in Spanish read to me by my Russian grandmother?"

For Michelle Blackmon the idea of portraying women as positive models and rejecting stereotypes is particularly important. She has problems with scripts where black women are portrayed as "bitches and sluts" and tries to avoid those scripts at all costs, which can sometimes cost her employment. Blackmon also shows a sensitivity to how many women are onstage as well as how they are portrayed: "I try to specifically be sensitive to women's issues, and as a black woman, there are issues of positive role models. It's not that the types don't exist. It's that when you get to a point when that's all you see, what kind of role models are these for our young people? That becomes very important to me. As we all know, women get the real raw end of the deal on the stage. The best roles are written for men, and in most of the plays the balance of men and women is definitely tipped to the men. It's very frustrating, so I have a tendency to look at pieces that deal either with women's issues or in terms of numbers of characters."

As for Blackmon, quality, size, and number of female roles are concerns for Tisa Chang, in addition to her emphasis on ethnic considerations: "I've always chosen plays that have very strong and large women's roles because I used to be an actress. And I've really pushed the Asian American women. I've gone out my way simply because their works speak to me. It's not just a sisterhood solidarity thing, but it's also practical in the sense that I find there are more and better actresses with fewer opportunities than male actors. So I say, 'How can we even the equation?'"

Although she did not invoke the vocabulary of role models, Bea Kiyohara is also concerned with ethnic as well as gender issues in her play selection process and is equally concerned about how women are portrayed. She sees a need to be especially vigilant regarding the seemingly small moments in a play in which derogatory information can be imparted to an audience almost without it being apparent. In particular, Kiyohara is referring to the cultural differences that could lead to unwittingly perpetuating negative stereotypes of the submissive, compliant Asian female if a director is not careful. She believes women have the ability to be more sensitive to those moments, thus avoiding them: "I think as a woman you have to be sensitive to a lot more issues when you start examining a play. Every junction is some sort of tiny moral choice. 'What am I saying about women?' 'What am I saying about ethnics?' 'What am I saying about gays?' You have to continually come back to what I call those little moral interpretations and those choices. Women are much more in tune with that, coming from our own personal experiences, where a lot of people don't even think about them."

While ethnic issues were obviously in the thoughts of women of color, they were not absent from the concerns of the other women. Emily Mann and JoAnne Akalaitis, in particular, both speak of the need for today's theatre to be more inclusive of the voices of artists of color, and they are actively engaged in trying to bring those works to their audiences, even if the scripts are not always under their own direction. For all these women, regardless of other specific concerns, they definitely agree on the need to avoid perpetuating negative or limiting stereotypes as well as the desire to broaden and balance the perspective of their audiences.

Women's Perspectives on Male-Oriented Scripts

There are also times when gender considerations influence script selection in ways that are not about doing a "woman's play," per se, but instead reflect a specific interest in getting a woman's perspective on a "male-oriented" script. Melia Bensussen explains how this situation came to her and what the consequences were: "Right now I'm directing *Oleanna*, and the producer wanted a woman to direct it, which I think was a very good idea. I find that I am interpreting the text differently than I believe [author David] Mamet intended me to. I can tell by the clues set up. I'm not going against the text at all, but I'm using the text in a different fashion." She goes on to imply that the text uses very stereotypical notions about the differences between men and women, and she believes that she is able to resist the trap of seeing the relationship in only that one particular way.

Tori Haring-Smith has also had the experience of working on at least one particularly "male" play. She would like to do more and believes that the female perspective she brings to her interpretation of these kinds of scripts can create a balance in the production that might not be there if the director were a man. She talks first about a play she would like to do in the future: "I'm interested in *Buried Child*, by Sam Shepard. I have always thought it should be done by a woman. I really feel that the mother and the nurturing images are central to that play, and they haven't been understood in the conventionally masculine world Shepard lives in." Then she shares her experience with a past production of a play usually seen as quite masculine:

> When I directed *Speed of Darkness*, Stephen Tesich's play, it was gender that influenced that selection, even though it wasn't a woman's play. I sat and watched the play at Berkeley Rep, and it was not a play that I thought I would like to direct. But when the house lights went up at the end, most of the women were getting up and leaving and most of the men in the house were sitting and weeping. It fascinated me. I said, "I've never seen a play affect men like this. I really want to do this play, I really want to understand this play." Usually it's the men who get up and say, "Let's have a beer," and it's the women who are getting out the Kleenexes and tidying the makeup. I wanted to get inside the male response to Tesich's play. Because it was specifically not a female play, I wanted to see how it worked. I think my *Speed of Darkness* was such an extremely successful production because for me it inevitably became a female play. I was most interested in the mother and daughter, but the husband was so strongly written by the playwright that the resulting production was really balanced. I think it surprises people when I succeed, especially with a male script. *Speed of Darkness* really surprised people because it is a very male

script. It's about Viet Nam vets and guns, what it means to be infertile as a male, and what it means to know that your daughter isn't your daughter.

It's clear that a number of these women not only want to broaden the kinds of scripts they are able to work on, but they also believe they can bring something special to the interpretation of plays people might not immediately associate with a woman director.

Finding Gender Influence After the Fact

Although many of the other directors create their own works at times, Maria Irene Fornes is arguably better known as a playwright than a director and is most often directing her own works. Therefore, our conversation about script selection evolved into a discussion of whether gender was a conscious influence on the subjects about which she chooses to write. Just as she insists she is not aware of gender when she directs, Fornes says she does not think about it when she writes, but afterwards can definitely identify its influence. When she sits down to write, she doesn't write about themes. She merely starts with small details and lets the story evolve through exploration of those details. Her focus on women seems to evolve in a similar, nonconscious way:

> I've never set out to write a play that's a feminist play, and yet I feel all my plays are feminist. A lot of feminists think that my work is not feminist anymore, that I wrote my feminist play [*Fefu and her Friends*], because they don't realize that the most feminist thing that you can do is write a play where the female character is the main character, where a female character just takes over and you experience the woman as the center of the universe. I start writing a play and I don't care who is the central character or what other characters are there, and it seems that the male may be a stronger character in the first scene, and without my noticing, without knowing how it happened, the female character has become the character that's central, and that has happened because I'm a woman.

Although brought up here primarily in the context of playwriting, the issue of the centrality of women becomes an important one for many women directors because most of them, regardless of the context of their work or their conscious consideration of gender issues, do try to give women characters, if not centrality, then at least a subjectivity and completeness often previously denied them.

OTHER INFLUENCES ON SCRIPT SELECTION

No Conscious Gender Influence

While the preceding responses have explored various ways women believe gender influences their script selection process, fully one-third of the women

Tori Haring-Smith (right) directs actors (from left) Phyllis Kay, Allen Oliver, and Richard Donelly in Tom Grady's *American Cocktail* at the Trinity Repertory Company (1994). Photo by Robert R. Haring-Smith.

interviewed insist they are not consciously influenced by gender in their script selection process, citing other concerns. For example, Brenda Hubbard thinks other issues are more important, especially a need to balance a season and appeal to her constituent audience. Victoria Parker wants to illuminate challenging social issues while avoiding anything overtly political. Alana Byington looks for plays with issues of moral ambiguity and multiple viewpoints. Rita Giomi believes that as a woman she may be sensitive to different issues in a script but makes her choices based on what the piece has to say to an audience, style of writing, character treatment, and desire for variety. JoAnne Akalaitis says she looks for great art regardless of the gender of the writer, although it could obviously be argued that defining greatness in art is a gendered activity based on a historically male-dominated sense of aesthetic values.

The women I spoke with who want to reject conscious gender identification as a consideration in their script selection process and who support the concept of the artist as a genderless being, believe it to be highly advantageous for them as professionals to resist thinking of themselves as women directors, perhaps in part to avoid being stuck with those "girl's scripts" or having to compete with other women for that "woman's slot." This point of view fits a liberal feminist model in that these women have found success by avoiding issues of gender and participating in a male-dominated system that was already in place when they began their careers. In an early work, Sue-Ellen Case saw danger in the need to detach from gender identification and posed the argument that perhaps women might be excluded from the dramatic experience altogether.[4] Jill Dolan echoed this caution to liberal feminists, warning that they may have have "acquiese[d] to their erasure as women" because the universal standard they apply is still based on a male model.[5] While it is not my intent to pit theory against practice, it should be noted that this tension does exist between the two elements.

In fact, some of the women I spoke with were quite aware of this tension and were beginning to wrestle with it in their work. While she celebrates the fact that women have taken enormous strides in their careers in the last few decades, Liz Huddle believes that "succeeding by simply becoming men" is a very bad solution for women directors. She acknowledges, however, that someone looking at her career and the projects she has selected over the years could perhaps draw that conclusion but says her awareness is now changing. Fontaine Syer says she is always looking for personal challenge and a good play that says something she is interested in communicating to the world. Syer does, however, admit that gender might be an influence, just not a conscious one.

Gloria Muzio also believes gender is not a conscious influence. She seems to be more comfortable than Syer in saying it could be influential in script selection, but she does deemphasize its prominence in her personal process, placing more importance on the sum of an artist's life experiences: "I think that in reading scripts, I respond to them in a different way because of the different issues on my mind. You can't avoid having a gender response to a script because it's part of your experience. What you're doing is taking a piece of material and interpreting it and being as true to the playwright as you can, but it's still your soul you're putting into that play to bring it to life when you're creating a production. I guess it's not conscious, it's just part of who you are—gender."

While fascinated by the question of gender's possible influence, Zelda Fichandler insists her interests are in humanist concerns and even while calling herself a feminist, she is careful to note that she sees her feminism as an aspect of being a humanist. For her, humanist issues are irrevokably linked to an idea often invoked by others when describing a "woman's" play: "I'm trying to think if it's gender related, since so many of the great plays are about families. The microcosm of the society is the family. I would say I'm interested in family plays, but most of the great plays are family plays." As Jill Dolan points out, however, not all family plays have been considered great plays and gender bias clearly seems to have some influence in this difference in reception on the part of the critics. In particular, Dolan contrasts the differences in critical reception between Arthur Miller's *Death of a Salesman* and Marsha Norman's *'night, Mother*, where "in the change from male writer to female and father/son focus to mother/daughter, domestic drama is reduced to kitchen drama, which is considered specific rather than universal, and melodramatic rather than tragic. ... While Miller can write about the family and be canonized, Norman's attempt to tackle similar issues is seen as evidence of the preoccupations of her gender class."[6]

Fichandler also relates that reviewers have often commented that she is particularly good with plays about men, but unlike Haring-Smith, who sees directing these plays as a way to balance gender issues, Fichandler places more emphasis on some kind of universal humanist vision:

> I don't know that it has to do with gender. I think it has to do with a very deep interest in psychology, in the basic psychological root of a play, what the characters want and how they get it. Generally I'm interested in plays in the humanist tradition, which I guess all plays are. When I did *Death of a Salesman*, the reviewers said I always display a great understanding of father/son relationships, or male bonding relationships, or something like that. I don't know what that means. That means that I'm interested in human relationships. That's how I feel about work. It isn't gender related, it's what's being revealed that appeals to me. I mean, if you asked a psychoanalyst if they are more interested in men or women, would they be able to answer you?

Anne Bogart is another director who believes how she chooses her projects is not influenced by gender. She is at a point in her career where she is rarely offered specific scripts of any kind, much less only "women's" scripts. Theatres that wish to work with her usually ask her what production she would like to do for them, which is a rather unique position for any director and one Bogart has fought long and hard to achieve. While being very aware of her identity as a woman in the theatre and very articulate about gender's influence in other parts of her working process, Bogart insists gender is not an influence in script selection. She explains how she makes her script choices:

> Interest to me is a very intangible and tangible thing at the same time. It's the only thing we have to work with, it's our only tool. I think men and women are equally guided, if they're any good, by their genuine interest. I think interest changes all the time. I went through a period where I was obsessed with male/female relationships on the stage. Being homosexual, it's a really odd thing that I'm fascinated by a man and a woman standing on stage. It says everything to me. I went through that stage, and now I'm on to other things. I think that the interests I've had, and the choice of projects which is determined by that interest, I found pretty universal and not gender specific.

Julie Taymor doesn't see gender as a significant influence on the stories she chooses to work on, although, like a number of the others, she points out the difficulty in being certain just what the exact influences are: "I pick and choose what I want to do. Sometimes people offer me jobs and I either like them or I don't, but I don't get women's plays. I develop my own work, mostly. I would like to do female stories, and if I find something then I'll do it. I do think there is room for better stories where the females are the leads. It doesn't have to be about being tough, or being a woman. I don't want to show that women have had it rough. I just want to tell a story that interests me, where I can identify with the characters." As a visual artist and writer, Taymor usually creates or adapts her own scripts and concerns herself with issues of the outsider, the person dispossessed. One might make a case that gender could have a significant influence on this theme, but to date, Taymor's protagonists have usually been male, not female. It would, of course, be possible to make a case for unconscious gender influences in the processes of any of these women. Their own perceptions lead them to conclude, however, that gender issues are, in fact, insignificant or nonexistent in their personal script selection process.

OVERCOMING PERCEIVED LIMITATIONS

Breaking Out of the Woman's Slot

Even in their differing circumstances, it does seem that the potentially confining influence of the "woman's slot" can affect most women directors to some degree, regardless of their stature and experience. If they do not choose to embrace the designation, the ways women break out of the "woman's slot" are varied. One way mentioned above is to create original scripts. Another is to start or run a theatre, thereby gaining more artistic control. Mary Robinson describes how she tried during her tenure at Philadelphia Drama Guild to reverse her perceived early career limitations: "I was a little bit typed. I never got the large classics I was eager to do, and as artistic director I'm trying to rectify that. I'm trying to make up for the plays I didn't get to do for a number of years, being type cast the way actors and directors and all artists are—and perhaps part of the typing was because I was a woman."

For the women who free-lance and are usually offered scripts by others, breaking away from expectations of what a woman should direct involves somehow changing the expectations of others, the ones with the scripts to offer. Gloria Muzio describes with a combination of frustration and relief how a successful production of one particular play has changed the kinds of scripts she is now offered:

I used to only get offered the relationship plays, the sisters plays, the mother/ daughter plays, and the divorce plays—you know, the plays that people think women are going to respond to. After seeing *Other People's Money* [a hard-edged play about Wall Street power], the first thing people would say would be, "I can't believe that a woman directed that play!" And that used to infuriate me because I never knew what it meant. Did it mean it wasn't soft enough for a woman to direct? Or the play was very tough and they were surprised that a woman had directed it? Or it was so good and they were surprised that a woman directed it? It's trying to find the play that's going to break that image of a woman doing something soft. And frankly, I like a lot of those soft plays, but it's also nice to be considered to do plays that don't just have to do with women's issues. Men don't direct plays that just have to do with men's issues. It's always been important and crucial to me to be thought of as a good director and not as a good woman director. It's also important to me to maintain what is me, which includes being a woman.

Echoing issues brought up earlier by Tori Haring-Smith, Muzio goes on to explain why she pursued the job of directing *Other People's Money* and why she believes the production was so successful, thus allowing her to break away from the expectations of others:

What interested me was that it seemed to be a power play between a man and a woman. I was more tuned into that dynamic, having felt that, having worked that, having been through that from the woman's point of view. I know what it's like when you walk into an office and there's a powerful man, and you can't help but be aware that you're a woman dealing with a very powerful man. You try to say it doesn't matter, but there is something different. I don't mean that it's awful or wonderful. I don't have a judgment on it. But there is something different, and you can't ignore it. Why I responded to that play had a lot to do with that woman lawyer taking on the biggest case of her career facing this very powerful man. I really responded to that, and I think that's part of what my focus in directing that play was. It was certainly true to the play, but I wasn't interested at all in the machinations of Wall Street. I was much more interested in the personal dynamic that was going on because of my personal experience. Perhaps if I weren't a woman, I wouldn't have focused so much or have felt so strongly about that woman's plight. I think that's what made that play as successful as it was; part of it was that it was a real human dilemma and not just a story about Wall Street. Something happened with *Other People's Money* because there were a lot of men in the play, it was about business. The leading character was a very tough, unlikable guy, and scripts that came to me after that were of a broader range.

Because of gendered expectations, it seems women have to earn the right to a broader selection of scripts as Muzio has done, but Seret Scott expresses a frustration shared by many about the fragility of the situation: "As I work more and more, it doesn't need to be that gender or ethnic issue anymore. I have proven myself in so many other areas. But everybody gets tired of having to prove themselves every time."

Confronting Internal Limitations

Another influence in the process of breaking away from expectations is confronting the sometimes limiting notions women carry within themselves as they respond to the expectations they routinely encounter from others. More specifically, a few women talked about how easy it was to accept the limitations put on them by others, especially early in a career before an artistic identity has solidified and matured. Melia Bensussen definitely ties the gender expectations to the point in her career rather than her real desires regarding the making of art:

> I do think my answers about script selection would have been different ten years ago and assume they'll be very different ten years from now. I find that I am drawn to what might be termed messy scripts—big, ambitious, maybe not fully resolved, not black and white, not cleanly packaged resolutions, ambiguous, where it's more open to interpretation, where I can take more liberties. I don't know if this is gender; part of me senses that it is. This is starting to change for me, but I would say that the emotional tone of an evening, the overall ideas, the big picture of it was often more important to me than the neatness of shape and form in the text. It seemed better to me to have a more complex, less defined moment than a simpler, more delineated one. My heart would leap when there was a dark, messy, ambiguous, difficult play, and I would not get excited by the neat and tidy. I wonder if it's not connected to notions of career. I saw myself career-wise as an underdog. This is perhaps an image that I'm shedding—"I'm young, I'm a woman, I'm never going to be a success so I can direct all these messy plays." I don't have to worry about which show is a hit, so perhaps I choose plays that aren't finished but they're interesting to me, whereas I see my male colleagues—who are, I have to say, doing much better than I am career-wise—having chosen texts that were going to be hits. I don't know if that's personality. I don't know what that is.

While seeing oneself as not having to worry about commercial success because of being an underdog can obviously be seen as a limitation, it can also give some advantage in that the director can be free to make more interesting and exciting artistic choices. It does become a kind of "Catch-22," however, as women try to build up their careers and to develop an ongoing body of work.

Building a Body of Work

Emily Mann is one director who said she initially believed gender was not a conscious factor in her script selection process, but she has, after many years of working, now identified a pattern of influence in the body of her work over the years. It's a pattern she is comfortable with, and she is glad to become more conscious of it:

I produce what I love and feel I must see done. It's just recently that people started to tell me that there was a pattern to it that they had noticed—that it was often about women, even if it was written by men. It's almost like building up a body of work of how to perceive women in the great works of literature—American and European literature and African American literature. I wasn't that aware of it, I just knew I was doing what I needed to do. I will be more often interested in seeing a new look at a female character or a female story. How could I not? I'm glad to be more conscious of it. I want to make sure that I track it intelligently. I think the more we see women starting to build that body of work, the more we really begin to be able to study what it is. Many men who think they are sensitive to women say, "You didn't have this percentage of women writers." But I believe you produce what you love and what you connect with. If the men are producing more stories about men, that makes a lot of sense to me. They're doing what they feel inside of them they've got to see done. They might in their heads say, "Wait a minute, we should have more representation of black people or women, or Latinos, or whatever," but some of that is from the head, it isn't always from the gut. I'm much more interested in Black African and African American theatre than most people, and also things that have to do with Jews and ethnicity and questions of American identity. There are things that I have interests in that I will be more open to. I think every single artistic director is like that. I'm so pleased to be in a place where I can build a body of work that is unique to what it is I'm obsessed with, what I need to put out both as a director and as a writer, and also in producing the work of my colleagues. I think I'm going to find out a lot about what I believe in. I think I'm going to find out and grow as I can watch a body of work develop.

This building of a body of work is still a very problematic issue for women directors. If the body of work is built without conscious intent and with an unspoken acceptance of the perceived limitations on women directors, then what use is it? It seems, however, as if there are definitely more women working now to build a body of work with very conscious intent.

Summary

While there are many factors that go into a personal script selection process for any director, the main issue connecting gender and script selection seems to be the limited perception of others. This perception can lead to a woman director being considered only for the "woman's slot" or plays about women's issues. Only a few women in this book want to maintain an exclusive focus on women's scripts or gender issues, however. Although there are some who can control their own script selection, most of these women want to be able to consider a broader range of scripts than are usually offered to them by others. Ways of overcoming this perceived limitation can include finding ways to direct a project that breaks the ongoing expectations of others, creating your own scripts or being otherwise involved with the development of new scripts, or running your own theatre. In spite of their rejection of the limitations inherent in the "woman's slot," most of the directors inter-viewed believe they have a special sensitivity to women's issues and the por-trayal of women on stage as well as an interest in trying to get more women's voices on stage. They also believe that bringing a woman's perspective to a male-oriented script can create more balance and insight for the audience. One-third of the directors say gender plays no role at all in their script selec-tion process; they look instead for what they identify as more humanist con-cerns. Many of the directors seem rooted in the humanist belief that although society does control gender identity to a significant degree, there still exists a universal human experience that can be communicated to an audience. The difference is that they firmly believe this universality can and must be pre-sented through the experiences of women as well as men.

9. WORKING WITH ACTORS

Although the chapters on leadership and collaboration encompass many of the ways these directors work with their actors during the rehearsal process, many of the women interviewed believe there is something special in the way they work with actors. These differences seemed most evident in the audition and casting process and in their work on character interpretation and development.

CASTING ISSUES

The Personal Nature of the Casting Process

All of the directing texts emphasize the importance of good casting choices, saying casting can represent anywhere from half to three-quarters of the work of putting together a successful production. While all directors have their own styles in auditions, there are certain structural commonalities identified in the texts, such as prepared auditions, cold readings, special auditions for singing, dancing, or other special requirements, and callbacks resulting in final casting choices. Some of the texts describe or recommend various possible ways of arriving at those final choices, but it seems clear that a director makes the critical decisions based on a very personal sense of what might be right for a given situation or production. There are obviously no absolute formulas for casting.

Anne Bogart states her strong belief in the personal nature of casting choices but says gender is not a significant factor for her. She is influenced by "level of talent, taste, eroticism, surprise. You're always attracted to something that you'd like to be, so you see that in another person. Casting is a very complicated issue, but I find it highly personal. I would imagine that each individual, whether you're a man or a woman, would respond to it very personally." Like Bogart, Mary Robinson wants to be surprised by the auditioners but believes this openness to be simply good directing: "I sometimes have very specific ideas about the roles, but I'm also willing to be and interested in being surprised. I certainly look for actors who will fit into an ensemble and be collaborative with each other. That's very important to me. I don't think that's necessarily female. Most directors work that way, I believe."

Roberta Levitow is another director who believes at this point in her career that gender has no influence in her casting process. "I was a casting director at the Los Angeles Theatre Center for about a year, and I saw so many actors that I think whatever inclination I had to be warm and friendly in casting went away. It's pretty scientific for me at this point." It's interesting to note that at first her comment might seem to imply that being warm and friendly at auditions could have something to do with gender, although Levitow later clarified her meaning by saying, "I changed my behavior because I was seeing hundreds of actors and [was] inundated with demands for attention. The process became more mechanical, not more male. A male or a female in the same situation might shift from gracious, personal attention to a more businesslike approach."

Seret Scott believes she takes a different approach to casting than do most directors because of her willingness to consider a person's potential over the specific audition they have given. She is quite adamant, however, that this has nothing to do with being a woman, rather much more to do with being an actress for many years before becoming a director: "In the audition and casting process, I find I take into consideration what this person's potential may be. They may not have given a good audition, they may not have been able to get what I want, but I know this is the right person. I think, being an actress, I know the kind of stress you're under in the audition process. A lot of actors who audition for me know me as an actress. They feel more stress when they come in because they feel they're auditioning for a friend. I do cast the best person possible. That means I'm not going to cast a good friend just because they need a job. I will cast them if they're the best person possible."

Unusual Casting Choices

Aside from an occasional reference to intuitive casting, taking more time with actors to put them at their ease, or making an effort to access the emotional availability or potential of an actor, the main comments about the difference women perceive in their casting process concerns an openness and willingness to look at casting choices differently than they believe a man might. The first issue identified as part of this openness is a widely held belief that women are more open to unusual or different choices—casting against type, so to speak.

Rita Giomi brought up the issue of a special openness in casting in the early moments of her interview, but only in very general terms: "I would say casting is actually one of the largest places gender affects my process because I think I look for different things in actors. This is not qualitative at all, not in terms of being better because of gender. I just think there's a huge difference. Everything's going to sound like generalizations, but I think women are tuned to subtleties in personality that men may not be conscious of, because of the way we've been raised, and what it is we look for, and what our own personal experiences are. Not that we're necessarily tuned to better things, just different things." Michelle Blackmon, like Giomi, believes she is able to see people differently, saying that is because she is used to being outside the mainstream. She translates this to a desire to work against obvious types: "I want to allow actors to give me what they can give me, as opposed to saying it has to be this type of person. Because of my experience of being a black actor, I try to look at people a little more broadly."

Pamela Hendrick is more specific about what casting against type means in her process: "I think I look for something different than physical appearance in casting a role. I almost never think in terms of what a character looks like. I'm much more interested in a quality of representation. I'm looking for a personality quality that's not even all that definable to me, but I know it when I see it—an energy level, a quality, something that's more ephemeral. I rarely go into an audition looking for a specific physical type. I'm not particularly interested in plays that are about people's external physical appearances." Melia Bensussen also addresses the issue of physical appearance at auditions:

> I think my notions of what attractiveness is are affected by gender and what is interesting in a person if a script calls for a beautiful woman. I think there's a complexity in how, as a woman, one views these things, because you know what is conventionally viewed as attractive, then you know what you find attractive, and then you know what the men find attractive. There are layers there. Yes, she's conventionally beautiful, but is she really beautiful? I don't know if those are questions men ask or not. I would think ultimately that all of these things are connected with making art in a sophisticated way. We keep all sides of the picture open at those stages because you need them in order to make intelligent choices. There are times I feel very male when I'm casting. In auditions, I feel like a man quite often—oh, this is so sexist to say— when I am very, very clear about physical appearance. There is something about judging by physical appearance that feels male to me, something I can absolutely tap into. I can think horrible things about women and men based on their physical appearances—not horrible, really, but what I'm thinking is what this body reads like on stage. I see that as male. I see that as placing a priority on the physical.

Of course, in the realm of feminist theory, the gaze that defines its object in terms of conventional physical, sexual attractiveness is thought of as culturally male. It is also the gaze that keeps women at the margins of the

Melia Bensussen (center) with actresses Christina Haag (left) and Deborah Kipp (right) on the set of Brian Friel's *Dancing at Lughnasa* at the Cleveland Playhouse (1994). Photo by Faye Sholitan.

stage and defined by outward appearance over other considerations. "Typing" seems, however, to be a common experience in theatre for both male and female actors, but it may be the women directors who think they are doing the most to eliminate this unfortunate tendency.

Timothy Near provides a personal anecdote to illustrate her belief that she is more open to unusual casting choices than she believes her male counterparts to be: "I think regarding shapes and sizes I'm not as traditional because I'm very tall, and when I was an actress I felt there were many times when people thought they couldn't cast me because I was tall. They think an ingenue wouldn't be tall. Well, I'm living proof that an ingenue was tall. So I always try to take in any shape and size that comes in to see if that is a possibility, whereas I think maybe men might not do that as much." Emily Mann, however, has known Near for years and disagrees with her self-analysis. Mann believes Near's openness has more to do with her political convictions than her gender. "I agree with her on a lot of things, and I can't imagine Timothy not being female, but I don't think that's why she's so open. It's that her whole life she's lived a consistent set of politics." Mann identifies herself as having similar values and is equally open to nontraditional casting choices. She uses her production of Strindberg's *Miss Julie* as an example:

> I made the part of Kristin much bigger, and I made her very sexy, and very earthy, a real sexual threat to Miss Julie because she had her own sexuality, her own life. Why does the cook have to be ugly and cold? There's a good thing going on there between Kristen and Jean. If you play that first scene right, there's a real relationship, a good relationship there before Miss Julie enters. Then Julie's needs are such and Jean's needs are such that other things occur. How I directed the show was more like a Rorschach test about sexuality. When Ingmar Bergman had Miss Julie come back after going in to make love with Jean, he had blood streaming down her legs and she went out the door and threw up. I did the opposite. I had them coming out enthralled; there's an afterglow. It was good. I don't understand why she would stay if she'd been raped or abused. What are the next two acts of the play about? This is a woman who is awakened sexually and had the most incredible experience. Otherwise you just have a victim and a scoundrel. That doesn't interest me. Now maybe because I'm a woman, I see it this way. I think it's often impossible for guys to think that this woman loved making love. She's a highly charged sexual being. Interpretation and casting are utterly linked. I'm sure being a woman infects and informs every moment that's on the stage because I have a personal stake in what's going on at every moment. I really truly cannot separate myself from that, especially when it comes to emotion, sexuality, love between people, hate between people, relationships between people.

Mann attributes some of her openness, specifically the casting of the role of Kristen and the nature of the relationship between Jean and Julie, to being a woman, but in general places more emphasis on her personal and political beliefs as the stronger influences, especially when talking about the decision she made to cast a black actor in the male role of Jean in this same production.

Nontraditional and Cross-Gender Casting

This openness to unusual or unexpected shapes, sizes, and colors can also extend to an openness to nontraditional casting of women in traditionally male roles when it seems possible and appropriate. Timothy Near used female singer/actor Ronnie Gilbert as Teresias in a production of *Oedipus* because she was easily able to conceptualize a seer and visionary as a woman without changing the other values of the play. Tisa Chang often looks for ways to use cross-gender casting because she has so many strong actresses connected with her company. She also describes how she uses cross-gender doubling to undercut certain stereotypes:

> When we take roles from existing Chinese literature, very often I will have a heroine, who's always soft and sinewy, also double in the warrior roles. I go out of my way to create balance. I wonder is that part of my political advocacy, a little bit of my militancy, or is that the way I see the natural rounding of a character? I really don't see women only in the role of housewives, or eligible brides, which is how they are portrayed throughout the Chinese fables. Ultimately, I feel that they do something else. They also are conjurers, wizards, witches, beings with power. I think this has a lot to do with my being an empowered woman. Certainly when I was growing up, this was something the world didn't recognize. These dualities always have appealed to me, so I try to put them in my stage works.

Like many others I spoke with, Liz Diamond is open to casting women in roles traditionally played by men, but she also cautions against some possible traps in cross-gender casting:

> I'm much more likely to wonder whether a role could be played by a woman than perhaps a man might. At the same time, last year when I was working on *Julius Caesar* with Doug Hughes, he was really interested in the possibility of Cassius being played by a woman. I wasn't at all convinced that it was a good idea, particularly because of the sort of ambiguous love that flows between Cassius and Brutus which I thought was complex and beautiful. I did not want to create a sort of Lady Macbeth character out of Cassius. By doing a nontraditional casting in that case, I felt we would have been playing into a boring theatrical stereotype. I know that was influenced by gender.

Other directors say they try to use nontraditional casting as often as possible to allow more women to be involved in their productions. This response is particularly common in directors from academic environments, who often have more female students than male ones and are always looking for ways to involve female actors.

Only a small number of the women are actively engaged in cross-gender casting in order to foreground the arbitrariness of gender roles in our culture. One who is consistently committed to cross-gender casting is Diana Marré, who believes the use of drag in a show is one of the best theatrical tools for breaking down stereotypical notions of gender socialization. She uses the device in many of her shows, especially when she works on the classics. Although she insists that she can "still direct men to be men and women to be women," she finds using cross-gender casting to be highly theatrical and lots of fun for everyone involved:

> It's fun to coach, and the students have fun with it. I'm interested in break-
> ing down stereotypes, doing a lot of body work, and getting them to move
> differently. It helps as an acting exercise, and it really helps pump up the the-
> atricality in a show. In *Comedy of Errors* it was just fun to make those com-
> ments on the politics of the town. It got the actors out of playing those old,
> boring, iambic pentameter "dum-dee-dum-dee's." It made them use another
> voice and another body. It brought life into what they were doing because
> they were doing an impersonation, and for some reason it just made that lan-
> guage work. Those characters had less trouble with the verse than the char-
> acters that I cast to type.

Although most of the other women stop short of the idea of this kind of foregrounding in cross-gender casting, the idea of playing against or break-ing down stereotypes is important in their casting choices.

CHARACTER DEVELOPMENT ISSUES

Expanding the Range

Many women say playing against or breaking down stereotypes is equally important in their work on character development. Pamela Hendrick often uses cross-gender casting to open up the possibilities of more roles for her female students, but she is much more explicit about her use of cross-gender work in rehearsal to expand the range of her actors, both male and female:

> One of the things I definitely try to get my actors to do is to investigate alter-
> native modes of self-expression. I try to get my female actors to investigate
> the world of gesture and vocalization that might have eluded them because
> it seems masculine to them, and I try to get men to investigate the feminine
> as well. I think that our culture is very gender dimorphic, and we want to
> identify, we expect to, and in fact do identify the gender of a stranger within
> seconds of meeting them. I know there are thousands of complex signals that
> we give off, and I find often that by really trying to pinpoint what some of
> those gendered differences are, we can open up to performers a more dynamic
> world of investigating character. We can get a lot more levels of performance
> out of a man, for instance, if he's willing to add dynamism to his voice, to use
> his head voice, and to loosen his spine a bit. We can get far more powerful
> performances from a woman if we encourage her to claim more physical space
> with her body, to find a more powerful center of gravity. I definitely and very
> consciously apply gender to the exploration of character with my actors.

Looking for more levels in a performance is clearly not limited to an exploration of gender behaviors, but many of the directors believe women are more sensitive to this kind of deep character exploration, possibly for gender-related reasons. Roberta Levitow definitely sees working on character development as a significant place in her process where gender influences manifest. She speaks about having certain insights because of being a woman and describes the differences in her level of confidence and exploration between working on a play about male behavior and another with a central female character she was easily able to identify with. This kind of comment can be dangerous in the assumption that "you have to be one to understand one," but Levitow clearly believes one can learn about the other in the process of the work and does not want to be limited by only doing things she understands from personal experience. In fact, acting is usually based on the assumption that a performer can learn to identify with a character *as if* they are that person, whether the character is from another culture, historical era, social class, or physical circumstance, so why not another gender? It's interesting that some of the assumptions about what directors should know and do sometimes seem to be more limiting than what we routinely expect actors to do. After all, directors always do research in preparation for a production, and why shouldn't that research involve gender behavior? Levitow discusses her own experience in this regard:

> As imaginative as I can be, and as much of a student of human nature that I hope I am, there is a limited pool of what I know and what I can imagine and what I can identify with based on my own experience. For example, when I was working on *Speed-the-Plow*, I read everything I could possibly read that David Mamet had written about these characters and about his analysis of how men interact. I talked a lot to the men in the cast about giving me verbs and some sort of shorthand for some of the codes of behavior that Mamet was trying to illuminate. I believe he's a genius at describing the way men interact in a contemporary American setting. I did know that, but I was educated to it. It had not been part of my experience to actually behave that way. Although I have a lot of insight into what the characters were doing, there definitely was a rubicon I had not crossed. I had to turn to these guys and very openly say, "What's going on here? I can tell something's happening. What is it? What names would you give to this interaction?" They would have to tell me, and it was actually really fun and fascinating. When I did *Hedda Gabler*, I felt absolutely certain I knew exactly how and why Hedda was behaving the way she did. I had tremendous confidence about that particular production because I felt I really knew it. Somehow a man had written it so that it was absolutely true to my perception. I don't think we're all the same, personally. I think we're different in many distinctive ways, and we are different by gender.

While Levitow shares specific examples about the gender influence in a particular production, others simply bring up a general avoidance of stereotypes and simplistic or obvious character types as the starting point for their discussion of work on character development, a point with which Levitow is in complete agreement.

Special Sensitivity to Negative or Underdeveloped Female Characters

The issue of trying to avoid stereotyping of characters, particularly female ones, was also part of earlier discussions in regards to script selection, especially the awareness that character interpretation actually begins with the script choice. Rita Giomi addresses the need to flesh out characters, usually female ones, that are not well defined by the author: "I think you need to do that as a director anyway, making sure you're finding the balance of the character. With female characters, you do it because quite often male playwrights unwittingly leave out the other half of women. I'm not saying that all men don't understand women, but they're writing from their own perspective, and the chances are better that the men will be more rounded than the women."

Bea Kiyohara explains that because there is a great deal of truth to certain of the stereotypes about Asian women, she thinks she has to be particularly sensitive to discovering unspoken or even unwritten strengths as she is working on female characters. This need to complete a character or give her something that is not immediately obvious in the script in order to create a more complete and nonstereotypical portrayal is also very important to Adele Prandini. She is particularly aware of how she might approach negative female characters such as villains or victims: "Even if I'm working with a woman who is a villain onstage, there is something about empowerment that has to be present for me, particularly when I'm dealing with material that is about what we call women's issues. I'm not going to put somebody out there as a victim. I'm not going to put somebody out there without access to some kind of power. I take great care to assure there's something new here, something different here, so that the woman in the audience is not re-raped or re-abused, but can look at this and experience this in a new and different way."

Mary Robinson also sees the need to balance the villainous characters but attributes that tendency more to good directing than to gender behavior. She uses the example of work with the actor playing Iago in her production of *Othello*, which was in rehearsal at the time of our interview:

> I think that in bringing out the best in actors we are simply doing our jobs. What we're both looking for is where the audience will connect with him. Not because we're trying to make him sympathetic or lovable, but because I think the really disturbing thing about Iago is that there's an Iago in all of us. I don't want the audience to sit back and fold their arms and say, "What a horrible human being." I want them to say, "Oh my god, he's fascinating, and I can see where he's coming from in a weird way." I don't know if that's particularly female. I think that's what a director should do. I think that's what Shakespeare intended, as opposed to Goneril or Regan or characters who are more evil incarnate.

It's intriguing to note that the characters Robinson describes as intended by Shakespeare to be "evil incarnate" are the female villains. At first, she did not really address what she might do when working on the negative female images. In a later conversation, however, Robinson related that she believes she's not ready to direct *King Lear* because she doesn't yet know how to balance those particular characters. She goes on to point out that when directing *Macbeth* she worked hard to "humanize" both Macbeth and Lady Macbeth.

A Different Approach to Male Characters

Interestingly enough, for a few women the need to approach characters in new and nonstereotypical ways is more clearly defined in the way they work with male characters. Victoria Parker talks about how she works more closely with the male characters because she believes from her experience as an actor that a woman already knows how to flesh out a role for herself, whereas a male actor may need help in exploring the more sensitive side of his character:

> I approach the male characters differently. I am aware of that. I have a tendency to go for the male character's vulnerabilities and work on those. I figure if a woman's playing a woman's role and I just let her do what she knows is real and true, she's going to be fine. A female actor generally can sense what needs to be pulled forward if the author of the piece hasn't overtly revealed human vulnerabilities and courage. They'll usually find those elements if you give them the right environment. But a lot of times, male actors are so protected that you really have to work on them to go deeply into character. Even if the author hasn't provided a male character who's deeply sensitive, I'll always work to find it. I feel working with men you're more likely to get the surface picture of a thing. But the male characters in a play who are oppressors or aggressors, I want to get in there and find out about their vulnerability so that people can understand something about aggression, or something about that behavior. I don't leave that alone. But I do tend to leave women alone.

Rita Giomi also feels a need to balance male characters as part of the process of exploring all sides of any character, male or female. She is also aware of occasionally attempting to avoid any sense of backlash against male characters, especially negative ones. She wants to be sure that she will not ever be accused of man bashing, especially when directing a male villain. That's not her only reason, however: "I think that painting any character, male or female, as purely black or white does a great disservice to the playwright and the audience. It's not simply fear of backlash, it's fear of shallow work." Tori Haring-Smith shares Giomi's concern about backlash but tells how her intentions backfired when a critic misread her reasons for softening a villainous character:

When I least expect it, I always discover that somebody has misinterpreted my intentions. For example, I did *Vinegar Tom* by Caryl Churchill—a feminist play which I saw through feminist eyes. In it, there's a witch hunter, a man who tortures women, and he figures rather largely in the story. In terms of telling the story, I was really interested in making him well intentioned, not an automatically evil person. When I cast the part, I wanted somebody who could be powerful as a speaker, but at the same time would not be seen as a mustache-twirling villain. I chose a man who was small and slight—not physically overwhelming—and who had a real gentleness behind the strength in his voice. Most people really liked the play, but one particular critic (a man) felt I was so interested in bashing the patriarchy that I had cast this "wimp" as the strong man—I had "emasculated" him—which, of course, was exactly what I was trying to avoid. I was trying to play against the male stereotype, but I played right into it. It seemed like there was nothing I could do to challenge this critic's values and assumptions.

Julie Taymor has had a similar experience in the way some critics responded negatively to her attempts to balance a villanous character in her recent production of *Titus Andronicus*. She describes the play as "a very maligned play and very ahead of its time in its nihilism and its godlessness, in its ability to have no heroes and really no villains" and says her purpose in the production was to try to get her audience to change their perspective:

> I read a review saying that the actor playing Aaron the Moor isn't evil enough. We deliberately understated his way of speaking the most devilish lines, because evil doesn't come in evil forms. Evil comes in the most benign forms sometimes. "Oh my god, he killed and strangled all these people, that nice little clerk!" It's just this silly presumption that you should be obviously evil. It's very confusing because you're attracted to him, and yet he's doing the most heinous things and your understanding is that he's very personable. It was a choice not to make it "stock." None of the characters were meant to be one dimensional. Even Tamora, this seemingly evil woman, has a reason for her vengeance, a very strong one. So my interpretation was completely concocted to not have you pick a side. I'm not interested in trying to shock people and upset things. If you don't have something of some importance, of some depth to say, it does not interest me. I don't ever do a violent thing because I'm attracted to violence, but I'm very good at finding ways to show violence so that you're either distanced from it or brought into it. I like to play with the spectator's consciousness of their role in watching. I make them shift perspective.

Wanting to shift the audience perspective on certain kinds of characters and situations seems to be a common trait among many of these directors.

Looking for the Whole Human Being

Other women also speak of the need for finding balance in both male and female characters. Penny Metropulos is aware of always looking for the vulnerabilities in male characters and the strengths in female ones, and she wants to explore characters in as much depth and complexity as possible, to find as many sides to the story as she can. She attributes this more to her background as an actor, however, than to her gender: "I'd like to think it's because I'm a whole human being, or at least trying to be. I'm aware that it's a strength I have, being able to pull out lots of levels from people. I think a lot of that comes because of the kind of actor I have been. I explore a lot. It's important to me to find as many sides to something as I possibly can. It seems to me to be the only way we as a species will ever catch up to what we have as potential in our makeup, we must see and understand that everyone has all of these things in them." Timothy Near explains this same tendency in terms of wanting to know as much about a character as possible, a desire she thinks might be more common to women directors:

> I view the world from a woman's eyes, and I do think perhaps there is some difference in terms of wanting to understand, not just who somebody is in a play, for example, but why they are that way. I know with my experience with men in general that I am much more interested in explaining why something is happening, and the details and specifics of a feeling. It's been a long time since I've acted, but trying to remember back to the male directors I worked with, I don't feel that they were as interested in that as I am. I think that is to some extent the woman part of me. It's that I don't want to just say, "That woman's a bitch" or "That guy is vicious." I want to go back and really find out why the actions occurred, why this seemingly evil character was created. You go back to the child, the child that didn't have any of those awful, mean things, and see how it layered on to make them a bad person or an evil person. I find actors being surprised that I always want to go back to the good part and then begin to layer on what happened to make them a bad person. I think that's gender related. Also, it could be my upbringing and basic theory that people do start out good and then life affects them, and part of what is affecting them is their gender, their sexual roles.

Although she's not sure it's attributable solely to gender differences, in her experience, Julie Taymor finds being able to look at both sides of a character seems to come easier to women:

> Quite often when men are good at having an edge, of being dark, they don't have the other side, and I find that a lot of women do. For example, I'm directing *Titus Andronicus*, and people say, "How do you as a woman direct them in such a violent play?" What I find is I have no fear of the most brute imagery. That's not what makes a male or a female. But there's always the ability to find the other side in the work, looking for the other part of the story, not just looking to shock or to be tough, but to find the subtle edge that comes on the other side, the more personal or more sensitive or more delicate side of it. I don't know if that has anything to do with being a woman.

Taymor also tries to give the victim character more strength and believes that her experiences as a woman, as well as the experiences of her actress, bring a fresh perspective to the character:

I had some really fabulous discussions with Miriam Healy-Louie, the actress working on Lavinia, who is the victim character in *Titus* that has her tongue cut out, her hands cut off, and is raped. Her father kills her in the end because one shouldn't be shamed by a daughter who has been raped. It was wonderful to work on the challenge of how do you show this and not just have her be this messy victim. Where is the strength? How do you maintain the character that was there before this happened to her? What does it mean when it says in the stage direction, "She puts the stick in her mouth?" I'm sure a lot of feelings come with that image. We know exactly what that means to put the stick in the mouth, it's a dick in your mouth. I'm not sure a man would come to that conclusion right away unless the actress brought that to his attention and said she couldn't do that. So there are definitely advantages to telling the story with feminine experience behind you.

Liz Diamond, however, presents an opposing viewpoint about trying to balance evil characters in her directing process: "I love villains; I love bad guys and bad women. I'm much more interested in really getting my teeth into a real bad guy. Quite frankly, I think actors are only too good at finding the mitigating circumstances and rationalizing evil in an attempt to be loved by the audience. I often find on the contrary that it's my job to say, 'Look, this is an opportunity for you to have a really great time on stage doing heinous things that you would never do in your life. Go for it. Make me hate you.' I don't know whether this is influenced by gender or not. Probably. I was a good little girl."

Other Ways of Working with Actors

Some of the women also acknowledge having a very individual approach to this work based on personal connections to the characters or the needs of the individual actors. Most who work this way, however, identify it as having more to do with their background as actors than any perceived gender behaviors. Roberta Levitow feels a need to treat actors as equal collaborators, but even though she thinks her experiences as an actor were far more formative for her process than her gender, she does recognize the complexity of the issue and how the emotional terrain of the actor can create gendered responses in spite of the best intentions: "I am prejudiced towards the idea—having been a performer for many years myself—that actors should be spoken to as equal collaborators, not as children or strange creatures. I try to the best of my ability, but I often feel that there are actors who do not find it conducive to their process to speak too objectively about what they're going through, that somehow want to maintain a certain kind of suspension of their own disbelief so they can do the work they do. I feel that it's within the actor territory that it gets more complicated personally and emotionally, which tends to bring up gender issues, because of what people assign to that landscape."

Seret Scott believes her collaborative way of working has much more to do with her history as an actor than with her identity as a woman: "I try to work in the way the actor works, but if you have a cast of six people and you're trying to work in individual ways, you make it very difficult and stressful on yourself. I have worked in productions where the director said, 'This is the way I do things, this is the way it's going to be done here.' As an actor, I could have given more to a production had a director been able to speak to me in the way that I work. That's the reason I do that." She also describes how she allows actors to discover their own direction, especially as they work through difficult moments or those that are not progressing well, and in spite of already knowing exactly what she wants them to do to fix the problem. She firmly believes that by working this way, the actor has more sense of ownership in the role and may, in fact, finally realize how she has been steering them in that same direction. Once again she firmly attributes this to an acting background rather than gender.

Liz Diamond links her way of working with actors more to an interest in poetry, rhythmic speech, and heightened language on stage:

> For me the stage is a sort of reverberating poem. I think we listen better when we hear familiar words in strange and fascinating ways, and when they come at us in rhythmic ways. Similarly, I'm very interested in the physical life of the character on the stage as it expresses the poetics of that person's soul. Perhaps I am as much of an outside-in director as an inside-out director. I'm always looking for the ways in which the body of the actor becomes a kind of calligraphic sign. The work I do is very physical, and I'm always looking for the actor to find ways to put it into the body. That's influenced by Brecht, it's influenced by Beckett, it's influenced by Matisse, it's influenced by the surrealists, and it is profoundly influenced by the theatre I witnessed in Africa. I'm less interested in empathy on stage than I am in understanding. I am interested in having the audience recoil in horror at someone, but understand that reaction. I'm as interested in having an audience understand why they want to cry or laugh as I am in having them laugh or cry.

JoAnne Akalaitis also works very physically with her actors, asking them to move rhythmically to music she finds evocative of the script she is working with. She spends a lot of time on exploration without fixing an interpretation of the text until very late in the process, trusting her intuitions at every step of the exploration. She seems convinced, however, that gender has little, if anything, to do with her methods. On the other hand, Adele Prandini says her physical approach to acting is very influenced by gender. She sees the special empowerment an actor can feel from being able to use the body in new ways as a way for women in particular to find personal power and liberation:

> The most important task that a director faces is to realize the full body of a script. Toward this goal we work to liberate the imagination and creativity of

the cast. I place a tremendous importance on helping actors discover the truths which their bodies hold. We know that we can alter our thoughts and emotional experience by changing the ways we use our bodies. I offer that we can also discover hidden feelings and meaning through the exploration of our physical selves. This is not accomplished through superficial warm up but through the study of physical techniques. I have studied modern dance, motivity, low flying trapeze, Decroux mime and Alexander technique as well as stilt walking and juggling. I use elements of these different forms every day in rehearsal. When actors challenge their physical boundaries a new knowledge emerges, resulting in a renewed creative spirit and the ability to exercise newfound power.

Several of the women identified a technique of self-disclosure which they use in helping actors find ideas for characters, believing that it might be a way of working which could be more accessible to women. I observed this use of self-disclosure in both Sharon Ott's and Susana Tubert's rehearsals. Tubert's cast was all women, so it was particular to female characters in this situation, although she says her work with all actors is similar regardless of the project or their gender. In Ott's process, her self-disclosure is used to share information and insights with both male and female actors, but during her interview, she explains that this technique is not always typical of her process. It simply seems to be more useful in this particular play because the subject matter is so closely identified with her own life interests.

A Woman's Aesthetic

Anne Bogart, while adamant that gender has no influence on casting, does identify the way she works on character and scene development as one she considers quintessentially female. Starting with a description of a film called *Night Shift*, which she believes to be emblematic of a woman's way of storytelling, she describes her process of working with actors:

> AB: When I saw the film I thought, "This is completely a woman's film. This film was made by a woman, it is the woman's aesthetic. It couldn't be made by a man." Why not? Well, for one thing—here comes that horrible, stereotypical word—it's cyclical, it's based on that type of structure. I find the idea of a woman downstairs and all these rooms with no central focus upstairs to be entirely female. This idea of a nonlinear narrative is essentially feminine. I relate to that and I work like that. It determines the order in which I work on scenes. It determines the way I think of the audience perceiving the event. It's a sense of accumulation as opposed to a straight line. It's like filo pastry, there's a layering. I don't try to finish every scene and then go to the next. I layer one thing on and then go to the next, come back, layer another thing on and then go to the next. Endless layering, and by the end, it's a very complex network inside the scene. As opposed to settling things in a scene, I try to open them up. The whole question of character is not obvious for women, whereas I think it's obvious for men. I find men are much more likely to say

a character is made up of XYZ, under control, handleable. More women are open to the character being not reductive or controllable but something not understandable.

RD: Do you find that you work with your actors differently in character development as a result of that belief?

AB: I don't know if I can speak for all women. I can speak for myself on this. I don't tell them what to do, I try to provoke them to do something. The end product of what they do is not interesting to me. I don't have a picture of what the character is. All I'm trying to do is to set something into motion which feels true, and I can't tell what the truth is until I can see it in front of me, or feel it. But it's very difficult to generalize for all women.

In the course of this discussion, Bogart also brought up the notion of a subversive female aesthetic. A friend had suggested to her that the mainstream, commercial theatre operated exclusively from a male bias and that there could never be a truly female production on Broadway because the female aesthetic was always subversive, never commercial:

AB: I think there's something very true there in that women tend, in a kind of Brechtian way, to put something out and subvert it at the same time. In the same way, I can't say a commanding sentence with a sense of the fact that I am using power. You can hear it in my voice. I'll say, "Move down right," but there's a sense of doubt in the sentence. In the same way, any moment I put on the stage usually has a consciousness of its opposite, so an image that I put forth is subverted quite often. The other thing about a female aesthetic was actually pointed out to me by Oskar Eustis. I've known him for years, and he once said the difference between our work is that in his work you have to go from A to B to get to C to get to D and finally E and so forth to Z. It goes that way. He feels in my work—and I would suggest that it is a gender issue—that each particular moment is a microcosm of the whole play, that you could take a particular slice, that any slice has in it all the possible elements of the whole.

RD: Do you think that's gender as opposed to just good directing?

AB: I do, I really do. I think the idea of subverting something is feminine, but I think Brecht had a very strong feminine streak in him, so this gets ambiguous.

Once again we come head to head with the notion that gender boundaries in the theatre seem so much more permeable, more moveable, to many artists. For every part of the process that one person insists has a gender influence, another individual can and will present an exception or a differing insight.

Summary

Many of the women I spoke with believe there is something special in the way they work with actors. One of the issues they identify is a special openness in the casting process, whether it is a willingness to consider potential as much as the audition itself, an interest in casting against obvious type, or making unusual or cross-gender casting choices more often than a man might. There are also issues identified in connection with working on character development, especially the conscious breaking down of stereotypes, having special sensitivity to negative female characters, working to find ways to humanize villainous characters, male or female, and a strong desire to balance and represent the whole human being by looking at all sides of the personality. A couple of general rehearsal techniques were brought up as particularly female, especially the use of self-disclosure in rehearsal and a nonlinear process of layering character details rather than looking for a finished interpretation. Some directors also talk about their work with language or the body, although gender influence is somewhat less clear in this area. These women believe that they do work with actors in unique ways, but the reasons for this seem to be varied, with gender being identified as only one of many factors. Some believe their own background as actors has more significance, and a number think that the way they work with actors results from simply trying to adhere to the principles of good directing.

10. TECHNICAL
AND SPATIAL ISSUES
INFLUENCED BY GENDER

While script selection and working with actors were the portions of the directing process most often referred to in the interviews without specific prompting, some issues regarding the technical elements of a production were occasionally also brought up, usually in the context of resistance to women directors. Furthermore, one specific question about the use of space was part of all interviews, giving entry into the technical areas not always discussed in connection with gender expectations.

TECHNICAL CONSIDERATIONS

A Need to Maintain Authority

In the exercise of their authority, some of the women identified certain situations that seem to involve gender issues more often than others. Nikki Appino is particularly aware of the technical portion of the production process, which seems to her to require more masculine attributes in order to maintain a position of authority. She had recently been an observer at a particularly complicated technical rehearsal with an all-male crew and a male director. She believes that in similar circumstances a woman would encounter greater difficulties and be faced with negative criticism for exercising her authority over others, perhaps because of a perception that she lacked technical awareness and authority or was too aggressive. She explains her own approach to those same kinds of rehearsals:

> I was working with a male director at one of the major theatres during my TCG residency. It's a huge space, a union house, a union crew. It interested

174

me to watch him run the show and deal with these guys, essentially technically. As I was sitting there watching, I was remarking to myself, "I do not think that a woman would have as easy a job doing what he's doing right now," which was essentially running a very complex and difficult tech with an all-male crew. Because of what it takes to run a technical rehearsal, that's where women are called bitches [and other unprintable and derogatory names]. That's where resistance comes out. I find myself having to play that same circumstance out, and I will put myself into a male role, meaning that I will adopt a certain attitude or that certain attitude will come on to me. It's very hard to say how conscious this is.

While she does not explicitly adopt what Appino calls a "male attitude" in dealing with technical or design matters, Roberta Levitow is very aware of the need to first clarify the interaction as peer artists with no gender connotations:

I think with most designers, because the work itself is external, the communication tends to be more direct. It's difficult to bat your eyes into a good set design. You have to create some kind of rapport and egalitarian communication, and that sometimes does take a little work. For example, there was a male designer I worked with recently, and I think we had a little wrestling to do in our first meeting or two to clarify what was going to be male/female about our interaction and what was going to be two peer artists about our interaction. My idea was that we were going to be peer artists and we were going to get there as quickly as we could. Once there's some kind of relief on that score, I think design work tends to be a lot easier than working with actors, because it's the external product rather than personal feelings and emotions.

Alana Byington attributes her sense of intimidation regarding visual and technical methods to being female, although she admits with wry humor that because of her social conditioning, "it's easy sometimes to think of all your weaknesses as female weakness." Especially since she is sometimes unsure, she believes others attribute this lack of certainty to being female and start to doubt her authority because of it. It's easy to see how the confusion between internal and external factors make it hard to determine where the lines are really drawn.

Understanding Technical Needs

Several directors admit to being somewhat uneasy in regards to the technical portion of the process because of their lack of familiarity with technical vocabulary and requirements. Most of these women say, however, that once they understand what is being presented by designers, they have no trouble responding authoritatively. The problem they identify is often one of being treated as if they don't understand. Patricia Blem describes this kind of situation as happening more often with designers who have never worked with her before: "If it's an all-male group of designers and I'm the only female, I do feel sometimes that my opinion is looked at with a grain of salt, even though I'm the director. It's usually with people who don't know me where I have to prove that I know what I'm talking about. It's not with the people I've worked with. Once they've worked with me, I have not had that same feeling."

Seret Scott notes that if a male set designer does not know her style of work, it is sometimes assumed she doesn't really know what she wants because of her preference for asking designers to come up with their own ideas rather than imposing her own in a more authoritarian way. She believes that when she offers them a chance to be creative, they sometimes hear it as ignorance on her part, believing that she doesn't really know what she wants:

> I've had to say on occasion to some designers, "Never mistake my allowing you to be creative for ignorance on my part." From some of the feedback I get from designers, I think I am more collaborative than most male directors. My being collaborative has a lot to do with wanting the designer to be creatively involved and not just give me exactly what I tell them to do. I really want the designer to walk away from the show saying, "I made some choices that did a great deal for the production." When that is called into question because they say, "You don't know what you want because you're saying I can be creative here," then I say, "That is not it at all, but I can see I'm going to have to give you what I want every step of the way." The designer is saying that he or she cannot think on their own.

Scott says that although she occasionally has this kind of difficulty with a designer, which she attributes to gender expectations, she doesn't have the same kind of problem with artistic directors "because for them to even contact me means they are usually looking for a double minority and the female issue is already out of the way. My competence is called into question for being black as opposed to female in that case." She also identifies two other areas of technical support where she occasionally feels some resistance to her work—the crew and the office staff:

> I do a lot of regional, and I find, frankly, that I get into a new place and the crew has more trouble with it than anybody else until they realize I know what I'm doing. They come to a run through and see how solid the product is, then they became more involved in the physical support of the production. Sometimes the crew acts like I'm not there, not part of the process. They say to me quicker than to somebody else, "You can't do that, it doesn't work." I'll say, "It does, and this is how you do it." Then they get upset, but they could have done it themselves in the first place. Sometimes the theatre administration, especially in smaller places, will act as if they're doing me a favor.

Although she clearly felt intimidated by technical concerns early in her career, Melia Bensussen describes with delight how something she first presumed to be a female failing was transformed into a career skill: "Three years ago I did a production of *The Matchmaker* with a big cast, and it was enormously technical. I loved doing it and that surprised me. Suddenly I thought, 'Wow, I love the technical work. I like being this precise. I like having it be fun and successful, commercial and straightforward.' It takes such skill and I think those were skills I always had, but I undervalued them to some extent and was more concerned with the big emotional, intuitive work, which I suppose is very female."

Gender in the Eye of the Beholder

Perception of certain kinds of visual imagery as masculine or feminine can be a very tricky business, as Timothy Near illustrates with an anecdote about two different situations where gender imagery was consciously utilized in the scenic design, but in one case thoroughly misinterpreted by a theatre critic:

> A woman designer designed a set that we felt was very feminine. It had a ramp and a stairway that were like big arms that wrapped around the stage and seemed to be nurturing, kind, protective of the actor. It was a one-woman show that was very personal, and we wanted her to feel safe. We designed something that felt, not womblike, but more like nestling in the curve of a mountain. So we defined it in that way. I also worked with a male designer doing *Little Foxes* on a thrust stage, and we decided to take a very masculine approach. The play is very muscular, it doesn't pull any punches. Regina had to take on a masculinity about her to just survive with these brothers and this father. So the stairway thrust straight from upstage center right at the audience, and we thought it was very phallic. Then the critic came and did an article about the very female sexual organ quality of this play. He thought the set resembled ovaries and fallopian tubes. A lot of them don't know Timothy is a woman when they write about these things, but he knew who I was. Maybe because I was a woman and this was a play about a woman, he took everything that we had meant to be very phallic to be very female.

Near's reaction following the publication of this article was that perhaps it doesn't really make much difference after all; perhaps gender is in the eye of the beholder.

USE OF SPACE

Eliminating the Fourth Wall

Of the few who perceive a distinct gender influence in their use of theatre space, Tori Haring-Smith is quick to define the difference in the way she deals with the fourth wall. Perhaps because of her work in feminist theory, she is extremely aware of the implications in the audience gaze and adjusts her staging accordingly: "I think my use of the space is very different. The fourth wall drives me nuts, absolutely bonkers. I think it has to do with the notion of the gaze, and that to gaze at someone without that person being able to gaze back is essentially voyeuristic. The theatre is a conversation and the actor must be able to speak back to the audience, so I always move the fourth wall out to the walls of the theatre. Whether I do that literally or whether the actors simply talk to the audience, I think it really makes the show more demonstrative. I like the show to include the audience so that there is no exclusive, one-way gaze."

Haring-Smith also says that she dislikes realistic sets and suspects there may be some kind of gender influence there, but she does not elaborate. Although Pamela Hendrick did not seem to apply this necessarily to the action on stage during a performance, like Haring-Smith, she is aware of the outside gaze and separation between actor and audience as something she wants to eliminate, especially during her rehearsal process: "I think the way that I set up my rehearsal room might reveal something about gender. I always tend to put discussions in circles. I tend to have a rehearsal room that's set so that it can comfortably accommodate the rehearsal, and when the rehearsal is over, can bring people back into a circle format so that I'm no longer on the outside watching. I feel the need at the end of rehearsal to break that audience/performer split, to bring everybody together in a space for the closing of rehearsal."

Creating Whole and Harmonious Pictures

Tori Haring-Smith likes a strong visual image and uses space in an extremely visual way, but she does not feel there is a gender influence in that regard. Seret Scott, however, does connect her visual use of space to being a woman: "I use more space than men. From the work I've seen by women, we all do. We move through space more, we bring the space with us more. We tighten it up in a large space, widen it in a smaller space. We make it work higher, make it work lower. It's the chance to paint all over, not just these very small pictures. It seems that women are more encompassing in each picture that they paint than men. Men seem to let the edges fall away and concentrate on a little area, make the whole thing play out there. I find the women incorporate more of the wholeness of the picture."

Others identify another issue in relation to composition that they believe might be applicable to women, the creation of balanced and harmonious stage pictures instead of more dramatic ones. Brenda Hubbard explores this concern:

> I think I tend, because I am a woman, to create harmonious pictures. I think that sometimes is a challenge to me as a director because not all plays are harmonious. I tend to look for and create some sort of balance and harmony

in the way things look and come across. I am less comfortable with jagged, raw edges. In our society, women are expected to balance the family, keep everything together, and make sure that people don't ever get too far out of their boundaries. I think that can be limiting to me. I think that has an influence on how I use the space. I create harmony sometimes where I should allow things to be more visually conflicted. I'm talking in terms of composition, and color, and all of that. I tend to make things pretty, as opposed to dramatic.

Melia Bensussen talks about a similar concern but believes that she is now getting more comfortable with a lack of harmonious pictures. She identifies the issue more with career development than with gender, although she does imply an early gender conditioning in her creation of a comfortable atmosphere:

I'm learning to be much bolder in my use of space. When I was younger, I was more comfortable with walls in the scenery, wanting a physical structure to contain things. To some extent, because of being young and female, there was a stronger instinct of wanting to recreate a homey atmosphere. I'm getting more comfortable with discomfort as I get older. Some of the men I knew when I was younger were braver earlier. Some of the women were, too. JoAnne Akalaitis is someone who I see as always having been so bold with space, in fact making that the concern, not the comfort level, not the human interaction level. I think my own journey has been one where now, after ten years of a professional career, I start to really feel like I can make actors uncomfortable in space and that's okay. The scenery, the design ideas do not have to make actors feel comfortable.

The conscious use of accepted principles of composition and picturization seems consistent among the directors, but occasionally these principles seem to manifest a gender influence in the assumptions of outside observers. Although she does not believe there are gender influences in the way she moves people around the stage space, Zelda Fichandler recalls that occasionally she hears from others that she moves actors through space as a man might have done. When asked why she thought those assumptions were made, Fichandler replies:

Because they're strong choices, because thought is an active ingredient. I think thought is the basis of behavior. To change behavior, you have to change thinking. So I'm very into what people are thinking. Feeling follows from what you think, and what you think often defines who you are. Thought causes feelings. The connection of thought and feeling is the basis that I work with. Where does thought/feeling make you want to move, and what does it make you want to do? Psycho-physical actions is what Stanislavski called them. "I'm thirsty, I want a glass of water, so I reach for the water." "I want to leave, but I still want to stay. I'd like to have the strength to go, but I really love you so I don't want to leave." That tells you how you're moving, two directions at once. I don't think that has any masculine or feminine connotations.

Tisa Chang identifies a strong cultural influence on the way she moves actors through space which has a great deal of gender influence in its basic assumptions: "In Asian theatre everything is not a direct route. Motion is circular. You go around, and you don't confront something straight on. It's much more successful if that energy curves. I have always used space with that in mind. There are more curves and ellipses than straight lines or sharp actions, unless it's used as a specific contrast to emphasize a point or a moment. I think that is a feminine characteristic. Certainly in the yin/yang theory, short, direct, percussive movements or beats would be considered masculine, whereas more languid lines or curves would be considered a feminine symbol."

Patricia Blem believes creating the wholeness of the picture to be technique, pure and simple. "You want to make a stage alive, you want to utilize your space, you want to make sure that the environment that you create, you use. I will use every place on stage at least once because if I don't use it, then it doesn't need to be there." Blem does have a tendency, however, to equate technique and use of logic with male energy rather than female energy, which she associates more often with creativity and inspiration.

Preference for Intimate Spaces

Michelle Blackmon uses her preference for the intimate experience to make one of the most specific comparisons between male and female approaches to space:

> Women have a tendency to be more intimate, to be more one-on-one, and the types of spaces I like are small, intimate theatres where you really reach out and grab an individual in the audience. I like those individual one-on-one connections, and I think that's a much more feminine quality. Men have a tendency to distance themselves from people. They like the presentational, and I think men have a tendency to go more for the technical aspects of theatre, the sense of the spectacle—how grand the set can be, how wonderful the costumes can be, how bright the lights can be, how exciting the effects. I think women are more into the presentation of the artist, the human behind all of that. I listen to what is being said onstage, and I think that is very much a gender thing. Women have a tendency to listen more and to hear what people are saying, whereas men are into the visual.

Although Blackmon sees it as a gender tendency, several other women wryly point out that perhaps women directors' comfort with and preference for intimate spaces could arise because they are not often given the opportunity to direct large spectacles. Perhaps the influence really is more in the perception by others of gender capabilities rather than any actual difference in ways of directing. Penny Metropulos believes that others might characterize the kinds of spaces she prefers as feminine, but in addition to her acting experience, she identifies two men as her strongest early influences regarding this preference: "I think that the kinds of spaces I like to work in are definitely what would be considered feminine spaces because they're open and free form and nonstructural. But early in my career, I was tremendously influenced by an open space designed by a man as well as the work of a male director whose whole philosophy of directing was to explore space, find out how space is cut and used and how sound in space works and that sort of thing. I do love large, nonstructured spaces, and I tend not to like literal sets. A lot of that has to do with being an actor. I want as few obstacles between the story and the action as possible."

Mary Robinson cites early career differences rather than gender differences in her preference for working on intimate stages and talks about how, once she got used to working in the larger space, she saw no other influences operating there except youth and inexperience:

> Having stated my preference for working on intimate projects, the first time I had to direct a play in a big space was quite difficult for me. I was uncomfortable moving people around in the space because I felt I was having to treat them as inanimate objects. That was at least ten years ago, and I have since become very comfortable doing that. It's just a part of the job. You do that for a day, and the next day you get to work on the other things again. I don't think I'd be very comfortable doing a play where that's all there was to it, just moving bodies around and playing traffic cop. I think I've become very comfortable in a huge space, but sometimes I think I'd love to vary that occasionally with a more intimate space.

Although she also sees her use of space as mostly defined by the play itself as well as her available resources, Adele Prandini's first response to the inquiry about any influence of gender on her use of space is a caustic one. "It keeps me out of a lot of them. Let's start there. That's just plain old sexism, which is very gender based. It keeps you from getting jobs." Liz Diamond also acknowledges that her gender has kept her in the intimate spaces for many years, but now that she is starting to work in bigger theatres she has discovered other challenges in making that transition. She is not at all sure, however, that there is any gender influence in meeting those challenges. In fact, she suspects there is none:

> I adore large scale projects. It's so much fun. It's symphonic, and addressing that big a canvas, marshalling that number of variables in a volume of space, is so fascinating to me. Sonic, visual, I love it. Yet, I still have a deep abiding love for the intimacy of small arenas. It has to do with the immediacy of the interaction between spectator and performer which I find so crucial. Something happens to the scale of an individual performance in a big space. I love turning up the volume on the audience and having them have a kind of "sense-around" experience. I find that the number of times you take a big project out of a rehearsal hall and put it into a big theatre, only to watch the juice go out of it as it gets up onto the gorgeous, fabulous proscenium stage with the mauve

seats in the house, and the carpeting, really scares me. I don't think it necessarily has only to do with size of space, it also has to do with roughness. A
rehearsal hall is a rough place. The seats aren't comfortable. The air doesn't
circulate. It's tight and it's live and visceral in a way that some of these big
proscenium houses aren't. I'm really interested in that right now because I am
being invited to work in these places, and I'd like to find out how to address
and solve that problem. I don't know if it can be done, but I'm interested in
that. But is it a gender thing about small versus big? No.

Most of the women who express a preference for intimate spaces discuss it in terms of the impact on the audience and emphasis on the human
experience. They ultimately believe, however, that it is not a concern unique
to women, simply part of a good theatrical experience.

Other Influences on the Use of
Space and Space Preferences

By far the most common response among the directors is that the use of
theatrical space is a learned technical capacity, one of the basic requirements
of the director's job. Furthermore, very few of the directors have the luxury
of stating a preference for any particular kind of stage or theatre space because
they often have to make do with what is available to them. Pamela Hendrick,
in spite of her comments about the rehearsal space, points out, "My use of
space has always been dictated by my resources, so I've had very little choice
in the kinds of spaces I've had to work in." Bea Kiyohara, however, voices the
belief that women might be more negotiable, flexible, and practical when
dealing with those kind of "make-do" spaces.

Emily Mann talks about the pleasure of working in different kinds of
spaces and does not want to declare any kind of space preference, whether
influenced by gender or not: "I just love to fit an event to a space and have
the space talk back to me about what an event can be. I love playing with the
different sizes and shapes and kinds of spaces. And then discovering what is
the connection, the combustion of a live event, what is that about in that place.
That's what I'm always doing. But I wouldn't say I prefer small to large or
large to small or round to straight. None of that." Susan Finque also likes
fitting an event to a space, and for her that translates to location-specific work
which emphasizes the "uniqueness of space." Nikki Appino, who is starting
to create more of her own work, is always looking for the "atmosphere" of a
space and is always looking at any space as a potential home for the work
that she does.

When expressing their general preferences for spaces or ways of working with space, many of the women could clearly identify other significant
influences besides gender, ranging from an experience or awareness of other
cultures to an appreciation of architecture and interior design, to a specific

Liz Diamond (left) with actors Jane Eden and Paul Giamatti in rehearsal for Bertolt Brecht's *St. Joan of the Stockyards* at the Yale Repertory Theatre (1993). Photo by Denise Hudson.

location influence, to a background in acting, dance or other movement styles, to painting and other visual imagery. Having grown up in the desert Southwest, Rita Giomi finds that "the thing I love to do most is have the least onstage. I'm always looking for the single element that will tell the story." Gloria Muzio, who had seriously considered a career in scene design before moving into directing, has a strong affinity for visual imagery, but she reiterates her confusion about where the influences lie in her relationship with creating and using the performance space: "The most important thing to me in beginning work on a play, except for working with a playwright, is working with a set designer. To me creating that space is crucial. I can't do anything until I've gone through those meetings with the set designer and have seen a model and all the design details. I don't know what that has to do with me being a woman so much as me being a visual person. I know that I'm very tuned into space and visual imagery and what the production looks like. That's just who I am."

Summary

Although very few women brought up the use of space as a gender issue on their own, the ones who did often identified a preference for intimate theatre spaces and a dislike of working on large visual spectacles as issues they believe might be seen as particular to women, although it is not clear whether this is a true preference or simply comfort with familiar kinds of theatre in which they have most often been invited to direct. As the question was probed further, however, it became clear that unlike some of the other issues discussed, almost none of the directors had thought about their use of space in gender terms before the question was posed. Aside from an awareness of the need to maintain authority, especially in the face of male designers or crew who presume technical ignorance on the part of a woman director, those few directors who did perceive a gender influence in their use of space identify the following issues as significant for women directors: the desire to change the spectator/performer relationship to bring them closer together, a tendency to create stage pictures more whole and harmonious than dramatic and edgy, and a stronger emphasis on the emotional immediacy provided by more intimate spaces. Furthermore, after considering the issue, a majority of the directors believe that there is very little gender influence in their preferences; they believe they can comfortably work in any kind of space, depending on the project, and they think that differences in the way they use space are defined more by the context of the project than by any other factor.

11. Economic and Career Considerations

Although artistic considerations were often difficult for the women to evaluate in terms of gender influences, there was little problem in identifying more concrete influences in the area of career development. Some areas of awareness emerged from the interviews which are obviously not unique to theatre but seem to be common to many professional women in various fields. While no questions were ever directly asked about the obstacles women encountered during their careers, it is obviously an area women associate with gender issues, and most of the directors addressed the issue in one way or another. The focus of the interviews was primarily on the artistic process itself, and I tried as much as possible to avoid developing a political perspective about women's position in the theatre, except insofar as it influences artistic or interpretive events. Since these issues are clearly of importance to many of the women interviewed, however, it would be remiss not to include them.

Family Demands

Life in the Theatre

Issues of struggling to build a satisfactory career as a director came up for many of the women. Liz Diamond sees the expectation of the theatre lifestyle making it difficult for any young artist to consider a career in the theatre:

> LD: The way we've constructed theatre and a career, the way we make our life in the theatre in this country, makes it very difficult to live a whole, rounded life. I think it's very difficult for men and women—journeyman directors—to think about family, to have family. I don't think we make room for

185

children in the theatre. We don't make room for children in this country. I think to the extent that the theatre is a mirror we hold up to life, the way our institutions are constructed is an absolute reflection of the state of this country's relationship to the notion of nurturing the next generation. We don't provide money for daycare, for men or women and their children. We have not constructed our working lives as artists to accommodate a happier rhythm and flow between the personal/private and the public/working. I struggle with that. I think that men struggle with that. I think it prevents many men and women from going into the theatre. I don't know what the theatre can do about that, but as artists we should be leading the way. We should be looking for ways to make it possible for artists—actors, directors, designers—to raise their kids, maintain their relationships at home and work. This is a very big issue. We've become a country of workaholics, and the workplace is more the place where we find community than the home.

RD: Do you think that as a woman artist you are in a better position to address that issue because of women's traditional concern with the family, perhaps being able to bring the two together in a way that a man is not conditioned to deal with?

LD: Yes, I think we have to take responsibility for it because I don't think the men are going to take responsibility for it any more than they've taken responsibility for raising children. There are a number of good men out there who are equal partners in the raising of their children, but I think that women need to be in the vanguard of public policy with regard to child care, child leave, health care, and so on, for the simple reason that it's in our interest to do so.

Melia Bensussen points out that the given assumptions inherent in the theatre life-style are "utterly male created, centuries old" and much harder on a woman:

> There is an assumption about what you're supposed to feel about your career and your art. I think those are male ideas, designed by people who had someone at home running a family. You're supposed to sacrifice everything for your art. Yes, there's the working mother guilt regardless of the career, but I feel like in the arts, and especially in the theatre because of the working hours, it hits in spades. I think that's very slowly starting to change as more directors are working mothers. Why don't theatres have daycare? You get an intern and you get an extra rehearsal room, not a big deal. I understand all the economic issues, but I do think the basic thing still happening is an assumption that if you really love your work, if you really want to be taken seriously as a theatre artist, then your work is all that matters to you. If you ask for time off to be with a spouse, if you say you need two days off for a holiday to spend with family, all of this is frowned on and you're not taken as seriously. That, I think, is an old male idea because there was the wife.

Time and Travel Demands

Tori Haring-Smith links the difficulties to traditional family role models as well as to the need for directors to be constantly traveling for their work. She talks about wanting to start a theatre of her own—not to move on to bigger and better things, but simply to be able to stay home and still do the kind of work she wants to do:

> I think there are so few women directors because it's so hard to direct and have a family—no matter what accommodations you try to make. I know men have families, too, but their roles must be different. In my marriage, for example, we have completely switched the traditional duties. My husband does the laundry, he does the cleaning, he does the cooking. We have a fifties marriage, and he's the housewife. And I still feel guilty whenever I travel. If a woman wants to have a family and children, I think it is harder as a female than as a male to maintain a professional directing career because you have to be prepared to go hither and thither whenever you get the call. Maybe men find all the travel just as hard, but talking to a lot of professional male directors, I doubt it. Society approves of their travel—not of ours. No one tells a man he *ought* to be at home raising his kids. You can't make a living as a director if you stay in one place—unless you are an artistic director or work in television. So you either have to have an academic appointment, which I have, or you have to be willing to start your own theatre. It's extremely difficult and limiting. I think that's why so many women start theatres. It's a good way to get work. I'm thinking right now that I want to start my own theatre. I'm ready to do that in order to get a consistent source of work that I want to do. I'm turning down work almost monthly, but I'm not getting the work I want, the freedom I want. I think we have to do something in this country so that women can be influential in the arts and not have to travel everywhere. The notion of hiring somebody, expecting them to pick up and go across the continent within two months, stay for six weeks, and then leave, is appalling. People should be allowed to do art and have stable family lives as well—can't art grow out of family life?

Seret Scott talks about bringing family concerns to the rehearsal hall and agrees about the difficulties traveling imposes on her family situation:

> I'm a wife and a mother. I don't leave that outside of the rehearsal hall. I bring everything, all the elements, into the rehearsal space. I feel it is a family as well. Because I work out of town virtually all the time, it's really tough on my family. I have a husband and one child, and they're very good about my having to be gone so much. I have strong guilt feelings about that. Sometimes it gets very difficult. Every time the phone rings, it's a job somewhere else. On the one hand I need this job, on the other hand it's going to keep me away. As an actress, when I signed on for a job I was gone for ten weeks, but as a director, I'm gone maybe four weeks. It's a little easier, but I will be gone for another four weeks right after that, so it ends up being the same.

Rita Giomi, single at the time of our interview, laments the difficulties of finding and maintaining a relationship while living the free-lance life in the theatre:

> I hate what this business does to your personal life, the difficulty of finding someone who can understand what it's like to have the amount of work you

do. I'm not interested in involving myself with actors. I love actors, but bringing that dynamic home in a relationship has never worked for me, and almost the only people I ever meet are actors. I've been trying to balance my life, to find ways to slow down, but that's difficult for me because if I'm not working, no new offers come up. I don't have unemployment to fall back on, so I have to work as much as I do. My guess is that isn't necessarily because I'm a woman. It has to do with being a free-lance artist. Being out of town a lot takes a toll. I love going to different places, meeting new people, but when you stop to think that you haven't been in your own house for five months out of the year that makes it difficult. Just try to keep a relationship going while you're not there.

There is general agreement among the directors that the time and travel demands of a career in the theatre are extremely difficult for any artist to balance with personal and family concerns. Regardless of whether it is primarily a woman's problem, many do think that the realm of personal and family concerns come more often under their care.

CAREER DEVELOPMENT

It Takes Women Longer to Be Successful

Initially, she never perceived gender as a detriment, but in looking back over her career, Sue Lawless, who has one of the longest professional careers among these women, a career including some Broadway credits, is now able to discuss her situation in terms of gender discrimination. Recently another factor has also begun to emerge for her, the specter of ageism, which becomes a double threat for a woman. In one of her letters, she explains her feelings:

> It was only after years and years of directing that it dawned on me on no specific morning that if I were a man with my track record, I might be further ahead in the commercial theatre. It has only been within the last fifteen years or so that my personal awareness of others' perspective of a woman director became apparent to me. Now I can state letter and verse of what was clearly chauvinistic behavior to me, but dealing with all of it at those moments, one got through them and went on. I never perceived it as a struggle, or at least the struggle I perceived was just a personal one of trying to keep working and doing and creating. Now that my perception of gender behavior or prejudices has sharpened, I also attribute it to age. Why hire an "old" anybody if you can get the up and coming young! And now if that "old" happens to be a woman, let's think twice.[1]

Lawless says that sometimes her words on this subject have been interpreted as bitter. She, however, believes she is not bitter, simply matter-of-fact. Many others agree with Lawless's statement that it takes a woman much longer than a man to achieve professional acceptance and success. Although she seems more hopeful now, Emily Mann believes that not so very long ago it used to take women quite a bit longer to find success: "Women had to be better at the job than men who were peers, so clearly more successful, better artists, also probably even better at the box office, in order to get ahead. I used to say for young women that during those awful years when you're trying to go from student to professional and then from small theatre professional to main stage and mainstream, that on average it took women about five years longer at each stage than their male counterparts who were equally talented."

Julie Taymor speaks from her own personal experience about the difficulty in maintaining a successful career, and she clearly identifies the problem as prejudice, and not simply male prejudice: "Like a lot of women, I feel that if I were a man and had done what I have done, I would be in a very different position at this point. You look at the track record, you look at the reviews, you look at the response, and you say, 'Why am I unemployed now? I shouldn't be hustling for work at this point. Not with the kind of work that I've done and the success rate.' I think that there is still that prejudice. Women are as bad at trusting women as men. I don't think there's any difference."

Liz Diamond makes it very clear that she believes it will definitely take women longer to achieve succcess but thinks perhaps that's not such a bad thing after all: "It takes a woman longer to be trusted with a big production than a man. Unquestionably. I think the reasons that happens are subtle and difficult to pinpoint. These are very deep unconscious impulses operating. Big play, big director. Kings, a lot of sword fights, you need to get a man. I don't think it ever hits the level of conscious thought, and that's why it happens. But I think that's changing. I think that's the power of all of these liberation movements. But success in art is a problematic concept. Are you successful if you get rich? In worldly terms, yes, but in artistic terms? Given the still dominant equation of masculine value with income, many male directors put pressure on themselves to do more commercial work."

Lack of Support and Tokenism

Brenda Hubbard has clearly had a recent negative experience and has come to believe that women can be set up to fail by not being given the support they need: "I wish some of the things I've said were not true. I have real sense of discontent about where women are in this whole process. I can say very clearly that the reason I resigned from one job was because I was not given the appropriate support and backing that I needed, and it was because I was a woman. I have a lot of anger about that. I am definitely not happy with the status of women in the theatre today." Agreeing with Hubbard about the lack of support given to women, Nikki Appino believes that although she has not experienced direct problems, covert discrimination still persists. Echoing an early comment by Seret Scott in the context of the script selection discussion,

**Nikki Appino (left) with actress Amy Caton Ford on the set of Appino's original film,
Threshold (1994). Photo by Kiyo Marsh.**

Appino sees covert discrimination especially in the need for a woman to be
constantly proving herself in situations in which a man is more easily accepted
after his early successes.

Michelle Blackmon expresses resentment at discrimination and tokenism
which is tied to racial as well as gender issues:

> MB: We go up against that all the time in casting, trying to be thought of
> as an actor as opposed to a black actor. Those are the issues I deal with con-
> stantly. Now the buzz word is cultural diversity. So now everybody's trying

to find their little role that they're sticking some ethnic person into and calling their play culturally diverse. It doesn't mean anything. But those are things that happen all the time. It's very frustrating as an artist to know that when you get thought of, in terms of being cast in plays, generally it has to do with money, that you are being cast because they got a grant to do some sort of culturally diverse project.

RD: Do you encounter that as much in directing?

MB: Not in the same way. Only in the sense that you are occasionally the director of a project because the grant was to do the culturally diverse project in the first place. It's very frustrating.

This issue of not being accepted for who you are but because some program requires diversity is also a frustration for Diana Marré. As a lesbian, she often wonders if her work really matters or if she is successful in certain situations because "they need one of me so they can look good on diversity."

Being an Outsider May Not Be So Bad

The perceived discrimination and lack of support has often left women feeling like outsiders in the theatre. Maria Irene Fornes presents the notion that being an outsider may not be so bad, however. She sees acceptance by the system as a disadvantage to an artist, and while her comment is specific to writers, it clearly reflects her feelings as a director as well: "I think that writers who are accepted by the system don't have any advantage over writers who are not. They have a disadvantage because the writers who are accepted by the system are then dependent on the system. And because once they have a success even more is expected of them." When asked if she feels the pressure is more or less acute for women, Fornes says it would depend on the individual, but all other things being equal, she would say the pressure on women would be more: "Because a man can be walking around in frayed jeans and barefoot on the street, and he's just slumming or something, and I think a woman would appear more like a failure."

There are others who agree with Fornes, believing that the institutional system as it exists in American theatre is not something to aspire to. Nikki Appino challenges the disfunctional situations that she thinks exist in the current institutions in the American regional theatre, whether run by women or not. Appino feels that women and other outsiders can effect change only if the entire structure changes:

My belief is that the contribution that women and people of color will make is by virtue of the fact that we have not been inside of these institutions and therefore should have a certain flexibility and not too many preexisting ideas of what it's supposed to be and how it's supposed to run. Therefore, hopefully, we can start to reestablish the whole foundation of how an institution works. There's a mindset, there are certain awarenesses that come with being a subculture, that come with being outside of the mainstream. I think that the really positive side of that is, therefore, the systems that those mindsets create can somehow find a more inclusive way of operating, a less disfunctional way of working.

Being the outsider can have the disadvantage, however, of making it very hard to get the work initially. Although I stated at the outset that I was not looking into discrimination experienced in the workplace, several women could not resist bringing it up as a highly influential gender issue for them. Seret Scott says just getting hired is always the most difficult part of any job for her as a woman, and Julie Taymor emphatically agrees. Rita Giomi believes "the hustle is harder for women" because of the "good old boys network. It exists and theatre is certainly not the exception to the way society functions in that regard." Alana Byington attributes some of the difficulty she encounters with getting work with the more "feminine" behavior of being more passive, not aggressively going out to promote herself. She believes, however, that there are many men in similar positions.

Preference for Working with Other Women

The notion of collaboration seems to most clearly define any probable differences in the working process of women directors as they perceive themselves and their ways of working. Although many of the women agree that men are learning to work in much more collaborative ways, at least one third of the women brought up an emerging preference for working with women collaborators when possible. Timothy Near admits to trying to hire women as often as possible because of her awareness of the lack of opportunities for women in the theatre. Nikki Appino, who was starting a woman's performance cabaret at the time of our conversation, believes that women need to give each other more chances and has a strong preference for working with women whenever possible. Victoria Parker is quite specific regarding her reasons for this feeling: "I do notice lately when I work as an actor I have a greater trust in women directors than I do men. I don't know why that is. It may be because of shared sensibility. It may be because we are becoming more clear sighted. Male/female communication is sometimes an obstacle course. Women have always known how to speak to one another, so it's a little bit easier for me to work with women. I trust them more. I trust them to be clear." Several others also speak of the difference in their comfort level when working with women.

Brenda Hubbard has clearly had some negative experiences with men, resulting in a preference for working with women designers: "When you work with male set designers, they sometimes tend to talk down to you about technical elements, assuming that you may not understand certain things because you've not spent a lot of time in a wood shop, or whatever. Sometimes that's true, and sometimes it's not. When I was actually hiring people and had control over the choice of people I worked with, I would tend to choose men that were more easygoing, more on the passive side, than men who were strongly opinionated as set designers. I like working with women designers best. I just like the collaboration; I like the way of communicating. I have sometimes found that same effective communication in working with gay men."

Perhaps it is a lack of sexual tension that leads to a feeling of more comfortable collaboration. Although she did not identify any specific negative experiences with men, Tisa Chang clearly thinks she works better with female collaborators: "I work very well with women. I've brought many women designers into the field, or have particularly sought them out, simply because we work very well together. They buy very readily into my ideal, into what I'm trying to accomplish. I find that they have been most supportive and receptive, so I don't have to struggle so hard."

While working with women collaborators is not common to her experience, the few times it has happened have been rewarding ones for Seret Scott because of the ease in communication: "I've worked with one female set designer out of all the shows I've done, and I do feel like even though I didn't know her very well, there was a little more shorthand than I have with some of the guys. I had one woman as a lighting designer. She was one of the top ones in the country, and she knew just what to give me. I didn't have to say anything, what I needed was just there."

Pamela Hendrick has quite a bit of experience with female collaborators and is very positive about the results:

> I will definitely say that the theatre productions I've been involved in that have been the most exemplary forms of collaboration have been all-women projects because it took very little time to set the group dynamic and to aim it towards collaboration. Everybody was at ease with it very quickly. The rule of group dynamics says that once a group is set up, somebody in the group will generally assume the role of undermining the leadership of the group. I think that does tend to be true, but it seems not to happen or to happen so much more subtly and more manageably when it's an all-woman group working together. Setting aside those differences and setting aside that fight for hierarchical status seems to quickly take a back seat to setting common goals and to working collaboratively. It seems to happen with great ease.

The entire design team for *Dream of a Common Language* was female, as was the playwright. Its director, Sharon Ott, is clearly trying to hire women as often as possible. It is not always easy, however, and some of the obstacles can be internal. One day at rehearsal there was a discussion regarding a moment in the play when one of the characters tries to explain the ambivalence and doubt that constantly plague her as an artist. She believes that women somehow are not entitled to their successes, that they can never really be as good as men. This causes her to secretly doubt her own talent as well as that of other women, even while fighting for recognition as an artist. The scene is based on an experience from the life of a friend of the playwright, a situation which caused this woman to question the legitimacy of the accomplishments of a fellow woman scientist. Nearly every woman in the room had a similar story to share. One of the ways this ambivalence manifested for Ott herself, especially when she first took over at the Berkeley Rep, was in an unconscious pull to surround herself with men because of the sense of authority they project, which then gave her a sense of validation and protection for her own authority. In her growing awareness of this trap, Ott found she has to be very consciously careful to hire women in order to counteract the unspoken and almost unconscious conditioning that whispers women are not worthy of success.

Julia Miles was especially critical of women who did not hire other women whenever possible. "I think they should stop and think how hard it was for them and have a little compassion. At the Women's Project we still sometimes use male directors because you have to train playwrights that women can direct. There are some women writers who still have trouble with that, although I'm happy to say it's fewer and fewer as time goes by and more women directors get their work out there. That's what it's all about; they should be allowed to work, the work should be good, the work should be recognized, people should see the work, and it speaks for itself." Whether or not the women in this book have any ambivalence about their right to success, most have found some measure of it in one way or another, although it is clearly arguable that they might be even more renowned if they were male.

Change Is Coming

Several of the directors saw welcome changes coming, especially because of the increased presence of women and artists of color in the theatre. JoAnne Akalaitis explains that although the theatre has been dominated by white men, she believes the institution is slowly changing. There are now more women artistic directors who are trying to create more open collaborations with associate artists and more of a concern with cultural pluralism in the major theatres. She still believes, however, that more work needs to be done because "the pressing issue in American culture is the people who have been left behind." Many others are in agreement on this point.

Some of the women commented during the interview that this kind of study really should be done every five years, perhaps more often. Perceptions in theatre are changing quickly, especially regarding women directors, and will continue to change as more women enter the profession. As women become more successful and gender boundaries less stringent, the concerns attributed to gender may become less problematical. Several women indicated that their responses to this study would have been quite different ten or perhaps even five years ago. This awareness of change is reiterated by Julianne Boyd, who sums up quite neatly why she believes women are finally making this progress:

> From when I started directing in nineteen-seventy to now, women have made substantial gains. It's not as great as I would have liked to have seen. The fact that there are still only one or two women directors on Broadway shows that. There are women directing in regional theatre and other venues where less money is at stake. I think the be-all and the end-all is not to direct on Broadway but to make a living in the theatre. However, Broadway success is the way people perceive directors where big money is at stake. I think we've made inroads and will make more inroads as more women direct in these venues and they have successful productions. We're making gains. There are more women artistic directors than there were five years ago. The number must have at least tripled, and those women are hiring women. In the past I found as much discrimination from women as I had from men in the hiring process, but it's changing because more women are becoming artistic directors who were free-lance directors and they know how hard it was. Emily Mann said a wonderful thing once, which was there are more women becoming artistic directors and having power positions in the theatre because as the amount of money one makes in theatre becomes less compared to other fields, especially film, theatre is perceived as a hobby or less of a serious profession, and only women can afford to do this. Who else is going to work for nothing?

When I asked Emily Mann to elaborate about this subject, she was not so emphatic about the point, insisting that it initially came out of anger:

> I was in a temper when I said that. There was a moment when suddenly a lot of women were given theatres. They were hired as artistic directors. I cynically said that was because the pay is at a level and the amount of work and time is at a level that if you're going to work that hard, you probably want to get rich. You can't do that in the theatre. A lot of the very talented men are going to film and television, or they're going into other forms of the business where they're going to make a lot of money. So, the theatre may see more and more women in power because the jobs are less and less seductive to men. Do I really believe that? I think there's a grain of truth to it. But I also think, on the positive side of things, that the boards of directors and the communities are very hungry for women's style right now. Or they were in the last three to five years, where we've seen a lot of the women come to prominence. They want leadership that cares about its community, that cares about the children, that cares about education, that wants to put work on the stage that is expansive of the human heart and spirit. I think a lot of the women happen to be of that ilk. It's rarer to find in a lot of the young men; they have a different agenda, and that agenda doesn't seem to be interesting to communities of the major regional houses right now.

Julia Miles also quotes Mann's infamous remark as she points to a study done in 1990 by the Women's Project which explores the issue of economics and its relationship to the gender of a director:

> I do think it has changed over the years as more women directors are working, but I still feel it's difficult. The main thing the study found was the lower the budget of the play, the more likely it was to be a woman directing. Women were doing a lot of Off Off Broadway or showcases. They were not getting very many large regional theatres or large theatres in New York or Broadway. I think there is a perception left over from the days when women were housebound that women don't know how to deal with great sums of money, and the men who have control of this were afraid they would blow it. That has to change, and it is changing slowly but truly. Of course, as Emily Mann said, "Now that all the boys have gone off to Hollywood and there's no money left, all the women are here to take over." It's such a hard task at this moment in history of the nonprofit theatre. It's a very good thing that women are getting some control because it will make it easier for everybody.[2]

As many of the directors were quick to point out, women are now making inroads to success in smaller venues and slowly graduating to larger institutions where more money and visibility are at stake.

Summary

While maintaining that theatre is still less discriminatory than many other professional fields, many of the women made comments about the discrimination they have nevertheless experienced, especially early in their careers. Most seem to believe that the situation is improving, however. Several issues were raised in this brief discussion of economic and career considerations. First, the expectations of the theatre life-style, especially the time and travel demands, are hard on any artist but especially difficult for women because of our cultural assumptions regarding the home and family still being primarily under a woman's care. Second, because of experiencing lack of support or direct resistance from male collaborators, or simply because of having such a positive experience with other women artists, a number of the women have a preference for working with female collaborators as often as possible. Finally, even women who seem quite successful believe it probably took them longer than men to achieve this success, to be trusted with larger budgets and bigger shows, although several women also think that the lack of the pressure and expectations that come to those who find commercial success may make them better artists. The directors are all hopeful about the increased presence of women directors in the theatre, especially as they see more and more women moving into positions of power and artistic control in more and larger theatres.

CONCLUSION

While a majority of the women directors I interviewed are not aware of a conscious emphasis on gender issues as they are working, when reflecting back on their working process, they can clearly identify several areas of probable influence. Perhaps the most obvious area of gender influence actually involves the perceptions of the other people they work with, who sometimes tend to see them as women first before they consider their talents as artists. These directors do not generally appreciate being identified as "women directors," preferring instead to be thought of simply as directors, and most are reluctant to make any generalities regarding gender differences at all. They prefer to view gender as simply an element, albeit a critical one, in a complex combination of influences which shapes their individual artistic identities. It seems that many of them consciously or unconsciouly see a career advantage in not foregrounding gender.

It is generally believed by these directors that the theatrical profession is by and large less discriminatory than other fields. Many also believe gender boundaries are much less clear in theatre than in other professions. Most of the women believe everyone has attributes in their personality which can be identified as both male and female and that gender identification comes through a combination of social conditioning and innate tendencies, with social conditioning accounting for a majority of the influences. While twenty-six out of thirty-five women interviewed consider themselves feminists, the remaining women seem to assume feminists are shrill, strident, victimized, or somehow limited in their perspective, and they prefer a designation of humanist or no identification at all. A majority of the directors interviewed would likely be classified as liberal feminists, those who have found success within the terms of a male-dominated theatrical establishment through playing by the established rules. Some of the more radical feminist theorists might look at these directors and see them as unwitting victims of the patriarchal values under which they are working. The women directors themselves, however, generally believe they are slowly and subtly changing the rules and assumptions about what good directors should be.

QUALITIES OF A GOOD DIRECTOR

It is in regard to the two major qualities of a good director that gender is perceived to have the most significant impact on the directing process. The qualities of leadership and collaboration are often presented as intertwined and of equal importance to the director. When we look at the issue of leadership, and especially how women are perceived in the position of artistic authority and vision, several trends can be identified. Leadership and power are often identified as behaviors which are socially valorized as masculine attributes. A clear majority of the women say, however, that they are not consciously aware of any internal gender influence in their own exercise of the director's power. Where they do encounter an awareness of leadership and power as a gender issue is in external resistance or challenge to their artistic authority. Although the circumstances and frequency of the incidents vary widely, almost everyone in this book has had at least one experience in her career in which she has met with resistance to her authority. The challenges are sometimes overt, sometimes covert, but are definitely believed to be a result of gender expectations or prejudices. The challenges come in various forms and most often require that she prove herself and the validity of her ideas or authority to the individual or group in question. Examples of overt resistance are seen most frequently in anecdotes about male actors, generally older ones, although one or two directors have experienced similar resistance from female actors. Resistance came most often in early career experiences and is becoming less frequent as each director establishes her professional reputation and becomes more comfortable with her own exercise of power.

There are also some possibilities of more covert resistance from producers or boards of directors. While it is sometimes difficult to determine exactly why a director might not be hired for a particular project, the consensus is that there is still a prevailing sense of apprehension regarding women in positions of authority, especially when the financial stakes of the project are high. Producers or artistic directors have sometimes actually been heard to wonder whether a woman would be strong enough to handle the challenges of the director's job. In other cases, one woman's failure has caused artistic directors to stop hiring other women, blaming the entire gender for the failure of one woman. As more women directors experience success, this concern begins to diminish, but it is by no means eliminated.

There are four other ways in which leadership issues manifest themselves. The first is in the area of behavior. Most of the directors believe that as women they have to be consistently on better behavior than male directors, especially when expressing anger, frustration, or dissatisfaction. The unfortunate stereo-type of the aggressive woman is still present in the way many women feel they are being perceived by others as a "dragon lady" or "bitch" whenever they are exacting or authoritative. This leads to regular behavior modification, especially a pressure to be careful not to express feelings of extreme anger or frustration, no matter how justified. This is not seen as a significant prob-lem, however, because most of the directors view a moderate style of leader-ship as an advantage because they believe it creates a better climate for col-laboration. The second issue concerns the feeling that because of a love for collaboration and an openness to getting input from other artists during the process, many women directors are perceived as lacking in decisiveness and leadership, whereas the women themselves believe they will have no trouble being decisive once all options have been explored. It's simply that they priv-ilege exploration over decision making until late in the process. The third issue is in relationship to personal appearance. Women who are considered sexy, attractive, petite, or especially feminine feel at a distinct disadvantage when dealing with issues of power, at least until they establish their authority in a particular situation. They believe that women often have to desexualize them-selves in order to wield their power successfully. Interestingly, there were a couple of exceptions who believe a nondescript, nonsexual appearance con-tributes to a perception of lack of authority. An attendant concern has to do with a woman's age. In a seemingly no-win situation, some of the younger women feel challenged by older, more experienced male artists, while one or two of the older, more experienced women feel passed over for younger tal-ent. The fourth issue is a personal, psychological one raised by only a few directors—an issue of insecurity in the position of artistic authority arising from a feeling of a lack of cultural entitlement to power. Even some of the most obviously successful women admit to a certain ambivalence about their success, usually because of the lack of social preparation for a role of power and influence.

It seems that the women are generally very aware of needing to take lead-ership and be the guiding visionary of the rehearsal process, and most seem quite comfortable with the necessary exercise of that power, even if they came to it with some difficulty. Most are much less concerned, however, with any external power structure or need to claim their authority and territory than they are with simply getting the job done well. One of the most consistent comments when talking about gender influences in their artistic process was that *perhaps* gender was an influence, but mostly they thought they were sim-ply following the principles of good directing as they understood them. They do speculate, however, that women might be inclined to pursue excellence in all parts of the process, even those areas where they feel some discomfort or difficulty, whereas male directors might simply give lip service in areas where they feel less comfortable, concentrating instead on their strengths.

The second major quality of a good director, and the other side of the leadership coin, is collaboration. All but one of these directors put a very high level of emphasis on the issue of open collaboration, and there was a generally held belief that women have a stronger propensity for working collaboratively and a different way of looking at a group artistic process, arising in large part from their social conditioning. Most believe women tend to be more concerned with what a group of artists can discover together than with simply realizing the preconceived vision of a director. They are less concerned with controlling the other artists and more concerned with freeing them to be as creative as possible within an environment of trust, intimacy, and sharing of feelings because they are convinced that this can often lead to a stronger, more creative result. Many seem to believe the stereotypical notion that women more often use a nurturing approach to collaboration with more openness to feelings, emotions, and intuitions. They also believe that group process is usually easier for a woman because of her social training as an observer and mediator within the family structure. They are careful, however, to point out that many male directors also use the same kind of open, nurturing approach and that it is clearly a learned behavior. It is simply that women have been encouraged to manifest that behavior more regularly in their lives. Although the directors generally look at collaboration as a very positive aspect of the directing process, there are a few women who perceive possible detriments, especially when an overemphasis on the collaborative process contributes to a less cohesive or finished final product.

In general, the majority of these directors are searching for a balance between effective but nonoppressive leadership and authority and an efficient and truly open method of collaboration. Images that emerge to describe this balance include the director at the center of a web or at the hub of a wheel. In these images, responsibility is shared more laterally than hierarchically, but all input is indeed focused towards the defining vision of the director, whose authority is more benign than autocratic, truly reflecting the notion of the director as the "first among equals." It seems that most of the male directors who dominated the field for decades, while acknowledging the need for both elements, were perhaps more comfortable with the leadership side of this required balance. Now, as women are entering the field in greater numbers, they are tending to emphasize the collaborative side rather than simply the leadership function. While a majority of the directors interviewed believe that women are more often concerned with open collaboration than with exerting their authority, almost every one of them could also point to an exception in their own experience. Just as there are definitely autocratic and highly controlling women directors, there are also many nurturing and highly collaborative male directors. Most directors, regardless of gender, agree that a mix of both is necessary for the good director.

ELEMENTS OF THE DIRECTING PROCESS

Secondary issues of concern for the directors focus on certain pragmatic elements of the directing process. A clear majority of the women are very concerned with gender issues in their script selection process, especially the ways in which women are portrayed on stage. This results in selecting scripts with strong women characters or with themes related to women's or gender issues as often as possible within their other consideration criteria. The directors also acknowledge, however, the trap that can come from privileging the woman's voice, and they decry the unfortunate tendency of producers and artistic directors to see women directors simply in terms of scripts about women. Many of these directors believe they have consistently been offered what they refer to as the "woman's slot" rather than having a broader selection of directing projects regularly made available to them. While women's issues are important to many of them, it is a career limitation most of the directors wish to reject, and they are actively involved in trying to overcome those perceived limitations, either by having more control over the selection process in some way or by trying to find projects which will help them break away from these gendered expectations. The directors also share a concern with how women characters are portrayed, regardless of the theme of the play. Perpetuation of gender stereotypes and derogatory portrayals of women are being actively rejected by a majority of the women interviewed. While there is some disagreement over whether a woman in a play should necessarily be a good role model, there is little disagreement that women should be entitled to a centrality and subjectivity previously denied them in dramatic literature.

While gender considerations are most often discussed in terms of script choices, they also seem to have some influence in casting as well as character development issues. At least half of the women believe they are more sensitive to nontraditional casting possibilities, especially ways in which roles which are not necessarily race or gender specific could be played by women or actors of color instead of by the usual white male actors. A few of the women occasionally make conscious gender switching a theatrical element in their interpretation of a play as a way to foreground the arbitrariness of gender distinctions. In character development there is a shared awareness by many of the directors that underdeveloped characters of both genders need to be fleshed out during the rehearsal process. This awareness usually begins with a discussion of female characters which are perceived as often underdeveloped by the writers, but it also includes male characters as well in an effort to break down stereotypical assumptions. Many of the women, especially those coming from acting careers and having unsatisfactory experiences with male directors in the past, believe they make a greater effort than their male counterparts to explore the whole human being. This translates to searching for vulnerabilities in a seemingly strong character and probing strengths in an apparently weak or victimized character. This exploration is undertaken regardless of the gender of the character, but is generally believed to be most necessary when presenting women in roles of villains or victims in order to explode the stereotypes as much as possible.

In terms of the visual and technical elements of a production, there is near unanimity regarding the belief that issues involved in the use of space have little or nothing to do with gender. As a learned technical behavior, it is considered pure "craft." None of the directors address, however, the issue of how the standards of this craft were developed; they simply accept them as neutral and strictly aesthetic in nature, a contention radical feminists might challenge. A few women also express a preference for intimate spaces. This, however, is more often attributed to the tendency for women to be given directing projects in smaller, more intimate locations, which in turn leads to a sense of comfort and confidence in those venues rather than any true preference. Another minor influence of gender expressed by several of the directors seems to be in the occasional feelings of inadequacy regarding their ability to deal with technical elements. This sense of inadequacy, usually felt early in a career, is generally thought, however, to arise more from lack of experience or training than from any innate lack of abilities on the part of women directors.

OTHER CAREER ISSUES

Other issues which are seen to be influenced by gender are more political and social than artistic. Virtually every woman has at least one anecdote to relate about experiencing some form of discrimination during her career. Most incidents were in the past and ranged from minor annoyances to extremely distasteful and disturbing incidents. Many of the women believe these incidents are now becoming less frequent. They do not know, however, whether it is because they are becoming more well known as directors as their careers progress or whether there is a general lessening of discrimination in the industry today. As many of the directors point out, women are now making inroads to success in smaller venues and slowly graduating to larger institutions where more money and visibility are at stake. With the rise of the free-lance director, increased participation from women in the field of theatre, and the lowering of the financial rewards in live theatre compared to other entertainment industries, one can clearly say that women's participation is in some ways transforming the profession of stage directing. Whether the transformation will be seen as a positive one in the eyes of the world or whether theatre will become a devalued and feminized art form in the eyes of a diminishing audience raised on the excesses and spectacle of television and film remains to be seen. The articulate and insightful responses of the women in my study indicate that the gain to the profession of directing by increased participation of women directors is extremely positive. Their presence in the American theatre cannot help but have some kind of long-term effect because they are obviously talented and committed artists, each one in her own unique way. It seems likely that whatever impact they will continue to have will be from a complex combination of attributes, not the least of which is gender.

The challenge, then, to women directors today is to somehow find ways to transcend both the gendered expectations of the ways women should work and the kinds of scripts they should direct as well as the potential traps of selecting or creating work based on a traditionally male-oriented way of working. This is obviously not an original idea, nor will it be a surprise to any woman director working in the theatre. The directors interviewed here, while generally successful in their careers, still have no easy answers for this particular dilemma, but they would like to be free to use their gender in their artistic work without feeling constrained or marginalized by it.

As the function of the director continues to grow in importance in the field of live theatre and as women enter the profession in greater numbers, the work of contemporary women directors has resonance for all theatre practitioners, male or female. Women's voices have often been overlooked in the past, but they have unique and valuable perspectives to add to our current body of knowledge in directing theory and pedagogy, as well as some very pragmatic approaches to problems and situations common for all directors, regardless of gender. Their increasing openness to true collaboration, combined with a willingness and ability to achieve a truly benevolent form of leadership, can maximize the creative contribution of all artists involved, leading to greater possibilities in the live theatre experience. In fact, women's perceptions of the directing process and their subsequent participation in it may well be instrumental in a transformation of that process and the realization of a new dominant model for directors of the future.

APPENDIX A: SIGNIFICANT INFLUENCES ON THE DIRECTORS' ARTISTIC IDENTITY AND PERSONAL DEVELOPMENT

FAMILY BACKGROUND

When talking about the role of family influences and upbringing in their artistic development, most of the women who consider this a strong influence on their development identify an encouraging, stimulating environment in their youth, one where they were not discouraged in their career aspiration because of their gender. Tisa Chang was influenced by her parents' love for drama when they were students in China and by her own early exposure to performing arts and literature. Several women identified their mothers as significant influences. Michelle Blackmon recalls her mother's strong will as the model that made her strong. Alana Byington had a physician mother and "grew up in a liberal household where women could really achieve anything." Fontaine Syer credits both her strong and encouraging mother and grandmother for her confidence in herself: "My mother told me from the time I was two years old I could do anything I put my mind on. I was grown before I ever heard 'No, you can't because you're a woman.' So rather than hearing it in your bones somewhere as you're growing up, it never occured to me until I was grown." Maria Irene Fornes identifies an incredible closeness with her mother as an early influence, and at the time of our interview, her mother, Carmen, was still traveling with Fornes even at age 100. Susana Tubert credits a free-spirited grandmother who left her husband behind in Argentina and traveled to Paris in the 1920s to pursue her studies in painting and sculpture as a significant influence in her early life: "She was the only woman in my family who was committed to her art in spite of everything." Pamela

Hendrick, Cynthia White, and Penny Metropulos all identified strong and influential fathers. In Hendrick's case, her English professor father's love of language and theatre was a strong factor in her early love of performing. White's father instilled in her a strong work ethic and the ability for rigorous self-evaluation, which she finds invaluable in her artistic success. Metropulos simply remembers her father's strong and nurturing influence in her childhood and also identifies her position as an only child in the family and being "the center of the universe" when growing up as the main reasons she feels no sense of limitations on her career aspirations.

Only two women mention any negative family influence. Gloria Muzio's comment is clearly not a negative reflection on her family, simply an acknowledgement of the confining tradition they represented for her. Raised in a traditional Italian Catholic family, Muzio believes that her experience of rebellion against the traditional role expected of her and the ensuing guilt she felt helped shape who she is today. Anne Bogart, while also rebelling against a confining tradition, is much more specific in her negative commentary on the gender constraints in her military family, identifying its influence on her development as "deprivation as a child, deprivation of love. I'm yearning for love, which influences everything I do. I was brought up in a navy family, which is all about the men. Girls weren't supposed to amount to anything. I think most of my career is based on revenge against my upbringing, of having nothing expected of me. It makes me so angry that I try to do a lot."

Influences identified with family background and upbringing also include a strong and defining sense of place for several of the directors. Rita Giomi describes being raised in the desert Southwest as a first generation American with European parents as the most important among her early influences. Tori Haring-Smith sees significant influence from her midwestern origins. Diana Marré credits her activism and dramatic flair to being raised in the conflict-ridden and racist South.

CULTURAL OR ETHNIC IDENTITY AND INFLUENCE

Prominent among other influences which have a profound effect on the artists are ethnicity and culture, both the culture of origin and cultures experienced through travel. Melia Bensussen identifies her travels to Asia and Israel as significant, but her culture of origin is a much stronger factor: "Having had Spanish as a first language, and growing up as a practicing Jew in Mexico City who always looked like an American, there's a foreignness and an outsider quality which I think has shaped many women directors. We all see ourselves as outsiders. For me, this was the literal place for that to begin." Born in Argentina of a Russian/Rumanian immigrant family, Susana Tubert is very aware of having a complex cultural identity with a lot of influences to draw on and no place to belong: "My father grew up in Paris, my mother lived in New York in her twenties. I grew up as a nonpracticing Jew in Catholic Argentina and every day felt a foreigner in my own country as a Spanish-speaking student at the American school. To my Argentine friends and cousins, I was the 'gringa' who could never fit in. No wonder my dance classes, which I started at age five, and my own 'living room plays' for my family were the only places where I felt at home." Tubert immigrated to the U.S. upon graduating from high school and in 1980 settled in New York to pursue act-ing: "All of a sudden I have a new label: I was Hispanic! It was too limiting and too frustrating. After ten years, I became a director."

Tisa Chang identifies culture, nationalism, and race as the strongest influences on her artistic work and personal development. Born in China and raised with strong Confucian values, then transplanted to the United States in the late 1950s with no possibility of returning to China because of the Communist revolution, Chang believes her determination to "go beyond what society had slotted for me because of my gender and ethnicity is particularly striking in everything I've done." Bea Kiyohara also lists ethnic concerns as high on her list of influences. Seret Scott identifies ethnic concerns as strongest among her influences, not necessarily in her true artistic identity but clearly in how others view her first and foremost as "a double minority, a black woman director." Although she identifies influences more personal than ethnic as significant in her artistic development, Michelle Blackmon is also very aware of being identified by others more often as an ethnic director than simply a director. Being a white woman raised in the South gave Diana Marré a strong awareness of ethnic issues, leading to her development as a scholar of Black American drama, especially the work of Lorraine Hansberry. As she defines it, much of her work "tries to foreground the issue of race." Barbara Ann Teer combines both creative and spiritual influences as she describes answering what to her is a "cultural calling" as an artist, a calling grounded in "the cul-ture of people of African descent."

Travel and experiences with other cultures were identified as formative for several of the directors. After finishing her undergraduate education, Liz Diamond lived in Burkina Faso, West Africa, teaching at the University of Ouagadougou and cofounding the Projet du Théâtre Rurale. The PTR was a fifteen-member ensemble that toured throughout the countryside, creating plays that addressed local social and political issues and explored traditional Arican performance forms. According to Diamond, this theatre was founded out of frustration over the "co-optation of traditional performance forms for purely folkloric ends. There seemed to be no real concerted effort to bring these rich aesthetic forms forward and to use them in ways that could really enrich the lives of contemporary African people." This experience had a profound effect on Diamond's political and aesthetic sensibilities. Julie Taymor lived in Indonesia for four years and credits that experience and her extensive travels to Japan and Eastern Europe as significant influences on her personal aesthetic. Sharon Ott was profoundly influenced by her travels to Japan, where she experienced a different cultural sense of the animate world. Alana Byington thinks her openness comes from living abroad for several years, traveling a lot throughout America and Europe, and being exposed to an incredible diversity in life-styles during her formative years.

EDUCATIONAL BACKGROUND

Education and intellectual pursuits are also high on many lists of influences. JoAnne Akalaitis identified the "life of the mind" as something of incredible importance to her. Several women identified love of reading or a particular kind of reading as a significant factor in their development. Melia Bensussen was influenced by reading the Old Testament in her youth, Tisa Chang by Chinese history, culture, and philosophy, and Mary Robinson especially by women authors. Although she did not identify a particular subject area, Pamela Hendrick says she has "always been a reader, and comes from a background that loves language." Tori Haring-Smith brought up her "intellectual interest in language that grows out of my lifelong study of language." Susan Finque articulates a fascination with language and how we communicate with each other. Gloria Muzio connects this fascination with communication very directly to her artistic development:

> Part of who I am and part of what has influenced me has to do with my focus on a humanist kind of connection to people, believing that the most important thing in the world is the connections between people. It's the communication of ideas, communication of feelings, communication of political thought. That's why I like to go to work with a bunch of people and work to tell a story to another bunch of people. You get together for five weeks and learn a story. I often think of it that way, that in those five weeks we're going to figure out what the story is and tell that the best way we can to a whole group of people. To me that passing on of feelings and ideas and thought is so important in terms of interconnections and has made it important to me to continue working, because that's the best way I know how, in terms of my training, to tell stories. To tell stories that are going to change people's lives or open up their eyes. That connection between people via storytelling is what has been my pursuit.

Besides the pursuit of knowledge or communication, several women also identified specific role models connected to their educational background. Anne Bogart credits a high school French teacher "who showed me art," Mary Robinson found support from a female high school drama teacher, and Fontaine Syer points to her "huge list of female role models" influential throughout her education, including the headmistress at her all-girls high school, the president and the head of the drama department at Mt. Holyoke College, and a female supervisor at a camp where she worked as a counselor for several summers. Liz Diamond cites a radical feminist professor of French at Wellesley College who "had an enormous influence on my thinking about the role of theatre in the world, and the role of art, and the responsibility of the intellectual to address moral and political issues."

POLITICAL OR SOCIAL CONCERNS

A number of the women identified social concerns and political issues as formative for their artistic identity. After discussing her influential professor, Diamond goes on to say that her studies of political science and history in college fed her "passion for theatre that raises issues of public and political moment. I'm much less interested in the private world than I am in the world of the polis. It's one of the reasons I love Shakespeare so much, because it's so big. The concerns extend from the most intimate confines of the heart to the whole world, and I love writing that operates on that scale." Both Melia Bensussen and Timothy Near identify growing up in families where strong commitment to social issues and ongoing political discussions were part of everyday life. Near, particularly, translates that background into a very specific desire to "promote a better world" through her artistic work. Susana Tubert also feels that her work is always "taking a political stand" because of the political and cultural environment in which she grew up. It's important for her to fight cultural stereotypes by "inviting others to see themselves in *our* stories." Several others also identify political concerns at the center of their artistic identity. In Adele Prandini's early career, she founded a theatre specifically devoted to women's and lesbian issues, and her work at the time of our interview was definitely focused on social concerns, including violence against women and AIDS. Susan Finque names "concern for the planet, especially an awareness of ecological and economic issues" as important in her work, and Seret Scott simply says she prefers "political theatre."

Although social concerns are very much a part of their work, other women directors prefer to define their focus as being on the individual. Victoria Parker is fascinated with issues of oppression and in her work tends to look for the strains, not just in plays but in character interactions and situations, that explore what she calls "living a life of less-ness" which leads to a sense of general malaise and anxiousness, a condition she thinks is all too common in our contemporary society. She is very careful, however, to say that she believes the message is best presented through stories that explore human oppression in general, rather than what she calls "platform" plays.

Maria Irene Fornes has consistently concerned herself with themes of justice and injustice as a writer. She concentrates on the private issues of individuals struggling with oppression and considers her work more humanist than political in nature. She admits that her plays can be perceived as political statements, but she is adamant that they are never written with overt political intent: "I am more interested in the individual than in politics, the individual as fighting oppression. In some way or another my work has to do with an oppression—by somebody, hardly ever by a government. That's why it's more humanistic than political, because I usually deal with the private rather than public, but then the individual is oppressed and even if a direct line to politics is not in the play, my plays end up being political for that reason. I am very concerned with justice and injustice."

Expressing a similar belief, but in a subtly different way, Emily Mann says she doesn't know how to separate the personal from the political because she believes that her work is "highly politically charged, but comes out of a personal need to tell that story." She goes on to define her primary influences as a complex combination of the social, the psychological, and the spiritual:

> I would say that's true of all the things that I have written and many I have directed; they are characterized as political pieces and yet to me they are very personal pieces. I live in the world. There's a sense always of a context in which we live, so certainly the social and the political inform the work. Yet I'm always looking for the spiritual center of any play, the emotional center of any play. Where I enter it is important to me. If it doesn't have all three ingredients, I'm probably not ready to direct it or write it. It's not what I need to be doing at that time, if those three things aren't operating.

Although Mann was the only one specifically to link particular influences in this way, it seems likely that others experienced their influences in various combinations as well.

RELIGIOUS OR SPIRITUAL INFLUENCES

Several women are quite specific about a spiritual influence being primary in their work. Some spoke of specific religious upbringings and the influence brought to bear on their later development. JoAnne Akalaitis was influenced by the rituals of the Catholic church, with their "seductive visuals" and their sense of the theatrical, and she has been involved with theatre from her Catholic high school days. Liz Huddle feels she is "indelibly stamped by the theatrical ritual of Catholicism. As a child you don't know it, but what you are seeing is grand theatre." Rita Giomi also identifies a Catholic upbringing as an important part of her development, as does Gloria Muzio, who sees its influence mostly in her resistance to the church's strictures. Melia Bensussen sees her Jewish background as a profound influence on her world view and artistic sensibilities, especially as she tends to bring Old rather than New

Testament imagery and allusions to her work with scripts. As an outsider to formal religious practice, be it her own Jewish heritage or the dominant Catholic culture of Argentina, Susana Tubert developed her own perception of spirituality: "Perhaps it's my own version of Magic Realism, but I am inevitably drawn to the fantastical in everyday life. Spiritual connections manifest themselves in my work without my looking for them. I suppose it's a very Latin American way of life."

Others see spirituality as a strong influence but are not so specific in defining its nature or identity. Although she did not identify a specific denomination in her background, Michelle Blackmon sees herself as a very spiritual person, one who is always exploring the nature of things. She attributes this focus to a strong influence from her mother, who taught her the power of positive thinking and to put her concerns out to the universe in prayer. Nikki Appino insists that a strong sense of spirituality informs all her work, regardless of its subject matter. Adele Prandini identifies a constant awareness of what she calls a sense of "synchronicity" in the world as an influence on her art, saying, "maybe at another point in time in our history they called it magic, or they called it religion, or they called it miracle." For Sharon Ott, the influence on her artistic identity is not an overt religious belief, but rather a "belief and a feeling that one is in a continuous spiritual universe." Barbara Ann Teer talks about her "spirit culture" and is clearly very spiritually connected to what she sees as its essence:

> I call it the "Science and Secret of Soul." Soul is a spiritual phenomenon that is often misinterpreted or taken lightly. The culture that I represent, that I'm born into, the values, the character, the ethics of the culture, is a spirit culture. It's an African tradition of practices that spring from a lineage that is very powerful. It's a very loving and caring tradition. I am answering a cultural calling to mount, to raise, to praise, to elevate, to inspire, to educate people who were born with this extraordinary gift of Soul. It's a very moving experience to be able to tap into that omnipresent force. That's why I do what I do. That's what moves me. Music is the language of God and so is dance and so are many of the creative impulses that come out of an African experience.

Patricia Blem unhesitatingly invokes the idea of the cosmos and spirituality as the strongest influence on her artistic identity. Although not conventionally religious, she sees her artistic work as a spiritual vocation, something she has been called to do. Her goal in the theatre work she does is to create beauty in the world. Penny Metropulos has a similar sense of her vocation. Although raised Anglican, in her youth she questioned the church and studied Eastern mysticism; she now has no denominational affiliation. She feels a strong sense of "soul connection" to her directing work, however. Once she began directing, she was sure she had found what it was she was meant to be doing in this world. She says quite passionately that it was as if "I had found my soul. My whole reason for being in the theatre was all about trying to find who I was as a person and in the world, and how my heart and spirit fit into all that." Metropulos also identifies her spirituality and her artistic renewal process as closely connected to nature, especially the mountains near her home in Ashland, Oregon.

OTHER ARTS AND DISCIPLINES

Strong influences also come from other creative art forms. First and foremost among these influences is literature. An appreciation for language, literature, and writing almost goes without saying for any stage director, and many of these women, in addition to their love of literature, also have strong identities as writers, either in doing original work or in adapting or translating other works. In fact, Maria Irene Fornes and Emily Mann are both as renowned for their playwriting as for their directing. Music also provided influence and inspiration. Penny Metropulos had a performing career as a professional singer by age nine. This exposure to music, especially jazz, and performing had a profound impact on her life and gave her a strong and secure sense of herself. Anne Bogart identifies theories of music as a strong influence. Tisa Chang was influenced by the physical presence of two particular performers, one in dance and one in the world of music. "Seeing Martha Graham perform as Clytemnestra was one of the turning points in my life. Seeing Leonard Bernstein conduct from the first row of old Carnegie Hall was another because he was a totally physically expressive conductor. He would rise on his tippy toes to a relevé, and then drop down and do a curve, then a contortion. He could be considered the first performance artist because he was so physically expressive." Visual arts were of significance to several of the directors. Julie Taymor looks to visual artists for influence and inspiration in her work. Maria Irene Fornes was a painter and studied textile design before entering the world of the theatre, and this sensibility is a strong part of her painterly approach to staging and stage pictures. Roberta Levitow unhesitatingly identified the visual arts as the strongest influence in her background:

> My parents were painters, and I spent most of my childhood in art museums and surrounded by art books. The idea of being an artist to me is the way visual artists are artists, finding a unique expression for the way one sees the world, creating some kind of controlled or harmonized rendering of it that other people look upon. Whenever it's best, that rendering is really resonant on many levels, on an aesthetic level, and on levels deeper or more varied than that, depending on the nature of the artwork. I've never thought, "I want to be a theatre person like Sarah Bernhardt." I've thought, "I want to be a great artist like Van Gogh." It's not been a very helpful comparison most of the time, the theater being what it is, but it certainly has been inspirational.

Other directors identified careers or studies in other disciplines before coming into the theatre as significant in their identity. JoAnne Akalaitis originally planned to become a doctor, then switched to philosophy, but while working in the graduate program in philosophy at Stanford, she became heavily involved with theatre. Zelda Fichandler was a premed student, has an undergraduate degree in Russian language and literature, and even did some work as a Russian translator before deciding to change her focus to the theatre. Rita Giomi cites her early training in science and engineering as formative and even draws a comparison between scientific principles and her work as a director: "All that training along the way has resonance in the work I do now, in terms of logic skills and in terms of science. So much of what science is is looking for order in chaos and I think that's what directing is." Sharon Ott, who began as a structural anthropology student and worked for the National Science Foundation for two years before deciding on a career in the theatre, is also very articulate about the continuing influence of her first career on her directing work:

> I really did serious anthropology for about five years, and that way of thinking did really affect who I am as an artist. I was interested in structural anthropology and the central unifying notion that there are structures that are common, even though the cultural manifestations above the structures are entirely different. People organize thoughts in a certain way, tend to organize them in binary opposition to each other. I still believe that, and it really ties in with directing a play. I look for the structure of the thinking, not specific behavioral manifestations, but what's under that.

All of these directors believe they bring unique awareness and insight to their creative work as a result of these other studies or careers.

INSPIRATIONAL ROLE MODELS

One of the most obvious influences on theatre artists is other theatre artists. Almost every one of these directors identified performers and directors, both living and dead, as well as a number of writers, both creative and theoretical, as significant influences on their artistic identity. In some cases the influence came from personal contact, in other cases from study about the work of others. The writer/theorist most often cited as a profound influence was Bertolt Brecht. Liz Diamond identifies him as a major influence among writers for the theatre. Pamela Hendrick's undergraduate theatre education was "very centered around Brecht, and that early exposure has remained a very strong influence in my choice of scripts, and in my approach towards the performer/audience relationship." Liz Huddle believes she has performed or directed "as much Brecht as any other person in the United States" and sees him as an enormous influence on her artistic identity, along with "an early and intense exposure to Shakespeare."

Although reading about or studying other theorists and practitioners, male and female, were also occasionally identified as influential, by far the most significant influence on most of these women in the realm of their theatre background seems to be the experience of working directly with or observing other inspirational, innovative, or encouraging directors. JoAnne Akalaitis left the doctoral program in philosophy at Stanford to work as an actor in San Francisco with Jules Irving and Herbert Blau before becoming a cofounder in 1969 of Mabou Mines, an experimental collaborative company recognized internationally as one of the most innovative in America. She credits these experiences, especially working with a strong collective of highly creative and innovative artists as among the most significant contributions to her identity as an artist. Melia Bensussen says she was strongly mentored in her career development and her identity as an artist by Joe Papp at the New York Public Theater. She also identifies another woman director, Mary Robinson, with encouraging and supporting her in a move to New York at an early stage of her career. Pamela Hendrick found inspiration and a sense of mutual support and development from the women who worked with her at Theatre Three, Cynthia White and Betsy Husting. White herself mentions strong support in securing early career directing opportunities from Mesrop Kesdeskian and Jack Clay, both faculty at Southern Methodist University, and from Jerry Turner, former artistic director at the Oregon Shakespeare Festival.

Roberta Levitow discovered a role model in June Moll, the first woman director she ever met, who opened her eyes to the fact that women could direct and direct effectively. Mary Robinson first became aware that women could direct by reading the inspirational biography of Margaret Webster, the best-known woman director in America in the 1940s. Robinson also cites the influence of director Stewart White (who died of AIDS in 1983), who "was the director who for many years I most wanted to emulate. He was extraordinarily sensitive with actors and a wonderful actor's director, although he was also able to stand back and get the big picture." Tori Haring-Smith discusses two directors whose work with actors had a significant impact on her development. "Richard Jenkins is an actor's director. I usually go at directing through a visual eye and an interpretive eye. He goes at it very internally through the actor, and he's really helped me bring out the actor in me. I think that my directing got markedly better during the five years I worked with him. I have an actor in me, but I wasn't accessing it as a director. Tina Packer influenced me in that respect, too. She also urged me to bring the actor out in the director, and I think that's really changed the way I think about things."

Sharon Ott also felt a profound influence from watching the work of other directors. Although she did not identify them by name, she did say these role models were all male: "You try to see the best, and then you allow it to enter you and hope that it becomes your own. All the impulses I have for my own directing come from other work I've seen. Not that I've tried to copy it, but I've certainly tried to absorb what made that work special." Maria Irene Fornes also agrees heartily and goes so far as to say that she sometimes learns more by watching others work than by trying to do it herself. Although she did not say if she had ever made personal contact with her idol, Anne Bogart found inspiration in the work of French director Ariane Mnouchkine. "She is a big influence, not so much her work, which some of it I like and some of it I don't, but her bravery. Whenever I've been in doubt and conflicted about what I'm doing, I think of her and I have the courage to do whatever it is I'm doing because she's gone before. She's my model of a woman of the generation before mine. She's created something that's uniquely what she needed to do, and that's always been a big influence."

Appendix B:
Theatrical Biographies
of the Directors

JoAnne Akalaitis

Joanne Akalaitis most recently directed *Suddenly Last Summer* and *The Poet* at Hartford Stage and *The Rover* by Aphra Behn at the Guthrie Theatre. Other credits include Jane Bowles' *In the Summer House* at Lincoln Center; John Ford's *Tis Pity She's a Whore* at the Goodman Theatre; *Cymbeline, Henry IV, Parts 1 and 2*, and *Woyzeck* at the New York Shakespeare Festival; *Dead End Kids*, Franz Xaver Kroetz's *Request Concert* (Drama Desk Award), *Through the Leaves* with Mabou Mines; Philip Glass's *The Photographer* at the BAM Next Wave Festival; *Endgame* and *The Balcony* at the American Repertory Theatre; *Green Card* at the Mark Taper Forum; and *Leon & Leon (and lenz)* and *The Screens* at the Guthrie Theater. Former artistic director for the New York Public Theater, Akalaitis is also the recipient of a 1993 Obie Award for Sustained Achievement, the 1993 Edwin Booth Award, four Obie Awards for Distinguished Direction and Production, a Guggenheim Fellowship for experimental theater, and Rockefeller and NEA grants for playwriting.

Nikki Appino

Nikki Appino just completed writing and directing her first film, *Threshold*, for a May 1995 premiere. *Sub Rosa* marks the fifth piece of original theatre work she has created or co-created. Other productions were *In, Djinn*, and *Dark Nights of Souls*. She is a graduate of the Experimental Theatre Wing at New York University and was the recipient of the 1990-91 TCG/NEA Directing Fellowship. Nikki has directed at A.C.T., the Group Theatre, Alice B. Theatre, Milwaukee Rep, Portland Rep, McCarter Theatre, Perseverance Theatre, and the Empty Space, and she is the founder of House of Dames.

Melia Bensussen

Melia Bensussen most recently directed *Twelfth Night* for the Oregon Shakespeare Festival. Other regional credits include productions at the Cleveland Playhouse, Berkshire Theatre Festival, Philadelphia Drama Guild, Portland Stage Company, and North Carolina Shakespeare Festival, among others. Among her New York credits are productions at the Manhattan Class Company, Primary Stages, Playwrights Horizons,

WPA, Women's Project, Ensemble Studio Theatre, Puerto Rican Traveling Theatre, and the New York Shakespeare Festival, where she was an associate artist for many years. In 1993 she was the recipient of the Princess Grace Statuette Award for Sustained Excellence. Previously she has received fellowships from the Princess Grace Foundation, the Drama League of New York, and the Theatre Communications Group. She is the editor of a newly released collection of translations of plays by Federico Garcia Lorca published by TCG.

Michelle Blackmon
Michelle Blackmon's directing credits include *The Best Christmas Pageant Ever* (Northwest Children's Theatre, Portland), *Bo* (Bushfire Theatre, Philadelphia), *Voices of Christmas* (Seattle GroupTheatre), *The Colored Museum* and *A Soldier's Play* (Interstate Firehouse Cultural Center, Portland), director/choreographer of *A...My Name Is Alice* (Oregon Stage Company), *Ain't Misbehavin'* and *Hair* (Evergreen Theatre Company, Seattle), and *The Wiz* (Langston Hughes Cultural Arts Center and Tacoma Little Theatre). Blackmon has extensive acting credits and has been choreographer for *A...My Name is Still Alice* (Seattle Group Theatre), an artist-in-residence and instructor for many Seattle-area schools, and has performed in Tashkent, Uzbekistan, in the former Soviet Union as part of the Seattle/Soviet Theatre Arts Exchange. She has an M.A. from American University and a B.F.A. in drama from Howard University.

Patricia Blem
Patricia Blem has worked as a director and actor in the Pacific Northwest for many years. Her directing credits include *Eleemosynary, Visions, Independence, In the Sweet Bye and Bye,* and *Childe Byron* for the Artists Repertory Theatre; *Quilters* for the Alaska Festival Theatre; and *Foursquare* for Triangle Productions. She served as production manager for Sumus Theatre and directed a number of shows there, including *A Thousand Clowns, Echoes, Of Mice and Men, The Rainmaker* and *Sister Mary Ignatius Explains It All for You.* She also directed the Oregon Trail Pageant for five summers. Patricia also has extensive acting credits in Portland and Spokane.

Anne Bogart
Anne Bogart is co-artistic director of the Saratoga International Theater Institute (SITI) founded with Japanese director Tadashi Suzuki in 1992. In January of 1995, she was honored with a mid-career celebration of her work by Actors Theatre of Louisville as part of their Modern Masters series. She is a recipient of two Obie Awards and a Bessie Award, and she was formerly artistic director at the Hartford Stage Company. Currently she is an associate professor at Columbia University. Recent productions include *Small Lives, Big Dreams,* American premiere September 1994 (Saratoga Springs, New York); *The Medium,* an original work based on the theories of Marshall McLuhan performed in Japan, Saratoga Springs, and the New York Theater Workshop; *Paradise* by Regina Taylor (Circle Rep); *The Women* by Clare Booth Luce (Hartford Stage); *Picnic* by William Inge (Actors Theater of Louisville); *Behavior In Public Places,* based on the theories of Erwin Goffman, produced by VIA Theater; *American Vaudeville,* created with Tina Landau at the Alley Theater in Houston, Texas; Paula Vogel's *The Baltimore Waltz* (Circle Rep); and Bertolt Brecht's *In the Jungle of Cities* (New York Shakespeare Festival).

Julianne Boyd
Julianne Boyd conceived and directed the Broadway musical hit, *Eubie!* a show based on the life of Eubie Blake which starred Gregory Hines and garnered three Tony

nominations. In 1980, Citicorp honored her with its Outstanding Young Entrepreneur award for reintroducing Eubie Blake's music to the public. She also conceived and directed (with Joan Micklin Silver) the award-winning Off-Broadway musical revues *A...My Name Is Alice* and *A...My Name Is Still Alice*. Over the past twenty-five years, she has worked extensively in New York and in regional theatres. Her Off-Broadway directing credits include Velina Hasu Houston's *Tea* at the Manhattan Theatre Club, Wendy Kesselman's *Maggie Magelita* at the Lamb's Theatre, and *Just So!* (which she also conceived and co-produced) at the Jack Lawrence Theatre. Regional credits include productions at the Old Globe Theatre, La Jolla Playhouse, McCarter Theatre, Syracuse Stage, Asolo Theatre, and the Coconut Grove Playhouse. From 1992 to 1994, she was artistic director at the Berkshire Theatre Festival, where she directed *Sweet and Hot: The Songs of Harold Arlen*, the world premiere of the musical *Brimstone* (soon to be released as a CD), and *Golf with Alan Shepard*. During her tenure there, she revitalized the Unicorn Theatre and produced the American premiere of Mark St. Germain's *Camping with Henry and Tom*, which is presently running Off-Broadway. Boyd taught at NYU, Baruch College, and John Jay College and holds a Ph.D. in theatre history from the CUNY Graduate Center. She is presently serving as president of the Society of Stage Directors and Choreographers, the first woman ever to hold that post. She is the founder and artistic director of the Barrington Stage Company (Great Barrington, Mass.), a theatre dedicated to producing new and rarely performed work.

Alana Byington
Alana Byington (formerly Alana Beth Lipp) has worked as a director and actor in the Portland area since 1979. She is currently associate director of the Oregon Stage Company, and her work there includes *The Holiday Broadcast of 1943*, *The Heidi Chronicles*, *Cat on a Hot Tin Roof*, *Smoke on the Mountain*, *The Misanthrope*, and the role of Sonia in *Uncle Vanya*. Other directing work in Portland theatres includes *A Lie of the Mind* and *Ten November* at Storefront; *Long Day's Journey into Night*, *Hedda Gabler*, *She Stoops to Conquer*, *Hay Fever*, *Talley's Folly*, and *Crimes of the Heart* at the New Rose Theatre; *The Mound Builders*, *Toys in the Attic*, and *Angels Fall* at the Artists Repertory Theatre; *Division Street* and *The Sound of a Voice* at the IFCC. Acting roles include Teresa in *Italian American Reconciliation*, Edward/Victoria in *Cloud Nine*, Ruth in *The Norman Conquests*, Stella in *A Streetcar Named Desire*, Dull Gret/Angie in *Top Girls*, Armande in *The Learned Ladies*, and Holly in *Uncommon Women and Others*. Byington has assisted at the Young Vic in London and the Actors Theatre of St. Paul. A graduate of the Professional Director Training Program at Ohio University, she recently returned there to teach the program for one quarter.

Tisa Chang
Tisa Chang is artistic/producing director and founder of the Pan Asian Repertory Theatre. Following an active dancing and acting career on Broadway (*The Basic Training of Pavlo Hummel*, *Lovely Ladies and Kind Gentlemen*) and Off-Broadway, in television and films (*Escape from Iran*, *Ambush Bay*), Chang began directing at LaMama ETC, where she adapted the ground-breaking Peking Opera and bilingual hit *The Return of the Phoenix*, which was later recreated for CBS-TV. Chang founded Pan Asian Rep in 1977 to provide sustained and significant professional opportunities for Asian American theatre artists and has guided the organization to become a leader among the nation's Asian American Arts groups. At Pan Asian Rep, Chang's intercultural direction includes the monumental epic, *Teahouse*, spanning 50 years of modern Chinese history, *Ghashiram Kotwal*, using Marathi music and theatre techniques,

and the music-theatre *Cambodia Agonistes*, currently on tour. She has also introduced audiences to the works of such notable playwrights as Wakako Yamauchi, Momoko Iko, and Laurence Yep. Chang has received numerous awards, including the 1991 Barnard Medal of Distinction, the Association of Asian Pacific American Artists' JIMMIE Award, and a 1988 Special Theatre World Award on behalf of Pan Asian Rep. She is active in public service and has been invited to China, Japan, India, Korea, and the former Soviet Union.

Liz Diamond

Liz Diamond is a resident director of the Yale Repertory Theatre, where, since 1991, she has staged Janusz Glowacki's *Antigone in New York*, Moliere's *School for Wives*, Suzan-Lori Parks's *The America Play* (which later moved to the Public in New York), Brecht's *St. Joan of the Stockyards*, and Parks' *The Death of The Last Black Man in the Whole Entire World*. Other recent work includes *Julius Caesar* at Seattle Repertory Theatre; *Dream of a Common Language* at the Women's Project; Parks' *Imperceptible Mutabilities in the Third Kingdom* at BACA Downtown; *Betting on the Dust Commander*, also by Parks, at the Working Theatre; Brecht's *Good Person of Sichuan* at Juilliard and *A Man's a Man* at Portland Stage; *Hamlet's Ghosts Perform Hamlet* at Home for Contemporary Theatre; *The Hypothesis* at La Mama ETC; and *The Dispute* at the New Theatre of Brooklyn. Diamond has translated works by Pavel Kohout and Ireneusz Iredinski, and in 1984 she adapted and staged the American premiere of Samuel Beckett's *Fizzles* at PS 122. Diamond's productions have won several Obie Awards and Connecticut Critics Circle Awards, including two for outstanding direction (for *Imperceptible Mutabilities* and *St. Joan* respectively). She has won directing fellowships from the National Endowment for the Arts, the New York State Council on the Arts, the Jerome and the SDC Foundations. She has served as artistic associate of the Women's Project and as resident director of New Dramatists in New York. She has taught at New York University and Fordham and is now on the faculty of the Yale School of Drama.

Zelda Fichandler

Zelda Fichandler was founding director of Arena Stage in Washington, D.C., in 1950 and was its producing director through the close of its 1990-91 fortieth anniversary season. Her visionary artistic leadership inspired Arena's creative evolution, and by her history-making example and eloquence, she has become a leading national figure in the performing arts. Under her guidance, Arena Stage became one of America's most innovative resident theatres and one of the leading companies in the world. She has always been attracted to plays with a conscience as well as artistic sensibility and has strived to create a vital tension between new works and works from earlier generations that speak to our own times. She directed more than 50 of Arena's productions, including *Mrs. Klein*, *The Three Sisters*, *Death of a Salesman*, *An Enemy of the People*, *Six Characters in Search of an Author*, *A Doll's House*, and the American premiers of new Eastern European works, *Duck Hunting*, *The Ascent of Mt. Fuji*, and *Screenplay*. Her *Inherit the Wind* toured Moscow and Leningrad in 1973, the company performed her *After the Fall* at the 1980 Hong Kong Arts Festival, and in 1987 her production of *The Crucible* appeared at the Israel Festival in Jerusalem. Her concern for the development of young actors led her, in 1984, to take on the role of artistic director of the graduate acting program at New York University's Tisch School of the Arts, and she served as the artistic director of the Acting Company from July 1991 to May 1994. The link between professional and educational theatre is important to her as a means "to attract young people to the benefits of company work and to train them to perform in the broadest repertory." She has also had an ongoing dedication to commissioning and giving voice to important new plays by young as well as established playwrights. Fichandler has received the Common Wealth Award, the Acting Company's John Houseman Award, the Margo Jones Award, Washingtonian of the Year Award, and the Ortho 21st Century Women Trailblazer Award. In 1976 the New York commercial theatre world awarded her Arena Stage the Antoinette Perry (Tony) Award, the first to be given to a company outside New York. She is currently president of the board of directors of the Theatre Communications Group, an organization that serves America's not-for-profit theatre institutions.

Susan Finque

Susan Finque is an actor, director, and educator based in Seattle, where she has lived and worked for ten years as an active member of the professional theatre community. She was a cofounder and artistic director of the Alice B. Theatre, Seattle's Gay and Lesbian Theatre for All People, where her acting and directing work was distinctive in its emphasis on ensemble collaboration, new work, and site-specific performance. She was a member of the acting company of the Bathhouse Theatre for two seasons, and her work has been seen on the stages of On the Boards, *Allegro!* Dance Festival, A Contemporary Theatre, Cornish College of the Arts, University of Washington, Seattle Mime Theatre, and the Annex Theatre, among others. She has toured the U.S. with a circus vaudeville troupe, has performed extensively inside women's prisons and jails, and her solo work on transsexuality has toured North American performance venues to critical acclaim. She has guest-directed for the Pomo Afro Homos, assisting in the development of their work *Dark Fruit* for its premiere at the New York Shakespeare Festival, along with directing company member Djola Branner in his solo piece *Sweet Sadie: Blues for Mama*. She is committed to the performing arts as an arena for social change and to developing theatre artists who are empowered by their craft. She has a B.A. from the University of California at Santa Cruz in Theatre and its Communities and has received awards, fellowships, and residencies from local, regional, state, and national arts commissions. Finque is currently an assistant professor at Antioch College in Yellow Springs, Ohio, where she is teaching Cross-Gender Performance, Site Specific Improvisation, and other acting courses, along with facilitating a directors' seminar.

Maria Irene Fornes

Maria Irene Fornes is the author of more than two dozen works for the stage, among which are *Promenade, The Successful Life of 3, Fefu and Her Friends, Eyes on the Harem, The Danube, Mud, The Conduct of Life, Abingdon Square*, and *What of the Night*. These plays are performed throughout the United States and Europe. She is the recipient of seven Obie Awards, one of which was for sustained achievement. She is also the recipient of a Distinguished Artist Award from the National Endowment for the Arts, a New York State Governor's Arts Award, Honorary Doctor of Letters Degree, Bates College, Lewiston, Maine, a Distinguished Director's Award from the San Diego Theatre Critics Circle, and an Award for Distinguished Achievements as an Artist and Educator from the Association for Theatre in Higher Education. She has received grants and fellowships from the Rockefeller Foundation, the John Simon Guggenheim Memorial Foundation, CINTAS, and NEA among others. At present she is the recipient of a Lila Wallace Readers' Digest Literary Award. Fornes conducts playwriting workshops in theaters and universities throughout the U.S. and abroad. From 1973 to 1979, she was managing director for the New York Theater Strategy. Besides directing most of her own plays, she has directed plays by Calderon,

Ibsen, Chekhov, and several contemporary authors. Two volumes of her plays have been published by PAJ Publications; other plays have been included in various anthologies. She is a member of the Dramatists Guild and the Society of Stage Directors and Choreographers.

Rita Giomi

Rita Giomi is a Seattle-based free-lance director. In the Seattle area, she has been privileged to direct for the Empty Space, Seattle Children's Theatre, Stark/Raving Theatre, Alice B. Theatre, and the Tacoma Actors Guild among others. In addition, her credits include work with companies in Alaska, California, New Mexico, Colorado, Louisiana and Oregon. Giomi received her M.F.A. in directing from the University of Washington.

Tori Haring-Smith

Tori Haring-Smith is the dramaturg at Trinity Repertory Company in Providence, Rhode Island, and a professor at Brown University, where she teaches acting, directing, dramaturgy, and dramatic literature. She has directed for several years throughout the Northeast. In New York, she directed at the Women's Workshop and assisted Joseph Chaikin with Susan Yankowitz's *Night Sky*, produced by the Women's Project and Productions. Most recently, she directed *The Country Wife* at the Jean Cocteau Rep in New York, *An American Cocktail* (world premiere) at Trinity, *The Swan* and *Speed of Darkness* at Alias Stage, and Constance Congdon's *Tales of the Lost Formicans* at Brown University. Her translations of Chekhov's *The Seagull* and Moliere's *The Miser* premiered at Trinity, and Olympia Dukakis directed her *Seagull* at the Arizona Theatre Company in 1994. In the summer of 1994, she was the American dramaturg for the Third International Conference of Women Playwrights in Adelaide, Australia. She has published several books and articles on writing, teaching, and theatre, including *From Farce to Metadrama: A Stage History of the Taming of the Shrew, 1594–1983* (Greenwood), *Writing Together* (HarperCollins), and, most recently, *Monologues for Women by Women* (Heinemann). Her new translation of Eduardo deFelippo's *Napoli Milionaria* premiered in New York in January 1995.

Pamela R. Hendrick

Pamela R. Hendrick is an assistant professor of theatre at Stockton College of New Jersey, where she directs campus productions and teaches acting, directing, and related theatre courses. She turned to a full-time career in academic theatre following graduate work at Northwestern University, where she earned her M.F.A. in directing in 1994. The first fifteen years of her professional life were spent in Minneapolis, Minnesota. There she acted in a variety of professional and amateur theatres and worked, first as an actor and later as a director, for the Playwrights' Center of Minneapolis. The Playwrights' Center served the development of new plays by holding workshops and staging readings of new scripts. In 1980, Hendrick founded Theatre Three along with Cynthia White and Betsy Husting, and she acted as its artistic co-director until it closed in 1990. Theatre Three was a small professional theatre dedicated to showcasing the work of women artists, including playwrights, designers, directors, actors, and choreographers. Hendrick has also applied her theatre background to teaching a number of courses outside the theatre community, including conflict resolution in Minnesota public schools and seminars in nonverbal communication for women in abusive relationships. Her teaching and directing process have been strongly influenced by this work. In recent years she has been exploring the role of gender in performance as it relates to movement, gesture, vocal pattern, and syntax.

Brenda Hubbard

Brenda Hubbard brings over 22 years of experience in the professional theatre to her position as assistant professor of Theatre Arts at Central Washington University. Originally from Yellow Springs, Ohio, Hubbard has lived all over the country including five years in Portland, Oregon, where she served as the artistic director of the city's oldest Equity theatre, Portland Repertory Theatre. During her tenure at the Rep, she produced over 30 shows, directing 15 of them. She was instrumental in upgrading the company to professional status and established new systems for operation as an Equity theatre. She also expanded the artistic programming and established a resident company of artists. In addition to her work as an administrator and director, she has also maintained an accomplished career as an actor performing with such notable companies as Seattle Repertory Theatre, A Contemporary Theatre, Empty Space, Tacoma Actor's Guild, San Jose Repertory Theatre Company, and the Oregon Shakespeare Festival, where she performed for two seasons. Her most recent appearances have been as Josie in *A Moon for the Misbegotten*, Masha in *Chekhov in Yalta*, and Evelyn in *Independence*. Her most recent directing assignments include the critically acclaimed *Master Harold...and the Boys* at Central Washington University, and the controversial multimedia production of *Coriolanus* at the University of Portland. At Central Washington University, she teaches acting, voice, and directing, among several other subjects. Hubbard's undergraduate work includes a B.F.A. from the Professional Actor's Training Program at the University of Washington and an M.F.A. in directing from the University of Portland. A recipient of the Willamette Week Award for outstanding direction, a Poncho Scholarship, and a University of Washington Fellowship, Hubbard has also appeared in over 100 radio and television commercials and several films. She is currently doing research for a writing project which examines the effects of gender on musical theatre.

Elizabeth Huddle

Elizabeth Huddle is currently the producing artistic director for Portland Center Stage in Portland, Oregon. For the last three decades, she has acted or directed with such distinguished organizations as San Francisco's American Conservatory Theatre, Repertory Theatre of Lincoln Center, Sundance Institute, Oregon Shakespeare Festival, San Francisco Opera, San Diego's Old Globe Theater, and the Mark Taper Forum in Los Angeles. She has also appeared on Broadway and guest-starred on numerous television programs. While working in Los Angeles, she received two Los Angeles Drama Critic Circle Awards, one for her work in *Second Lady*, which she also performed at the Fringe Festival in Edinburgh, Scotland; the other for her six-month run in the title role of *Sister Mary Explains It All for You*, directed by Warner Shook. Huddle was artistic director of Intiman Theatre in Seattle from 1986 through 1992, where she directed *A Streetcar Named Desire*, *A Midsummer Night's Dream*, *The Rivals*, *Arms and the Man*, *Hamlet*, *Born Yesterday*, *The Last Unicorn*, (world premiere), and *Man and Superman*. While there, she also established an acting internship program with the Cornish School of the Arts and produced the original production of the 1992 Pulitzer Prize–winning play *The Kentucky Cycle*. Following her tenure as artistic director, she returned to acting, appearing in Intiman's productions of *Hay Fever*, *How the Other Half Loves*, as Lady Bracknell in *The Importance of Being Earnest*, and as Martha in *Who's Afraid of Virginia Woolf?* She also directed *Intimate Exchanges*. Other professional experience includes serving on the advisory board of the Gathering at Bigfork, a playwrights' conference in Montana; serving as an appointee to the King County Arts Commission; directing at the Playwrights Workshop at the Sundance Institute, and contributing her considerable experience as an on-site evaluator and panelist on the National Endowment for the Arts Large Theater Grants Panel. As a member of several Theatre Arts Department faculties, she has taught courses at the University of California at Davis, the University of Washington, and at the ACT Conservatory in San Francisco.

Bea Kiyohara

Bea Kiyohara received her undergraduate degree in theater from the University of Washington. She has been performing, directing , and producing in the Seattle area for twenty years. She was the artistic director of the Northwest Asian American Theatre for fifteen years. She has served as chair of the King County Arts Commission, is presently on the Seattle Arts Commission, and has served on numerous panels and juries. Kiyohara has been an educator for over twenty-five years, teaching in the K–12 system as well as counseling at the University of Washington and at Seattle Central Community College. She is presently the dean of Student Development Services at Seattle Central Community College.

Roberta Levitow

Roberta Levitow most recently directed *Moe's Lucky Seven* by Marlane Meyer at Playwrights Horizons, *Electra* by Euripedes (translation: John Chioles) for Trinity University/Stieren Guest Artist, and Marlane Meyer's *Why Things Burn* at the Magic Theatre in San Francisco. New York credits include *Memory Tricks* by and with Marga Gomez for NYSF, *Little Egypt* by Lynn Siefert and *Miriam's Flowers* by Migdalia Cruz for Playwrights Horizons, *Each Day Dies with Sleep* by Jose Rivera for Circle Rep, and Marlane Meyer's *Etta Jenks* for the Women's Project. Regional works include Darrah Cloud's *The Stick Wife* at the Hartford Stage Company and Connie Congdon's *Tales of the Lost Formicans* for the Actors Theatre of Louisville (and the International Theatre Institute Festival in Helsinki, Finland), as well as plays by Gary Leon Hill, Eric Overmyer, Marlane Meyer, Josefina Lopez, and Donald Margulies for the Denver Center Theatre Company, South Coast Rep, Asolo Theatre and the L.A. Theatre Center. She has worked in new play development at LATC, Mark Taper Forum, Mid-West Playlabs, and the SCR Hispanic Playwrights Project. She is a graduate of Stanford University and the American Film Institute's Directing Workshop for Women. Levitow is a recipient of the Alan Schneider Award for directing, is a member of the Society of Stage Directors and Choreography, and serves on the board of SSDC and Theater Communications Group.

Emily Mann

Emily Mann is in her fifth season as artistic director of McCarter Theatre, where she directed the critically acclaimed productions of *The Matchmaker*, *The Perfectionist*, *Twilight: Los Angeles,1992*, *Three Sisters*, *Cat on a Hot Tin Roof*, and *The Glass Menagerie*, adapted and directed Strindberg's *Miss Julie*; and directed the rhythm and blues musical *Betsey Brown*, which she co-wrote with Ntozake Shange, with music by Baikida Carroll. Last season, she directed the world premiere production of Anna Deavere Smith's *Twilight: Los Angeles, 1992* at the Mark Taper Forum, which was hailed by Newsweek as "an American masterpiece." Mann began her professional career as a resident director for the Guthrie Theater and the BAM Theater Company and subsequently has directed at leading regional theaters throughout the country, including the Mark Taper Forum, Actors Theatre of Louisville, Goodman Theatre, La Jolla Playhouse, American Music Theatre Festival, and the Hartford Stage Company. An accomplished writer, she made her Broadway debut as both playwright and director of *Execution of Justice*, which was nominated for a Drama Desk Award for Outstanding

New Play and received the Bay Area Theatre Critics Circle Award, the HBO/USA Award, and the 1986 Playwriting Award from the Woman's Committee of the Dramatists Guild. Her first play, *Annulla, an Autobiography*, premiered at the Guthrie and was also produced at the New Theatre of Brooklyn featuring Linda Hunt. Her play *Still Life* premiered at the Goodman Theatre in Chicago and opened off-Broadway at the American Place Theatre under her direction in 1981, winning six Obie Awards, including Distinguished Playwriting, Distinguished Direction, and Best Production, as well as the Fringe First Award for Best Play at the Edinburgh Festival. *Still Life* has been presented at major theaters throughout the United States and Europe. Her current projects include the screenplay *You Strike a Woman, You Strike a Rock: The Story of Winnie Mandela* and two new works for the stage, *The Greensboro Massacre* and the stage adaptation of the best-selling autobiography *Having Our Say: The Delaney Sisters First 100 Years*, which will have its world premiere at McCarter this season, then move to Broadway. Her numerous awards include the Helen Hayes Award, a Guggenheim, a Playwright's Fellowship and Artistic Associate grant from the National Endowment for the Arts. She is an associate artist of Crossroads Theater and past vice president of the board of Theatre Communications Group.

Diana Marré

Diana Marré has directed over twenty productions for professional and university theaters. Her most recent was a double bill of Adrienne Kennedy's *Funnyhouse of a Negro* and Amiri Baraka's *Dutchman*. Her play, *Hired Hands*, has had over a dozen productions, and she has performed her one-woman show, *A Really Big Shoe*, in Seattle, San Francisco, Oakland, and Washington, D.C. Former chair of the Black Theater Association, Marré has a Ph.D. in dramatic art from the University of California, Berkeley. She is currently working on a novel, *A Dyke Like Me*, which will be published by Spectrum Press.

Penny Metropulos

Penny Metropulos began her career as an actress and singer. She started singing as a child in Dallas, Texas, and by the age of nine she had toured with the Ted Weems Band and sung with Duke Ellington. Later she joined the Dallas Theater Center, and she trained at the London Academy of Music and Dramatic Art. Her acting credits include seasons with the Oregon Shakespeare Festival, the Arizona Theatre Company, and the Manitoba Theatre Center. Since she began directing, she has worked for the Oregon Shakespeare Festival, where she directed Edward Bond's *Restoration* and Terrence McNally's *Lips Together, Teeth Apart*, for which she won a Portland Theatre Critics award as best director. In three consecutive seasons with the Bay Area's California Shakespeare Festival, her productions have included *Richard II*, *The Winter's Tale*, and a multiple Dramalogue Award–winning production of *Two Gentlemen of Verona*. This year she directed both *Light Up the Sky* and *A Christmas Carol* for the Alabama Shakespeare Festival. Some of her other credits include *Macbeth* and *Taming of the Shrew* for the Illinois Shakespeare Festival, Caryl Churchill's *Vinegar Tom* for Cornell University, *Serious Money* for Cornish Institute, and *The Cocktail Hour* and *A Shaina Maidel* at the Portland Repertory Theatre in Oregon. She has also directed several musical revues and a production of *Tosca* which she produced and staged at the Oregon Shakespeare Festival for the Rogue Opera Company. Metropulos has had a continuing interest in education and outreach for the arts. For the past seven years, she has helped to develop and direct programs for the Oregon Shakespeare Festival's extensive school visit program. She has also been an artist in residence at CalArts, Arizona State University, and Humboldt State University. While a member of the acting company at the Arizona Theatre Company, she founded and was executive director for their outreach program, *Encompass*. Metropulos will be directing *Merry Wives of Windsor* at the Oregon Shakespeare Festival for the 1995 season as well as *Much Ado About Nothing* for the California Shakespeare Festival. Currently she is directing *Othello* for the Acting Company in New York. She lives in Ashland, Oregon, with actor Richard Howard.

Gloria Muzio

Gloria Muzio has directed new plays and classics on and off Broadway and at regional theatres throughout the country. At the Roundabout Theatre on Broadway, Muzio directed *Candida*, starring Mary Steenburgen and Robert Sean Leonard, and Tom Stoppard's *Fifteen Minute Hamlet* and *The Real Inspector Hound*. Muzio was awarded the Joe A. Callaway Award and was nominated for an Outer Critics Circle Award for her direction of the long-running, Off-Broadway *Other People's Money*. Other NYC theatre includes the premiers of *Desdemona* by Paula Vogel and *The Truth-Teller* by Joyce Carol Oates at Circle Rep, the musical *Bubba Meises, Bubbe Stories* by Ellen Gould at the Cherry Lane (and its subsequent national tour), *Approximating Mother* by Kathleen Tolan at the Women's Project, *Price of Fame* by and starring Charles Grodin, several Young Playwrights Festivals at Playwrights Horizons (including most recently *Basement at the Bottom* by Nadine Graham), and *Dearly Departed* at the Second Stage. Regionally, she has directed classics and new plays at the Actors Theatre of Louisville (including the critically acclaimed *Below the Belt* by Richard Dresser and *Loving Daniel Boone*, aka *D. Boone*, by Marsha Norman), Hartford Stage Company, Long Wharf Theatre, Philadelphia Drama Guild, San Francisco's Magic Theatre, and others. She has also participated for several summers in the Sundance Institute's Playwright's Lab, where she has directed and helped develop several new plays. Muzio is a member of the Circle Repertory Company and an executive board member for the Society of Stage Directors and Choreographers. She was educated at Mount Holyoke College and has an M.F.A. in directing from Florida State University School of Theatre

Timothy Near

Timothy Near is in her eighth season as artistic director at San Jose Repertory Theatre. Her many directing credits at San Jose Rep include *The Caretaker, The Baby Dance, The Little Foxes, The 1940's Radio Hour, Oedipus the King, The Sea Gull*, and the world premiere of *Fire in the Rain ... Singer in the Storm*. She has recently added to her acting credits her San Jose Rep debut in the role of Anna in *Toys in the Attic*. She has acted and directed at numerous prestigious theatres, among them the Guthrie Theatre, Berkeley Rep, La Jolla Playhouse, Alliance Theatre in Atlanta, Mark Taper Forum in L.A., Ford's Theatre in Washington, D.C., Repertory Theatre of St. Louis, New York Shakespeare Festival, and Stage West in Massachusetts. She has received Hollywood Drama-Logue awards for her direction of *Ghost on Fire* at La Jolla Playhouse and *Fire in the Rain ... Singer in the Storm* at the Mark Taper Forum. A native of northern California, she is a graduate of San Francisco State University.

Sharon Ott

Sharon Ott is in her eleventh year as artistic director of the Berkeley Repertory Theatre. Last season she directed the Rep's world premiere production of *The Woman Warrior*, which was recently presented at the Huntington Theatre in Boston and which in February 1995 moved to the Center Theatre Group/Doolittle Theatre in Los Angeles. As artistic director, Ott has seen two plays of Philip Kan Gotanda to their premiere productions (*Yankee Dawg You Die*, which she directed, and *Fish Head Soup*, directed by Oskar Eustis), as well as premieres by Quincy Long, Jose Rivera, Laurence Yep, Neal Bell, Heather McDonald, and Geoff Hoyle. Ott has directed 20 plays at the Rep. Favorites include *The Lady from the Sea*, *The Illusion*, *Fuente Ovejuna*, *The Road To Mecca*, *Twelfth Night*, *The Tooth of Crime* and *Dream of a Common Language*. She has directed at theatres in Los Angeles, New York, Chicago, Milwaukee, Seattle, San Diego, Washington, D.C., and Boston and has received several Bay Area Theatre Critics Circle and Hollywood Drama-Logue awards as well as citations from the San Diego Theatre Critics Association and an Obie Award. Ott is former vice president of Theatre Communications Group and served as a panelist for the NEA, California Arts Council, and Center for the International Exchange of Scholars (Fulbright Fellowships).

Victoria Parker

Victoria Parker has over twenty years' experience as a performer and instructor, including twelve years' teaching experience at Portland State University. A graduate of the International Improvisation School in Calgary, Alberta, she has been associated with an international network of improvisational performers and trainers organized and licensed through International Theatre Sports®. She is a recognized trainer/director in this innovative improvisational form. In her six years as an artist in the schools with Young Audiences of Oregon, Parker has worked with diverse populations in grades K–12 as a performer and workshop leader. Most recently she has served as a resident artist with a special focus on programs for at-risk youth. Her directorial credits in Oregon and Washington include *When You Comin' Back, Red Ryder?* (for which she won a Willamette Week award for best direction), *Buried Child*, *For Colored Girls Who Have Considered Suicide When the Rainbow Is Enuff*, *A Life in the Theatre*, *Remember Where You Started From*, and *Shirley Valentine*. She is the founding co-director of Theatre Group for Humanity and a member of Waggie and Friends Improvisational Comedy Group. She also served one season as the artistic director of Storefront Actor's Theatre. She has been awarded the Portland Drama Critics Circle Awards for Best Supporting Actress and Best New Script (1991). Her current projects center around theatre communication in the context of social service and direction of theatre in small communities throughout the Pacific Northwest region.

Adele Prandini

Adele Prandini is in her fourth season as artistic director of Theatre Rhinoceros in San Francisco. She was the founder of It's Just a Stage, a lesbian theatre company, in 1974 and worked as a writer, director, and performer with IJAS until 1980. She is the author of *A Safe Light* (1984) and *Coconut* (1994). She is coauthor of *The Mountain is Stirring* (1980), written with Iris Landsberg, and *Pulp and Circumstance* (1987), written with Sue Zemel. Her monologue "Mama's Boy" was featured in *The AIDS Show* (1984) and *Unfinished Business* (1985). She has written two scripts for Make a Circus, which toured throughout California. Her directing credits include *Wild Blue* by Joe Pintauro, *Waiting for Godette* by Christian Huygen, *Queen of Swords* by Judy Grahn, *Pulp and Circumstances* by Prandini/Zemel, *Porcelain* by Chay Yew, and *Karla and Grif* by Vivienne Laxdal. She has been a recipient of Bay Area Theatre Critics Circle and Hollywood Drama-Logue awards. She was also the first artist recipient of the newly established LAVA award presented by Bay Area Career Women.

Mary B. Robinson

Mary B. Robinson is the former artistic director of the Philadelphia Drama Guild. The productions she directed for the Drama Guild include *Othello*, *Dancing at Lughnasa*,

Nora, The Misanthrope, A Moon for the Misbegotten, Macbeth, Boesman and Lena, and *A Midsummer Night's Dream*. Recently she also directed the premiere of Jeffrey Hatcher's *Three Viewings* at the Manhattan Theatre Club. From 1980 to 1985, she worked as associate artistic director at Hartford Stage, and in 1986 she received a Drama Desk nomination for her direction of Lanford Wilson's *Lemon Sky* (with Jeff Daniels and Jill Eikenberry) at Second Stage in New York. Her production of *A Shayna Maidel* ran for 15 months Off-Broadway. She has directed at regional theaters around the country and received national recognition as the first recipient of the Alan Schneider Award. She and her husband, playwright Erik Brogger, live in Philadelphia with their son Christopher.

Seret Scott

Seret Scott directed *A Raisin in the Sun* at the George Street Play House/Ford Theatre in 1995. In 1994 she directed *Zooman and the Sign* for the Second Stage Company in New York. Other directing credits include *Madam Mao's Memories* for the Old Globe Theatre, *My Children, My Africa* for Studio Arena Theatre, *So Long on Lonely Street* at the Alliance Theatre, *Shirley Valentine* for the Indiana Repertory Theatre, *Poof!* at the Humana Festival, *From the Mississippi Delta* at the Alley Theatre, the Old Globe Theatre, and the Virginia Stage Company, *Sweetbitter Baby* and *I'm Not Stupid* for the Young Playwright's Festival, *Fences* at the Capitol Repertory Company and New Mexico Repertory Theatre, *Some Sweet Day* at the Long Wharf Theatre, *Spooks* for the Crossroads Theatre Company, and *A Matter of Conscience* at the National Black Theatre.

Fontaine Syer

Fontaine Syer is the associate artistic director at the Oregon Shakespeare Festival. In two seasons, she has directed *Mad Forest, The Playboy of the Western World*, and *The Pool of Bethesda*. In other theatres she has directed *That Championship Season, As You Like It, Lenny, The Hostage, Waiting for Godot, Getting Out, A Taste of Honey, Loose Ends, Spoon River Anthology, A Child's Christmas in Wales, Butley, A Moon for the Misbegotten, Bent, Lone Star/Laundry and Bourbon, Translations, You Can't Take It With You, Footfalls, Rockaby, Painting Churches, Hamlet* (all at the Theatre Project Company, St. Louis); *Still Life* (Repertory Theatre of St. Louis); *Quilters* (Pennsylvania Centre Stage); *The Boys Next Door, Arsenic and Old Lace* (New American Theatre, Rockford); *The Voice of the Prairie, A Christmas Carol* (Alliance Theatre Company, Atlanta); *Takunda* (St. Louis Black Repertory Company); *A Streetcar Named Desire, A Midsummer Night's Dream, Arms and the Man* (Mount Holyoke College, South Hadley). Syer was cofounder and artistic director of the Theatre Project Company from 1975 to 1989; directed *Under Milkwood, A Christmas Memory* and *The Thanksgiving Visitor* for KWMU-FM (NPR) in St. Louis; taught acting, improvisation, and theatre history at Mount Holyoke College, acting and scene study at the University of Missouri (St. Louis), arts management at Washington University (St. Louis), master class and scene study at the Alliance Theatre Company. She holds an M.A. in directing and a B.A. in theatre arts from Mount Holyoke College.

Julie Taymor

Julie Taymor directs for theatre, opera, film, and television. For TFANA, she directed *The Tempest* and *The Taming of the Shrew*. She directed Mozart's *Die Zauberflote* for the Maggio Musicale in Florence, Zubin Mehta conducting. In 1992-93, she directed Stravinsky's *Oedipus Rex*, conducted by Seiji Ozawa and starring Jessye Norman, in Japan. The film of the opera aired on "Great Performances," as well as European and

Japanese television. She directed and adapted *Fool's Fire*, based on an Edgar Allan Poe story, for PBS's "American Playhouse." For the theatre, Taymor recently directed *Titus Andronicus* for the New York Shakespeare Festival and directed, designed, and co-wrote *Juan Darien* with Elliot Goldenthal (produced by the Music Theater Group). The recipient of two Obies as well as numerous other awards, it toured festivals in Edinburgh, France, Jerusalem, Montreal, and San Francisco. Other credits include *The Transposed Heads* at Lincoln Center; *Liberty's Taken* at Castle Hill Festival; and the upcoming film adaptations of *Juan Darien* and *The Transposed Heads*. Taymor's awards include the 1994 International Classical Music Award for Best Opera Production and a 1993 Emmy Award for *Oedipus Rex*; a 1988 Obie Award for *Juan Darien*; a 1985 Obie award for *Visual Magic*; the Brandeis Creative Arts Award; and the 1990 Dorothy Chandler Performing Arts Award. She was awarded a MacArthur Foundation Fellowship in 1992 and a Guggenheim Fellowship in 1990. In June of 1995, Taymor will be directing Strauss's *Salome* for the Kirov Opera in St. Petersburg, followed in September by Wagner's *The Flying Dutchman* for the Los Angeles Opera. Abrams is publishing a book on Taymor's work that will be available in the fall of 1995.

Barbara Ann Teer
Dr. Barbara Ann Teer and her National Black Theatre are a pioneering force in the world of culture, art, theatre, education, and business. Under Teer's guidance and direction, the National Black Theatre was established in 1968. During its 26 years in existence, Teer and her company toured Africa, South America, the Caribbean, and the United States as theatrical anthropologists documenting and articulating via theatrical performance the indigenous rituals and traditions of Africans of the diaspora. As an individual artist, Teer has studied abroad and is the recipient of numerous awards and citations. Her theatre has developed and emerged as an innovator in American theatre. Teer received a degree in dance education from the University of Illinois with highest honors and studied in Germany, Switzerland, and Paris. Her first show was choreographed by Agnes DeMille, and with Teer as dance captain, it won a Tony Award. She studied drama with, among other leading directors, Lloyd Richards, former dean of the Yale School of Drama. A recipient of 30 awards and citations, Teer is included in *Who's Who In America*. She performed on Broadway, was the cofounder, with actors Robert Hooks and Douglas Ward, of the Negro Ensemble Company, and contributed drama articles to numerous publications, including the *New York Times* and *Black World*. She has received honorary doctorate degrees in law and letters from the University of Rochester and the University of Southern Illinois.

Susana Tubert
Susana Tubert was awarded the 1991-92 Theatre Communications Group/National Endowment for the Arts Director Fellowship, presented to only six directors across the country. Since then, she's worked extensively at regional theatres and in NYC, where she resides. Regional credits include a workshop production of *Unmerciful Good Fortune* at Seattle Repertory Theatre and its premiere at the Victory Gardens/North Light Theatre Co. in Chicago, *Someone Who'll Watch Over Me* by Frank McGuiness at South Coast Rep (California), *Shakespeare Rock and Roles* by Jim Luigs at the Actors Theatre of Louisville (Kentucky), *Crumbs from the Table of Joy* by Lynne Nottage and *Migrant Moon* by James Farrell at the Sundance Institute (Utah), *The Last Living Newspaper* by Dale Worsley at the Theatre of the First Amendment/George Mason University (Virginia), *Accelerando* by Lisa Loomer and *Cultural Act* by Ignacio Cabrujas at the Gala Hispanic Theatre (D.C.), *Real Women Have Curves* by Josefina Lopez

at Seattle's Multicultural Theatre (Washington), at the Guadalupe Cultural Arts Center of San Antonio (Texas) and the American Theatre Festival (New Jersey), *Heroes and Saints* by Cherrie Moraga (opening production at the XVI Tenaz Chicano/Latino Theatre Festival), *We All Have the Same Story* by Dario Fo/Franca Rame at the National Theatre of Santo Domingo. New York credits include *And Now Miguel* by Lynne Alvarez at Lincoln Center Institute (residency at the Kennedy Center scheduled for spring 1995), *The Crossroads* by Juan Tovar, produced by Ensemble International Theatre at the Tribeca Performing Arts Center, *Real Women Have Curves* at Repertory Español, *The Road* by Eddie Sanchez, *Reinventing Daddy* by Gary Bonasorte and *Bad Boating* by Annie Evans at Circle Rep Lab, *but there are fires* by Caridad Svich at The Women's Project and Productions, *Picture Perfect* by Pablo Salinas at the Pearl Theatre, the musicals *Chinese Charade* and *The English Only Restaurant* at the Puerto Rican Traveling Theatre (the latter premiered at the Kennedy Center), and assistant to director Stanley Donan on the Broadway musical *The Red Shoes*. Tubert is a member of directors' forums at the Women's Project, Circle Rep Lab, NYTW, and has served on the N.Y. State Council on the Arts theatre panel for three years. As a writer/composer, she had two musicals for children, *A Day in the Life of a Robot* and *Let's Take Back Our Planet*, produced by the Don Quijote Experimental Children's Theatre. As a TCG/NEA Director Fellow, she assisted Harold Prince on *Kiss of the Spider Woman*, Peter Sellars on the opera *Saint Francois* at the Salzburg Music Festival, and Marshall Mason on Lanford Wilson's *Redwood Curtain*. Tubert teaches an ongoing actors' workshop through the Hispanic Organization of Latino Actors (HOLA) in NYC.

Cynthia White
Cynthia White is currently an associate director and director of new play development at the Oregon Shakespeare Festival, Ashland, Oregon. In nine seasons she has directed *A Midsummer Night's Dream, Toys in the Attic, Woman in Mind, The Voice of the Prairie*, and *Ballerina*, and as part of the 1995 season she will direct the premiere production of *Emma's Child* by Kristine Thatcher. Credits at other theatres include *Shadowlands* (Pioneer Theatre Company); *A Streetcar Named Desire* (Utah Shakespearean Festival); *Our Town* (Alabama Shakespeare Festival); *Blithe Spirit* and *Pack of Lies* (Portland Repertory Theatre); *The Merry Wives of Windsor* and *A Touch of the Poet* (Idaho Shakespeare Festival); *The Tempest* and *Cymbeline* (Virginia Shakespeare Festival); *A Shayna Maidel* (Actors' Project, Reno); *The Couch, Butler County, Native Speech* and *The Foreigner* (Stage #1, Dallas); *Spokesong* (New Arts Theatre, Dallas); *Mass Appeal* (New Stage Theatre, Jackson, Mississippi); *The Merchant of Venice, Lu Ann Hampton Laverty Oberlander* (University of Washington, Seattle); *A Midsummer Night's Dream* (Texas Shakespeare Festival); *The Comedy of Errors* (University of Evansville, Indiana); *The Taming of the Shrew* (Cornish College of the Arts, Seattle); *The Miss Firecracker Contest* and *Cloud Nine* (Southern Oregon State College, Ashland); *Toys in the Attic* and *Old Times* (Theatre Three, Minneapolis); *Misalliance, Sea Marks*, and *Hands Across the Sea* (Southern Methodist University, Dallas). White was a cofounder of Theatre Three (Minneapolis) with Pamela Hendrick and Betsy Husting. She has an M.F.A. in directing from Southern Methodist University and a B.A. in theatre arts from Lawrence University. White is currently president of the Shakespeare Theatre Association of America. A member of the Society of Stage Directors and Choreographers, she resides in Ashland with her husband, Dan Kremer, and their daughter Kate.

NOTES

Preface

1. Rebecca Daniels Adams, *Perceptions of Women Stage Directors Regarding the Influence of Gender in the Artistic Process*, diss., University of Oregon, 1992; Ann Arbor: UMI, 1993, 3517726.) Twenty-one women were interviewed for the original study between December 1991 and April 1992. Another fourteen interviews took place between March 1993 and October 1994 because of the generous grant sponsorship of St. Lawrence University, Canton, New York. I was also able to interview Julia Miles, artistic director of New York's Women's Project and Productions about her perceptions of the issues facing the women directors she has worked with as a producer. I also corresponded with two other directors, Diane Olson Dieter and Sue Lawless, who were not formally interviewed but whose opinions are included here.

2. Toby Cole and Helen Krich Chinoy, eds., *Directors on Directing*, rev. ed. (Indianapolis: Bobbs Merrill, 1963). Included are references to the work of Joan Littlewood (390–401) and Margaret Webster (418–20).

3. J. Robert Wills, ed., *The Director in a Changing Theatre: Essays on Theory and Practice, with New Plays for Performance* (Palo Alto: Mayfield, 1976).

4. Arthur Bartow, *The Director's Voice: Twenty-One Interviews* (New York: Theatre Communications Group, 1988). Included are interviews with JoAnne Akalaitis, Martha Clarke, and Zelda Fichandler.

5. Shirlee Hennigen, "Women Directors—The Early Years," *Women in the American Theatre*, rev. ed., eds. Helen Krich Chinoy and Linda Walsh Jenkins (New York: Theatre Communications Group, 1986), 203–6.

6. Susan Letzler Cole, *Directors in Rehearsal: A Hidden World* (New York: Routledge, Chapman and Hall, 1992). Directors featured include JoAnne Akalaitis, Maria Irene Fornes, Elizabeth Le Compte, Emily Mann, and Elinor Renfield.

7. Ellen Donkin and Susan Clement, eds., *Upstaging Big Daddy: Directing Theater as if Gender and Race Matter* (Ann Arbor: University of Michigan Press, 1993).

8. Helen Krich Chinoy, "Women Backstage and Out Front," in *Women in the American Theatre*, Chinoy and Jenkins, 358.

9. Jill Dolan, *The Feminist Spectator as Critic* (Ann Arbor: UMI Research Press, 1988), 3–16. Liberal feminism argues that working within the existing male-created structure will eventually create parity for women. Cultural or radical feminism sees clear and innate differences between men and women and proposes feminity as inherently superior to masculinity. Materialist feminism considers gender a social construct

231

for both women and men and looks at women as a class oppressed by material conditions and social relations.

10. Carol Gilligan, *In a Different Voice: Psychological Theory and Women's Development* (Cambridge: Harvard University Press, 1982), 14.

Chapter 1

1. Bartow, *Director's Voice*, xi–xii.
2. George Black, *Contemporary Stage Directing* (Fort Worth: Holt, Rinhart and Winston, 1991), v.
3. Joe Papp, "Staging Shakespeare: A Survey of Current Problems and Opinions," in *Directors on Directing*, Cole and Chinoy, 431.
4. Richard Trousdell, "Directing as Analysis of Situation," *Theatre Topics* vol. 2, no. 1 (March 1992): 25.
5. Robert Benedetti, *The Director at Work* (Englewood Cliffs, N.J.: Prentice-Hall, 1985), 3.
6. Robert Cohen and John Harrop, *Creative Play Direction*, 2d ed. (Englewood Cliffs, N.J.: Prentice-Hall, 1984), 10.
7. R. H. O'Neill and N. M. Boretz, *The Director as Artist: Play Direction Today* (New York: Holt, Rinehart and Winston, 1987), 1.
8. O'Neill and Boretz, *Director as Artist*, 282.
9. Douglas B. Hendel, "Actor Preferences for Director Behavior (Ph.D. diss., Bowling Green State University, 1986), 74.
10. I am indebted to Richard Trousdell's "Directing as Analysis of Situation" (*Theatre Topics* [March 1992]) and Brenda Marshall's dissertation "The Semiotic Phenomenology of Directing (South Illinois University, 1988) for corroboration of my own observations about the discernable patterns in the pedagogy of directing. I'm sure there are others who have ascertained the same patterns.
11. Cohen and Harrop, *Creative Play Direction*, 1.
12. Benedetti, *Director at Work*, 9.
13. O'Neill and Boretz, *Director as Artist*, xv–xviii.

Chapter 2

1. Carol Gilligan, *In a Different Voice: Psychological Theory and Women's Development* (Cambridge: Harvard University Press, 1982), 62.
2. Deborah Tannen, *You Just Don't Understand: Women and Men in Conversation* (New York: William Morrow, 1990), 26.

Chapter 3

1. This theme runs consistently through the writings of Sue-Ellen Case, *Feminism and Theatre* (New York: Methuen, 1988); Jill Dolan, *The Feminist Spectator as Critic* (Ann Arbor: UMI Research Press, 1988); and Toril Moi, *Sexual/Textual Politics: Feminist Literary Theory* (London: Routledge, 1985), among others.
2. Heather McDonald, *Dream of a Common Language* (New York: Samuel French, 1993), 55-56.
3. Michele Pierce, "Sharon Ott: Don't Fence Her In," *American Theatre* (May/June 1994): 20.

Chapter 4

1. Vladimir Nemirovich-Danchenko, "The Three Faces of the Director," in *Directors on Directing*, ed. Toby Cole and Helen Krich Chinoy, 120 (Indianapolis: Bobbs Merrill, 1963).

2. André Antoine, "Behind the Fourth Wall," in *Directors on Directing*, Cole and Chinoy, 89–102.

3. Jacques Copeau, "Dramatic Economy," in *Directors on Directing*, Cole and Chinoy, 214–225.

4. Alexander Tairov, "The Director," in *The Director in a Changing Theatre: Essays on Theory and Practice, with New Plays for Performance*, ed. J. Robert Wills, 54 (Palo Alto: Mayfield, 1976).

5. Gordon Craig, "The Artist of the Theatre," in *Directors on Directing*, Cole and Chinoy, 147–63.

6. Robert Cohen and John Harrop, *Creative Play Direction*, 2d. Ed. (Englewood Cliffs, N.J.: Prentice-Hall, 1984), 1.

7. Robert Benedetti, *The Director at Work* (Englewood Cliffs, N.J.: Prentice-Hall, 1985), 23–24.

8. Benedetti, *Director at Work*, 6.

9. R. H. O'Neill and N. M. Boretz, *The Director as Artist: Play Direction Today* (New York: Holt, Rinehart and Winston, 1987), 244.

10. Francis Hodge, *Play Directing: Analysis, Communication and Style* (Englewood Cliffs, N.J.: Prentice-Hall, 1971), 69–70.

11. Alexander Dean and Lawrence Carra, *Fundamentals of Play Directing*, 5th ed. (New York: Holt, Rinehart and Winston, 1989), 20.

12. Misha Berson, "Women at the Helm," *American Theatre* (May/June 1994): 66.

13. Simi Horwitz, "Inside the Secret Garden: Women Directors Make Inroads on Broadway," *Theatre Week*, 10 February 1992, 24.

14. Misha Berson, "What Makes Sharon Run?" *American Theatre* (July/August 1993): 17.

15. Berson, "Women at the Helm," 66.

Chapter 5

1. Julia Miles, personal interview, 26 March 1993. Although not working as a director herself, Julia Miles, founder and artistic director of the Women's Project and Productions in New York, was supportive and insightful in her discussion of issues for women directors in today's theatre. Her organization, which encourages and produces work by women in the theatre, including work by many of the women interviewed in this book, is currently in its seventeenth year. According to Miles, the Woman's Project was started primarily for women playwrights because that was the need she perceived at the time, but after a couple of years she also realized that there weren't very many women directors, so she also started working with women directors.

2. Miles interview.

3. Robert Coe, "The Once and Future Trinity," *American Theatre* (June 1990): 59–60.

4. Diane Olson Dieter, letter to the author, February 1992.

Chapter 6

1. Alexander Tairov, "The Director," in *The Director in a Changing Theatre: Essays on Theory and Practice, with New Plays for Performance*, ed. J. Robert Wills, (Indianapolis: Bobbs-Merrill, 1963) 53.
2. Jacques Copeau, "Dramatic Economy," in *Directors on Directing*, rev. ed., eds. Toby Cole and Helen Krich Chinoy, (Indianapolis: Bobbs-Merrill, 1963) 219.
3. Tyrone Guthrie, "An Audience of One," *Directors on Directing*, in Cole and Chinoy, 255–56.
4. Robert Benedetti, *The Director at Work* (Englewood Cliffs, N.J.: Prentice-Hall, 1985), 4.
5. Benedetti, *Director at Work*, 5-6.
6. Arthur Bartow, *The Director's Voice: Twenty-One Interviews* (New York: Theatre Communications Group, 1988), 114.
7. Benedetti, *Director at Work*, 109–10.
8. Robert Cohen and John Harrop, *Creative Play Direction*, 2d ed. (Englewood Cliffs, N.J.: Prentice-Hall, 1984), 9–10. The phrase "first among equals" is also attributed to Alan Schneider in R. H. O'Neill and N. M. Boretz, *The Director as Artist: Play Direction Today* (New York: Holt, Rinehart and Winston, 1987), 248.
9. Emily Mann as quoted by Hilary de Vries, "Creating a Theatre of Different American Voices," *New York Times*, 13 January 1991, S2, 26.
10. Carol Gilligan, *In a Different Voice: Psychological Theory and Women's Development* (Cambridge: Harvard University Press, 1982), 32. Gilligan uses a case study of two eleven-year-old children to contrast the boy's sense of hierarchical ordering (using imagery of winning and losing and potential for violence) with the girl's relational view of the same situation (using imagery of a network, a web of relationships that is sustained by a process of communication).
11. Julia Miles, interview with author, 26 March 1993.

Chapter 7

1. Clare Venables, "The Woman Director in the Theatre," *Theatre Quarterly* 10, no. 38 (summer 1980): 5.
2. Fichandler is referring to a landmark report compiled by Theatre Communications Group based on a series of nationwide meetings with artistic directors from America's regional theatres. Excerpts from the report can be found in "The Artistic Home: Discussions with Artistic Directors of America's Institutional Theatre," Todd London, *American Theatre* (March 1988).
3. Des McAnnuff, "The Time of Zelda Fichandler," *American Theatre* (March 1991): 61.
4. Sue Lawless as quoted in "Taking Vep in the Right Direction, *Front Row Center* (program for George Street Playhouse), February 1989.
5. Sue Lawless, letter to the author, March 11, 1992.

Chapter 8

1. Simi Horwitz, "Inside the Secret Garden: Women Directors Make Inroads on Broadway," *Theatre Week*, 10 February 1992, 22.
2. Sue-Ellen Case, *Feminism and Theatre* (New York: Methuen, 1988). Chapter Seven discusses the concerns of the new poetics in great detail.

3. Jill Dolan, *The Feminist Spectator as Critic* (Ann Arbor: UMI Research Press), 49.
4. Case, *Feminism and Theatre*, 18.
5. Dolan, *Feminist Spectator*, 5.
6. Dolan, *Feminist Spectator*, 33.

Chapter 11

1. Sue Lawless, letter to the author, 27 January 1992.
2. Julia Miles, personal interview, 26 March 1993.

BIBLIOGRAPHY

Adams, Rebecca Daniels. "Perceptions of Women Stage Directors Regarding the Influence of Gender in the Artistic Process." Ph.D. diss., University of Oregon, 1992. Ann Arbor: UMI, 1993.

Akalaitis, JoAnne. "Cross Currents in American Theatre." Reed College. Portland, 30 January 1992.

_____. Telephone interview. 2 April 1992.

Antoine, André. "Behind the Fourth Wall." In *Directors on Directing*, rev. ed., edited by Toby Cole and Helen Krich Chinoy, 89–102. Indianapolis: Bobbs Merrill, 1963.

Appino, Nikki. Personal interview. 19 December 1991.

Bartow, Arthur. *The Director's Voice: Twenty One Interviews*. New York: Theatre Communications Group, 1988.

Benedetti, Robert. *The Director at Work*. Englewood Cliffs, N.J.: Prentice-Hall, 1985.

Bensussen, Melia. Telephone interview. 10 March 1994.

Berson, Misha. "What Makes Sharon Run?" *American Theatre* (July/August 1993): 14-19.

_____. "Women at the Helm." *American Theatre* (May/June 1994): 14–21+.

Black, George. *Contemporary Stage Directing*. Fort Worth: Holt, Rinehart and Winston, 1991.

Blackmon, Michelle. Personal interview. 5 March 1992.

Blem, Patricia. Personal interview. 30 December 1991.

Bogart, Anne. Personal interview. 14 October 1994.

Boyd, Julianne. Telephone interview. 5 April 1992.

Bradby, David, and David Williams. *Directors' Theatre*. Houndmills: Macmillan, 1988.

Byington, Alana. Personal interview. 2 January 1992.

Case, Sue-Ellen. *Feminism and Theatre*. New York: Methuen, 1988.

Chang, Tisa. Personal interview. 13 October 1994.

Chinoy, Helen Krich. "The Emergence of the Director." Cole and Chinoy, 3–77.

_____. "Women Backstage and Out Front." Chinoy and Jenkins. 353–363.

Chinoy, Helen Krich, and Linda Walsh Jenkins, eds. *Women in American Theatre*. Rev. edition. New York: Theatre Communications Group, 1987.

Coe, Robert. "The Once and Future Trinity." *American Theatre* (June 1990): 12–21+.

Cole, Susan Letzler. *Directors in Rehearsal: A Hidden World*. New York: Routledge, Chapman and Hall, 1992.

Cole, Toby, and Helen Krich Chinoy, eds. *Directors on Directing*. Rev. ed. Indianapolis: Bobbs Merrill, 1963.

Copeau, Jacques. "Dramatic Economy." Cole and Chinoy, 214–25.
Craig, Gordon. "The Artist of the Theatre." Cole and Chinoy, 147–63.
Dean, Alexander, and Lawrence Carra. *Fundamentals of Play Directing.* 5th ed. New York: Holt, Rinehart and Winston, 1989.
deVries, Hilary. "Creating a Theatre of Different American Voices." *New York Times,* 13 January 1991, sec. 2, 5+.
Diamond, Liz. Personal interview. 25 March 1993.
Dieter, Diane Olson. Letter to the author, February 1992.
Dolan, Jill. *The Feminist Spectator as Critic.* Ann Arbor: UMI Research Press, 1988.
Donkin, Ellen and Susan Clement, eds. *Upstaging Big Daddy: Directing Theatre as if Race and Gender Matter.* Ann Arbor: University of Michigan Press, 1993.
Fichandler, Zelda. Personal interview. 24 March 1994.
Finque, Susan. Personal interview. 18 December 1991.
Fornes, Maria Irene. Personal interview. 17 February 1992.
Gilligan, Carol. *In a Different Voice: Psychological Theory and Women's Development.* Cambridge: Harvard University Press, 1982.
Giomi, Rita. Personal interview. 18 December 1991.
Guthrie, Tyrone. "An Audience of One." Cole and Chinoy, 245–56.
Haring-Smith, Tori. Personal interview. 5 March 1994.
Hendel, Douglas B. "Actor Preferences for Director Behavior." Ph.D. diss., Bowling Green State University, 1986.
Hendrick, Pamela. Personal interview. 8 October 1994.
Hennigen, Shirlee. "The Woman Director in the Contemporary Professional Theatre." Ph.D. diss., Washington State University, 1983.
____. "Women Directors—The Early Years." Chinoy and Jenkins, 203–6.
Hodge, Francis. *Play Directing: Analysis, Communication and Style.* Englewood Cliffs, N.J.: Prentice-Hall, 1971.
Horwitz, Simi. "Inside the Secret Garden: Women directors makes inroads on Broadway." *Theatre Week,* 10 February 1992, 22–27.
Hubbard, Brenda. Personal interview. 2 January 1992.
Huddle, Elizabeth. Telephone interview. 11 March 1992.
Kiyohara, Bea. Personal interview. 19 December 1991.
Langworthy, Douglas. "Timothy Near: Sailing Beautifully." *American Theatre* (May/June 1994): 19.
Lawless, Sue. Letters to the author, 27 January 1992 and 11 March 1992.
Levitow, Roberta. Letter to the author, 23 February 1992.
____. Telephone interview. 7 October 1994.
London, Todd. "The Artistic Home: Discussions with Artistic Directors of America's Institutional Theatre." *American Theatre* (March 1988):30–34+.
Malpede, Karen. "Producing & Directing: Theatre for the People (Diaries and Interviews—Hallie Flanagan, Judith Malina, and Barbara Teer)." In *Women in Theatre: Compassion and Hope,* edited by Karen Malpede, 179–230. New York: Drama Book Publishers, 1983.
Mann, Emily. Personal interview. 24 March 1993.
Marré, Diana. Personal interview. 19 December 1991.
Marshall, Brenda K. DeVore. "A Semiotic Phenomenology of Directing." Ph.D. diss., Southern Illinois University, 1988.
McAnuff, Des. "The Time of Zelda Fichandler." *American Theatre* (March 1991): 18–25+.
McDonald, Heather. *Dream of a Common Language.* New York: Samuel French, 1993.
Metropulos, Penny. Personal interview. 12 February 1992.

Miles, Julia. Personal interview. 26 March 1993.

Moi, Toril. *Sexual/Textual Politics: Feminist Literary Theory.* London: Routledge, 1985.

Muzio, Gloria. Personal interview. 24 March 1994.

Near, Timothy. Personal interview. 14 February 1992.

Nemirovich-Danchenko, Vladimir. "The Three Faces of the Director." Cole and Chinoy, 119–24.

O'Neill, R. H., and N. M. Boretz. *The Director as Artist: Play Direction Today.* New York: Holt, Rinehart and Winston, 1987.

O'Quinn, Jim. "Mary B. Robinson: She Knew What She Wanted." *American Theatre* (May/June 1994): 21.

Ott, Sharon. Personal interview. 20 February 1992.

Parker, Victoria. Personal interview. 31 December 1991.

Pierce, Michelle. "Sharon Ott: Don't Fence Her In." *American Theatre* (May/June 1994): 20.

Prandini, Adele. Personal interview. 14 February 1992.

Robinson, Mary. Personal interview. 22 March 1994.

Savran, David. Interview with Maria Irene Fornes. In *In Their Own Words: Contemporary American Playwrights,* 51-69. New York: Theatre Communications Group, 1988.

Scott, Seret. Personal interview. 23 March 1994.

Selznick, Daniel. "Theatrical Pilgrims Find a Road Less Traveled." *New York Times,* 13 May 1990, Sec. 2, 7+.

Sheehy, Margaret. "Why Aren't There More Women Directors?" *Drama: The Quarterly Theatre Review* 152 (1984):12.

Syer, Fontaine. Personal interview. 11 February 1992.

Tairov, Alexander. "The Director." Wills, 53–58.

"Taking Vep in the Right Direction," *Front Row Center* (program for George Street Playhouse), February 1989.

Tannen, Deborah. *You Just Don't Understand: Women and Men in Conversation.* New York: William Morrow, 1990.

Taymor, Julie. Personal interview. 25 March 1994.

Teer, Barbara Ann. Personal interview. 14 October 1994.

Todd, Susan, ed. *Women and Theatre: Calling the Shots.* London: Faber and Faber, 1984.

Trousdell, Richard. "Directing as Analysis of Situation." *Theatre Topics,* Vol. 2, no. 1 (March 1992): 25–39.

Tubert, Susana. Personal interview. 6 March 1992.

Venables, Clare. "The Woman Director in the Theatre." *Theatre Quarterly* 10, no. 38 (Summer 1980): 3–7.

White, Cynthia. Telephone interview. 12 March 1992.

Wills, J. Robert, ed. *The Director in a Changing Theatre.* Palo Alto: Mayfield, 1976.

INDEX

241